William Nanson Lettsom, William Sidney Walker

A Critical Examination of the Text of Shakespeare

Vol. I

William Nanson Lettsom, William Sidney Walker

A Critical Examination of the Text of Shakespeare
Vol. I

ISBN/EAN: 9783744709439

Printed in Europe, USA, Canada, Australia, Japan

Cover: Foto ©Thomas Meinert / pixelio.de

More available books at **www.hansebooks.com**

A CRITICAL EXAMINATION

OF THE

EXT OF SHAKESPEARE.

A CRITICAL EXAMINATION

OF THE

TEXT OF SHAKESPEARE,

WITH

REMARKS ON HIS LANGUAGE AND THAT

OF HIS CONTEMPORARIES,

TOGETHER WITH

NOTES ON HIS PLAYS AND POEMS.

BY

WILLIAM SIDNEY WALKER,

FORMERLY FELLOW OF TRINITY COLLEGE, CAMBRIDGE.

VOL. I.

LONDON:
JOHN RUSSELL SMITH,
36, SOHO SQUARE.
1860.

CONTENTS OF VOL. I.

PRELIMINARY NOTICE.

The present work, including the preface, was ready for the press, and indeed was partly printed, when Mr. N. E. S. A. Hamilton's letter, dated the 22nd of June, 1859, appeared in the *Times*. From that letter, as well as from others, afterwards published in the same paper, on the subject of Mr. Collier's annotated copy of the second folio of Shakespeare, there is reason to believe that that volume has been unduly tampered with, and moreover that it is not the book which was once possessed by Mr. F. C. Parry. In consequence of the new light thus thrown on this mysterious folio, I was at first in doubt whether I should not modify, if not altogether omit, that portion of my preface which relates to Mr. Collier's Old Corrector. As, however, the inquiry is scarcely yet brought to a final close, as the circumstances, which at present appear so suspicious, may be hereafter satisfactorily explained, and as, at any rate, most of my observations on Mr. Collier's Old Corrector are applicable to the other Old Correctors, who are known to have annotated other folios, though their labours have as yet been only partially exhibited to the public, I have left that portion of my preface as it originally stood.

It is not superfluous to remark, that, whatever may be the results of the investigation at the British Museum, or of any other investigations, which may be hereafter instituted, they cannot materially affect the criticism of Shakespeare. This is quite a different case from that of the Ireland papers. The latter were partly legal documents with dates, partly literary compositions professedly written with Shakespeare's own hand. Among them (not to mention the play of Vortigern) were autograph copies of all King Lear, and of a small portion of Hamlet. If these papers had been genuine, they must have been admitted as authorities of the highest possible value: autograph copies must of course supersede all others. But if it should be hereafter shown that the writing in Mr. Collier's annotated folio is not feigned, if palæographers should finally agree that it belongs not to the nineteenth but to the seventeenth century, would that raise the Old Corrector to the rank of an authority?—should we know any thing more of him then than we know at present, namely that he wrote after 1632, and consequently must have been later than the editor of the second folio, and may have been much later? —would more deference be due to him than to that editor, who yet is not admitted as an authority by the most competent critics?—should we know more than we do now what was his object in altering the text, whether it was to restore the genuine words of Shakespeare, or to render his plays more intelligible to a later audience by occasionally modernising the phraseology, or whether he had sometimes the former object in view, sometimes the latter? Surely no competent and impartial editor could safely adopt his readings except for their intrinsic probability, and it would be his duty to do the same with the most recent conjectures, whether given with the real names of their proposers, or brought forward under an unwarrantable disguise.

W. Nanson Lettsom.

PREFACE.

I AM afraid that Walker's friends must be much surprised, and indeed, it is a source of no small regret to myself, that so long a time has been occupied in preparing the following work for publication. It is now no less than five years since the treatise on *Shakespeare's Versification* was published, and it may no doubt be reasonably supposed that a much shorter interval would have been amply sufficient to prepare for the press the contents of three duodecimo volumes. The time, however, requisite for such an operation, must depend not merely upon the leisure and qualifications of the editor, or the nature of the work itself, but also upon the state in which it had been left by the author. As to myself, I have not only been repeatedly interrupted by other matters, but have been delayed throughout by my original inexperience, which it required no little time to remove. Any person who had spent his life in the constant habit of literary exertion might have easily performed in a comparatively short time the task which I have got through with difficulty in a long one; if, in particular, he had been accustomed to the critical study of our old authors, he might have passed rapidly over the path, where I was obliged to plod slowly along, learning my duty in the discharge of it. Such a person, moreover, would, in all probability, not merely have finished his task much earlier, but have done it infinitely better. I have indeed, to solicit the reader, not merely to pardon delays, but to overlook unavoidable blunders in performance. I am conscious that, in the notes, I have occasionally, for the sake of brevity, spoken confidently, where doubt and hesitation would have been more in place. Above all, I must beg particular indulgence for those portions, both of the notes and the preface, where I have been compelled by the subject to sit, as it were, in judgment on my superiors, and to criticise critics, without having any claim myself to that respectable title.

Let us now consider those impediments which may be attributed to the nature of the work, and to the state in which it was left by the author. The work is for the most part made up of quotations: and these, with a very few exceptions, I have verified by reference to the authors from whom they were taken. This alone occupied much time. Some people may think, that, as Walker was so eminent in verbal criticism, and must, therefore, have well known the value of accuracy in transcribing, I might have safely trusted to him on this point, and consequently, threw away time and trouble in thus testing his correctness. I soon found, however, that, though his own observations, when they occurred, were either originally written with accuracy, or were carefully corrected where they required correction, it was quite otherwise with the numerous quotations that form the bulk of these volumes. It is natural enough that mistakes should be made in numbering, particularly when passages are quoted from near the beginning or end of an act or scene; such mistakes are common enough in Walker's manuscript; but these are accompanied by others of an entirely different nature. From among the latter, I have noted down (partly from this work and partly from the *Versification*) about seventy, most of which resemble the blunders in the old copies of our Elizabethan dramatists, and consequently bear upon the revision of Shakespeare's text. Several of these, whimsically enough, confirm some of Walker's own opinions. I need only mention one of them here. At page 253 of the *Versification* the reader will find a well known passage from King John, ii. 1; it is thus written in the manuscript,—

> "St. George, that swing'd the dragon, and e'er since
> *Swings* on his horse' back at mine hostess' door."

Had this mistake occurred in the first folio, and had any poor editor proposed to substitute for *swings* the genuine word *sits*, his proposal would no doubt have been condemned as wanton and unnecessary, and the other reading would have been stoutly defended as an instance of Shakespeare's propensity to play on words. As it is, Walker's error gives support to Article xliii. of the present work.

Here and there (but very seldom) the manuscript exhibits discrepancies of another kind. Readings occur which may be thought improvements on the received text, and have the air of legitimate conjectures, but which, as they are put down without any observation, were probably slips either of Walker's pen or of his memory. I have not ventured to alter such variations from the printed texts of Shakespeare, but have adverted to them in the notes, whenever I have observed them.

One may be noticed here as a philological curiosity. It occurs at page 29 of the *Versification*. Walker there quotes a passage from Troilus and Cressida, iii. 3, thus,—

> "Keeps pace with thought, and almost like the Gods,
> Does thoughts unveil in their *dim* cradles,"

and immediately afterwards, proposing to cure the halting measure of the second line by a different arrangement, he again quotes the passage with the usual reading, *dumb*. The same passage is also quoted for another reason in Article xliii. of the present work, and there also it is given in the usual way. This discrepancy at least can have been nothing but a slip of the pen; yet *dim* makes as good sense as *dumb*, perhaps somewhat better; and if the one reading had appeared in the quarto, and the other in the folio, there would have been a reasonable ground for a difference of opinion as to which should be preferred. Mr. Collier, indeed, in his last edition, suggests *dim* as an emendation, though he has not placed it in the text, being of opinion that dumb could scarcely have been composed for *dim*, as the latter word was never spelt with a final *b*. *Dumb*, however, was occasionally spelt without that letter, and *dim* and *dum* may readily have been confounded. But however that may be, neither *dim* nor *dumb* affords any countenance to the *crudities* of the Old Corrector. I admit, with Walker and Mr. Collier, that the metre here is faulty, and I hold that it is part of an editor's duty to repair defective verses, when he can, by probable conjectures; but surely it is scarcely allowable to procure our materials for that laudable purpose by the destruction of the sense. In concluding this digression, I must apologise for my own negligence in not having detected Walker's oversight. That negligence was, indeed, all the more glaring, as I had occasion to write a note on the passage in question. But this only shows how easily errors escape detection, when the general sense is not affected by them. Even a certain degree of awkwardness in a sentence would not excite the suspicions of the same corrector, who would at once notice a piece of palpable nonsense. Such awkward passages abound in the original editions of our old dramatists, and demand the peculiar attention of modern editors. Unfortunately, too many of the latter have taken up the mischievous notion that a passage is never to be corrected as long as sense can be made out of it, and in consequence, go confidently to sleep just at the times when it is most incumbent upon them to be wide awake.

I have now to describe the state in which this work

was left by the author, and I cannot do this better than by comparing and contrasting its condition with that of the *Versification.* The latter was found divided into sixty regularly numbered articles; I ought, perhaps, rather to say fifty-nine, as there was no division or distinction between the second and the third; the proper title of every Article was placed at its head by Walker himself, and, after verifying the quotations, correcting literal errors, and pruning superfluities, the manuscript might at once have been handed over to the printer, but for two circumstances, which rendered it necessary to transcribe the whole. Almost every page, of the early portions at least, was crowded with interlineations of additional matter, while other additional matter was accommodated in additional pages distributed at irregular intervals, as occasion required. These additional pages were rather more numerous than the rest. I should add, that here and there were scattered other portions of additional matter, with directions where they should be placed. Fortunately, Walker wrote a very clear hand, so that it was less difficult than might be supposed to distinguish and arrange this mass of seeming confusion.

Much that I have just said of the *Versification* is applicable to the larger work. In this manuscript, however, the different parts were neither numbered, nor (except in a few cases) headed with their respective titles; and though it mostly appeared, from the general nature of the subjects, that Walker had intended to distribute the work, like its companion, into Articles, yet other portions, which consisted of short observations on particular passages, led to an exactly opposite conclusion. I noticed, however, that when Walker directed additions to be made to certain previous portions without specifying the page where the latter were to be found, he almost always referred to the subject, scarcely ever to the act and scene of a play. Occasionally, indeed, he was vague enough in this matter, sometimes referring merely to "a former note," sometimes to a page, leaving a gap for the number. I at last determined, after a good deal of doubt, to take the *Versification* for a model, as far as was practicable, in arranging the present work. I divided into one hundred and nineteen Articles all that part which treats of general matters, and added from a separate paper another Article, which seemed well adapted to form part of this treatise. As to the short notes on particular passages, which were scattered almost at random through every part of the manuscript, I separated them from the rest, and arranged them according to acts and scenes, following the order of the plays as given in the first folio. Some valuable general observations have been placed at the head of the notes on the plays to which they respectively relate. These separate notes form the third volume of this work; the other two are dedicated to the one hundred and twenty Articles. At the end of the second I have added, in a supplement, an account of some other remains of Walker's, which, for various reasons, it was unadvisable to publish at full. Though I have thus done a good deal in the way of arrangement, I have effected but little in the way of retrenchment. I found it impossible to do more in the latter respect without completely altering the character of the work, and, in my humble opinion, materially diminishing its value. Some readers, indeed, may suppose that, as Walker frequently quotes passages that others have quoted, and refers to emendations that others have made, occasionally even, through inadvertence, producing the latter as conjectures of his own, I might have cut away such portions of the work, not merely without injury, but even with positive advantage. It will, however, I believe, be found that such quotations and conjectures are essential either to support Walker's own positions, or to confirm the opinions of his predecessors; that he has either placed them in a new light, or given them quite a novel application. We have a remarkable instance of this in the well-known passage from Antony and Cleopatra, i. 5,—

> "Who neigh'd so high, that what I would have spoke
> Was beastly dumb'd by him,"

where *dumb'd*, the emendation of Theobald, has been received by most editors in the place of *dumbe*, the reading of the folio. Walker has placed this passage at the head of Article lxii., one of the most important in his work. In this article he has shown how frequently old copies confound the *e* and *d*, particularly at the ends of words. From the frequency and peculiarity of this error, he has inferred that there must have been something remarkable in the old handwriting, which would account for such a result. This, indeed, was the case, as any one may perceive by examining the facsimile of Massinger's writing placed opposite to p. 593, vol. iv., of Gifford's second edition of that poet's works. And Walker here traced out the truth, not by poring over old manuscripts, but by exercising critical sagacity; while others, who possessed the special knowledge which he wanted, but could afford to dispense with, were unable to apply it with the same effect. Nor is the proneness of the old printers to confound these letters a trifling matter, however it may seem so to uncritical readers. Some of the blunders, indeed, which proceed from this cause (as, for example, *white beares* for *white beards*) are so palpably ridiculous, that in these cases the most scrupulous editors have altered the old printed text. In other instances, and particularly in one most important class, in which the blunder merely produces a certain awkwardness by changing the tense, the earlier editors usually altered the text for the sake of correct grammar, while their successors have restored the expelled reading, out of deference to the old copies. Thus (not to mention innumerable other instanccs) in The Tempest, i. 2,—

> "———————— the fire, and cracks
> Of sulphurous roaring, the most mighty Neptune
> *Seeme* to besiege,"

and in Much Ado &c., iv. 1,—

> "You *seeme* to me as Diane in her Orbe,"

where most of the earlier editors read *seem'd*, the majority of the recent ones have reinstated *seem;* though it is clear from the context, that in both passages the present tense is altogether out of place. It is true we are told by some critics, that Shakespeare and his contemporaries were excessively irregular and licentious in their style, and confounded the active and passive, the past and present, ancient idioms and modern ones, in the most extraordinary manner. The truth, I suspect, is, that they had little regard for the rules of artificial grammar, but followed the dictates of natural grammar more faithfully than ourselves. I am afraid that too frequently our modern editors, with all their professed reverence for our old poets, ascribe to them incorrect phraseology, to save the credit of blundering printers. At any rate, on such points as that now under consideration, and on several others, the authority of the old copies is weak indeed: it would not, perhaps, be too much to say, that it is scarcely worth a straw.

The mention of old copies, and of early and recent editors, reminds me that it is now time to say something of the various editions of Shakespeare. I would rather leave for future notice the subject of the old copies, and confine myself for the present to giving a cursory account of those editions that bear the name of an editor. The first of these was published in 1709, by Rowe. He is said to have followed the text of the fourth folio, and this may have been the case in general, though in his dedication he complains of that edition, and certainly has restored some passages by the aid of the quartos. This part of his task, however, he seems to have discharged with great carelessness and inconsistency. Thus, for instance, he has inserted from the quartos all that part of Hamlet, iv. 4, which the folios omit; but he has followed the latter in omitting the whole of the beautiful scene, King Lear, iv. 3, which the quartos have preserved. We are indebted to him for several elegant emendations, but as his edition, like the old copies, is without notes, it can scarcely be called a critical one. It appears from Mr. Dyce's notes, that Rowe's second edition contains emendations not found in the first; consequently, as I am acquainted only with the latter, I may, in my notes to Walker's work, have attributed to Pope, conjectures that are the property of Rowe.

The first really critical edition was Pope's. This great man has shown in his remarkable preface that he had formed a just idea of the duties of an editor, and had estimated far more correctly than some recent critics have done the value of the old authorities for the text of his author. Unfortunately, his practice was too frequently not in accord with his professions. Instead of acting "with a religious abhorrence of all innovation, and without any indulgence to his private sense or conjecture," instead of altering nothing, except "*ex fide codicum*, upon authority," he has made repeated use of conjecture, sometimes, I admit, with great propriety, at other times in the most wanton manner, and (what is worst of all) has frequently changed the old text without giving notice to the reader. He has, indeed, been ranked by Malone with the editor of the second folio, as one of the two principal corrupters of Shakespeare's text, and certainly he has gone so far in the way of cutting and carving, that he was one of the last critics who should have sneered at

> "—— slashing Bentley with his desperate hook."

His successor and antagonist, Theobald, has gained a high reputation from the general excellence of his conjectures. He was a scholar, and, besides, possessed very considerable critical abilities. In cleverness and sagacity, however, the next editor, Hanmer, was quite his equal. Unfortunately for Hanmer's credit, he entirely neglected the old copies, and depended exclusively on conjecture for amending the text; Theobald, on the other hand, took the blunders of the old copies as the foundation of his conjectures; he was aware that a critical practitioner should trace disease to its source. Before quitting the subject of Hanmer, I may be allowed to state that one of his conjectures has been imperfectly reported by every succeeding editor who has mentioned it. In the passage near the end of Troilus and Cressida, which the first folio gives thus,—

> "Sit gods upon your throanes, and smile at Troy.
> I say at once, let your briefe plagues be mercy," &c.

Hanmer does not merely read *smite* for *smile:* he knew better: his reading is,—

> "Sit, Gods, upon your thrones, and *smile all* Troy
> I say at once; let" &c.

Smile, no doubt, is nonsense, and the words, "I say at once," are awkward, whether we take them with what goes before, or with what comes after. Perhaps we might reasonably read; partly with Hanmer,—

> "Sit, gods, upon your thrones, and *smite all* Troy;
> *Ay, slay* at once; let" &c.

Ay is almost always spelt *I* in the old copies.

Warburton, the last of the earlier editors, used the same license of conjecture as his predecessors. Some few of his emendations are remarkable for ingenuity; indeed, he appears to the more advantage the more desperate the corruption; but, for the most part, his alterations are not merely needless but absurd. Pope and Hanmer, by their sophistications, remove real or apparent difficulties; they leave an easy readable text even after their worst ravages; but Warburton exasperates asperities, deepens obscurity into darkness, and takes infinite pains to make passages altogether impassable, where nobody but himself had been sensible of an obstruction. His arrogance and presumption made him enemies, and at the same time laid him peculiarly open to attack. His edition was, in consequence, assailed by his contemporaries with merciless severity.

These early editors, however they might differ in other respects, were all addicted to alter rather than to explain; they were all, more or less, deficient in the knowledge of the old language, and consequently often thought the text corrupt, when, in truth, the editor was ignorant; and even when they consulted the old copies, which was the case principally with Pope and Theobald, they performed this essential duty with much carelessness and little discrimination. But, with all their faults, they were free from some mischievous errors of the wonderful nineteenth century. None of them (except Warburton) was addicted to harsh, forced, and contorted explanations; none of them imagined that, "all things considered, there never was a book so correctly printed as the first folio;" none of them were so frantic as to "believe that the text of no author in the world is so immaculate as that of our great national poet." They were all men of distinguished talents, and were utterly incapable of falling into such woful mistakes as these.

Before I proceed to speak of later editors, I wish to give a single specimen of the various changes which the text of Shakespeare has undergone. It will enable the reader to form some notion of the peculiar difference between the earlier and more recent schools of criticism. In the last scene of the first act of Cymbeline, the following passage is thus given by the three earliest folios,—

"——————— should I (damn'd then)
Slaver with lips as common as the stairs
That mount the Capitol: join gripes with hands
Made hard with hourly falsehood (falsehood as
With labour): then by peeping in an eye" &c.

The fourth folio, by an ordinary typographical blunder,

omitted the first *falsehood;* on which Rowe, who saw that both the metre and the syntax were at fault, instead of consulting the earlier folios, put matters (as he thought) to rights by the following conjectural reading and arrangement,—

> "Made hard with hourly falsehood as with labour?
> Then *glad myself* by peeping in an eye" &c.

This change was accepted by six following editors, including even Capell and Johnson. Capell, though he printed Rowe's interpolation in black letter, said nothing of the original reading; Johnson, however, mentioned the latter with approbation in a note, and at the same time proposed to read *lie* for *by*. His advice was taken in both cases by some succeeding editors, and it might have been expected that a passage, so successfully treated, might for the future have been left alone. But in the eyes of still later critics nothing is so terrible as the slightest conjecture, nothing so precious as an old typographical blunder. In every recent edition, Johnson's conjecture, so slight, so easy, and so indispensable, has been unceremoniously rejected, and the sore has been salved, not cured, with the help of a hyphen, by reading *by-peeping* or *bo-peeping*. Neither of these readings satisfies the construction. Mr. Knight is mistaken in saying that *by-peeping* is the reading of the old copy; the old copy omits the hyphen, the insertion of which is as much a conjecture as any other alteration. Not that I should object to this or any other conjecture, if I believed that it restored what the poet wrote. This I cannot think the case here. Johnson saw, what the more recent editors seem to have overlooked, that *slaver* and *join* require to be connected, not with a participle, but with another verb. The same error occurs in Goffe, Courageous Turk, ii. 1,—

> "Make him *by* snoring on a wanton breast,
> And suck the adulterate and spiced breath
> Of a lewd faíned (?) woman?"

and in Beaumont and Fletcher, Mad Lover, i. 1,—

> "—— your cold sallads without salt or vinegar
> *By* wambling in your stomachs,"

where Mr. Dyce properly adopts Sympson's correction, *Lie*, observing, "The first folio has *By* (a misprint for *Ly*); the second reads *Be*."

It is remarkable that the edition, which eclipsed, or at least deserved to eclipse, the labours of the preceding editors, was the work of one who neither excelled in the knowledge of Elizabethan idioms, nor possessed any brilliancy of talent, and, moreover, could scarcely write English so as to be understood. His style may be fairly described by parodying Johnson's panegyric on Addison. Whoever wishes to attain an English style uncouth without simplicity, obscure without conciseness, and slovenly without ease, must give his nights and days to the Notes of Capell. Capell, however, possessed two useful qualities, industry and good sense, without which more brilliant endowments can avail little, and sometimes are positively mischievous. He founded his text directly on the old copies, which he seems to have studied attentively, without shutting his eyes to their defects. By following this middle course, he avoided some errors both of earlier and later editors. Through a whimsical arrangement, Capell's Notes and Various Readings were not merely published ten years after the text, but when they did appear, appeared in a different form, being contained in three quarto volumes, while the text and preface fill ten small octavos. The two publications even now can only be bought separately, yet, as the references in the Notes and Various Readings are made not to the Acts and Scenes of the Plays, but to the volumes and pages of Capell's edition, it is necessary to procure the latter before the three quartos can be used with any convenience. One of Capell's merits should not be passed over. He had sounder notions of Shakespeare's versification than almost any other editor.

The editions that followed Capell's are so numerous, that it would be impossible, even if I possessed the requisite knowledge for such a task, to give so much as a cursory account of them. Johnson's first edition, which he executed alone, preceded Capell's; but he is so much better known as associated with Steevens, that we may speak of him as one of the later editors. Some passages of his preface exhibit, in its full development, that morbid horror of conjecture that has since raged like an epidemic among critics and commentators. "They," says he of the first publishers, "who had the copy before their eyes, were more likely to read it right, than we who read it only by imagination." But it is not true that we read the copy only by imagination. It might as well be said that a judge or jury sifts evidence only by imagination. We do not read the copy by imagination, but by the evidence of the printed book; it is our duty to sift that evidence, to reject what is probably false, to receive what is probably true, and to reconcile what at first sight may seem contradictory. Johnson, indeed, contradicts himself immediately after, for he goes on to say, "But it is evident that they have often made strange mistakes." How could we have any good reason to believe this, if we had no proof of it but the vague testimony of our imagination? We have, however, much better testimony,—the testimony of the old printed books themselves. By comparing one authority with another, when we have them to compare, and, when we have not, by comparing particular suspicious passages with the unsuspected context, we make the old printers give evidence for and against themselves, and thus arrive, not indeed at certain, but at probable results.

Johnson has certainly drawn a most exaggerated picture of the perils that beset conjectural criticism. "That a conjectural critic should often be mistaken, cannot be wonderful either to others or himself, if it be considered that in his art there is no system, no principal or axiomatical truth that regulates subordinate propositions." I am not sure that I fully comprehend this sentence. Axiomatical truths are simple matters, and such of them as are of general application can be applied to this study as easily as to any other. In conjectural criticism, as in other arts, observation has accumulated facts, and reason has deduced consequences; now these two processes lay the foundation of all practical systems. That conjectural critics are often mistaken, I admit, particularly when they are rash or ignorant, and sometimes when they are neither, for they are no more infallible than Popes or Philosophers; but here Johnson falls into an inconsistency, which since his time has become common enough. He speaks slightingly of this unfortunate art, and of all who have to do with it, and yet makes it matter of crimination that, like all other human arts, it is imperfect, and its professors are not more than men.

What follows is in a similar strain. "His chance of error is renewed at every attempt;" no doubt; and what lawyer ever conducted a cause, what general ever fought a battle, without running the risk of losing it from some unforeseen mishap? "An oblique view of the passage, a slight misapprehension of a phrase, a casual inattention to the parts connected, is sufficient to make him not merely fail, but fail ridiculously;" no doubt; and before now, from analogous causes, great philosophers have not merely failed, but failed ridiculously. In conjecture, as in other pursuits, trifling oversights occasionally produce serious consequences. "And when he succeeds best, he produces perhaps but one reading of many probable, and he that suggests another will always be able to dispute his claims." Now this is true only of certain cases; and, after all, it is no more than what actually happened to the two illustrious astronomers, who not long ago, finding that the received text of the celestial volume could not account for the irregularities in the motions of Uranus, introduced the weapon of conjecture into the armoury of the exact sciences, and ventured to interpolate a world. Their two hypothetical planets differed in their elements from one another, and also from the real one, which was immediately discovered; yet the names of Leverrier and Adams are justly immortalised for the sagacity and scientific boldness with which they sought and practically found the truth. Had an analogous case occurred in literature, had two editors suggested two probable emendations, and had then a newly-discovered manuscript revealed a similar but not the same reading, we should have been edified by homilies on the danger of conjecture and the fallibility of critics. The merit of detecting a corruption and approximating to the truth, would have been forgotten; it would only have been remembered that the emenders had not hit on the exact word that proceeded from the author; and it would have been made a reproach to them that probability is not certainty.

The same vein of exaggeration runs through Johnson's next paragraph. "The allurements of emendation are scarcely resistible. Conjecture has all the joy and all the pride of invention, and he that has once started a happy change, is too much delighted to consider what objections may rise against it." Now all this is just as applicable to ten thousand other matters as to conjecture. Everybody is too ready to take his own goose for a swan; everybody, who gets a crotchet into his head, is apt to overlook the objections that may be reasonably made to it. Prejudices and hasty decisions not merely corrupt texts, but ruin families and overthrow empires. Had Johnson, however, lived in our days, he would have seen the majority of critics resisting, with philosophic indifference, what he describes as scarcely resistible allurements, and deriving as much "joy and pride" from demolishing as from producing conjectures. Invention at present is far less busily employed in concocting new readings by conjecture, than in squeezing new senses out of old readings by forced interpretations.

Capell, though he frequently refers to the labours of his "moderns," rarely mentions them by name, and gives their opinions in his own peculiar phraseology. Johnson let his predecessors speak for themselves. His was the first Variorum Edition. It was several times reprinted, and gradually expanded under the editorship of Steevens and Reed, till, in 1813, it reached the formidable number of twenty-one volumes. I am not acquainted with any of these editions, except the first; but if the text which they offer at all resembles that which goes under the names of Steevens and Malone, it must differ essentially from the original text of Johnson, as well as from that which appears in the Variorum Edition of 1821. This edition, which was finished by Boswell, after the death of Malone, was the last and most complete of those edited by the latter critic. Malone, though quite as hostile to Capell as Steevens and Farmer were, was, like him, a pains-taking, plodding, industrious editor, without any unusual share of ability, but with an ample allowance of plain common sense. His knowledge of the old language was respectable, though in that department, Steevens, I suspect, was considerably his superior. The latter, however, seems so much under the influence of whim, and sometimes of worse impulses, that it is scarcely prudent to put full confidence in him.

The most remarkable occurrence, in a critical point of view, that distinguished the era of Steevens and Malone, was the controversy between them as to the authority of the second folio. In this dispute Malone had much the advantage. He at least proved that the second folio was not only most carelessly printed, but that it swarmed with palpable sophistications, introduced to remove real or supposed defects in metre or phraseology. Some of these alterations no doubt restore the genuine language of Shakespeare; some have been retained in modern texts; others may have been improperly rejected; and most of them are interesting, as probably representing the notions of the poet's versification and language, which prevailed in the time of Charles the First, but (with one or two exceptions) they have no appearance of being derived from any lost authority, and therefore they can only be safely regarded as the results of more or less successful conjecture.

During the long interval between the publication of Johnson's first edition and the completion of the last Variorum, the study of the Elizabethan dialect (if I may use the phrase) was diligently prosecuted; the most obscure and worthless works of Shakespeare's contemporaries were eagerly sought out and patiently read; and scarcely a heap of rubbish was left unsifted by the persevering critics, who sometimes as editors, sometimes as pamphleteers, and essayists, undertook to elucidate the text of the great poet. It so happened, however, that the most distinguished among the critics of this period confined himself to editing Shakespeare's contemporaries, and thus, though he largely extended the knowledge of the Elizabethan literature, illustrated Shakespeare himself only occasionally and indirectly. The reader will at once perceive that I allude to Gifford. Mr. Dyce, though he published many years ago an edition of Shakespeare's Poems, employed himself, till very lately, in editing the secondary dramatists whom Gifford had left untouched. The united labours of these two distinguished critics may be said to have reintroduced into the world a class of writers, some of whom had been all but forgotten, while the rest could only be read in corrupt old copies, or sophisticated modern editions. We can now peruse them in comparatively clear, pure, and intelligible texts, and can without difficulty study the language of Shakespeare in that of his contemporaries.

Shakespeare himself was not so fortunate as his fellow dramatists. After having been operated upon by sundry editors, whose labours however effected little, and made little impression on the public, he at last fell into the hands of Mr. Knight and Mr. Collier. The labours of these editors are so familiar to the public, that it is unnecessary to speak of them at any length. Each gave an entirely new text, Mr. Knight's being founded on the first folio, Mr. Collier's on the old copies in general. Mr. Collier, I think, scarcely did full justice to the first folio, and allowed something more than their due weight to the quartos; still the utmost that can be imputed to him under this head is a slight inclination to the latter, and an occasional want of judgment in particular passages. Mr. Knight, on the contrary, followed the first folio with the blindest partiality, even in those plays in which it was evidently printed from a preceding quarto, and repeatedly adopted from the folio the most palpable printer's blunders, when the quartos might have set him right. Both he and Mr. Collier had the most ludicrous horror of conjecture. In consequence, they ejected from the text many of the most certain emendations of their predecessors, and supplied their places with all sorts of corruptions from the old copies. This imposed on them the necessity of defending, by the most forced explanations, the nonsensical readings which they had restored, and as in various instances these old corruptions ruined the metre as well as destroyed the sense, both these editors were tempted to uphold metrical maxims as utterly erroneous as their strained and unwarrantable explanations. Their great object was evidently to keep out conjectures at any rate. In this sacred cause, they were ready to assert anything, not from wishing to deceive their readers, but because there was nothing which they were not themselves prone to believe. In the morbid aversion to conjecture, Mr. Collier went perhaps even further than Mr. Knight. Not that either he or Mr. Knight entirely excluded conjectures. No editor of Shakespeare has ventured on that, however he may have longed to do so. In fact, the most tight-laced of modern editors have been obliged, however reluctantly, to admit conjectures to an extent that would have been scarcely justifiable, had not the old copies been printed with extreme incorrectness.

The two editions just mentioned are the last of any note, published during Walker's life, and may possibly have exercised some influence on his mind. He occasionally alludes to Mr. Knight's labours, and I believe he had one of his editions at his elbow, but I rather think he was very slightly acquainted with Mr. Collier's edition. Otherwise, his attention would certainly have been attracted by the various readings contained in the foot notes; this collection is, in a critical point of view, the most valuable part of Mr. Collier's edition, and would have been of essential service to Walker.

Since the latter's death, both Mr. Knight and Mr. Collier have published editions which vary in several respects from those which I have noticed. Mr. Knight has excluded from his *Stratford Shakespeare* some absurd readings, which deformed his earlier editions, but has also introduced objectionable lections, from which his earlier editions are free: his critical notions remain as before. Mr. Collier also, in his recent edition, has occasionally improved on his former text. He has also altered it considerably by admitting many readings from his Old Corrector; but he has executed this part of his task with so little judgment, that he has too often rejected the best of these readings and admitted the worst. He has omitted much that was useful in his original notes, to make room for new matter only indirectly relating to Shakespeare; and indeed, in his recent annotations, has shown himself at least as intent on attacking his fellow editors as on illustrating his author.

Literature may have derived some other benefits from the critical labours of Mr. Knight and Mr. Collier, but the greatest and most essential of all should not be passed over in silence. Their editions induced Mr. Dyce to publish *Remarks* on them. Walker possessed this invaluable volume, and appears to have studied it with the greatest attention.

The editor of a work like the present can scarcely avoid saying something of Mr. Collier's Old Corrector, though the public, I suspect, must be by this time rather weary of the subject. I need not tell how Mr. Collier bought an old book for an old song, how the old book was found to be scribbled over from one end to the other with old writing, which must have detracted from the market value of the old book, and how consequently the separate value of the old writing must have been something less than nothing; I need not relate how some mysterious personage took counsel's opinion, and how counsel, "after due searching of the books and mature deliberation, returned" an answer, on which nobody has yet ventured to act. It is evident that there was a *will* to make a property of the Old Corrector, but somehow or other, in spite of the old proverb, a *way* was wanting. If the learned counsel had "duly searched" the editions of Shakespeare, he would have seen that many of the best of the readings in question had been first published by Rowe, Pope, and others down to our own day, and consequently could not be the property of Mr. Collier as first publisher. The fairest Circassians of this virgin Harem, which Mr. Collier had "purchased" for less than nothing, and which he proposed to protect by a guard of Bababalouks in wigs and gowns, had long been common to all the world. The choicest of his Cleopatras were every man's Cleopatras.

But Mr. Collier's singular proceedings should not affect our opinion of his Old Corrector. It was, indeed, unfortunate for the latter to be introduced to the world by a critic who was far more accustomed to the duties of an advocate than to those of a judge, one, indeed, who had past his time rather in defending at any rate and indiscriminately the best and worst readings of the old copies, than in estimating their merits calmly and dispassionately. Mr. Collier went upon his new and delicate task with his old zeal and ardour. The same lax system of interpretation, which he had found so useful in veiling the absurdities of the old copies, was now employed, whenever needed, to do the same kind office for the Old Corrector. But the old copies had numerous friends, who were disposed to wink at any vagaries of their defender; it was otherwise with the Old Corrector, when Mr. Collier brought him forward with a flourish of trumpets. The critics then chose to open their eyes, and treated the newly-found readings with as little ceremony as modern conjectures.

It is true that many of the best of these readings have been long before the public; that there is not a critic, from Rowe to Walker, who has proposed any considerable number of good conjectures, but has been anticipated in some of them by the Old Corrector. It has even been inferred from this that the latter was a mere recent impostor, who had simply copied the emendations that he appeared to anticipate. This notion, however, after the lapse of six years, still remains a mere suspicion. At any rate, the Old Corrector could not possibly have copied Walker's unpublished conjectures, yet he occasionally coincides with him, just as he does with the earlier editors. Nothing, in fact, is more common than such coincidences, because critical conjecture is an art, not a mere affair of chance;

and in that art, as in others, men setting out from the same premises, and applying the same rules, frequently arrive at the same conclusions; if they also not unfrequently differ, it is because different men apply the same rules with different degrees of skill. I have myself only recently discovered that an emendation which I thought my own, and have mentioned as such at note 17, vol. i., of this work (*sumd his pennons* for *suits Spenori*), is the property of Mr. Mitford. This, till lately, escaped my notice, the conjecture having been placed at the end of Mr. Dyce's edition of Greene, not under the passage (vol. i. p, 113) to which it applies.

The worst of the Old Corrector is, that we really *know* nothing about him. He is as mysterious a personage now, as he was when Mr. Dyce applied the phrase to him six years ago. Whether his readings rest on any authority; whether they are the sweepings of this or that actor's memory; whether they are mere conjectures, and, if so, whether they are the conjectures of one man, or of a dozen, or of a score, is mere matter of surmise. All we really *know* is, that some person or persons, some time *after* 1632, wrote down these readings in the margin of a book. Mr. Collier, indeed, tells us that the handwriting is the same throughout, though at one time he thought otherwise; and, moreover, that it is the handwriting of the time, that is, I presume, of about 1632. This, however, is merely his opinion, and I need not say that the testimony of a prejudiced witness in a matter of opinion is not worth much. One fact, however, is, perhaps, of some importance. The book, according to Mr. Collier, is not in its original binding; but it does not seem, from anything he says, that the marginal notes have anywhere suffered from the cutting of the second binder, though the copy is stated to be a short one. This looks as if the second binding was older than the marginal notes, and, consequently, the earliest of the latter must have been considerably, perhaps were very much, later than 1632.

The question of time is of importance in various ways, and particularly with reference to Mr. Collier's theory, that the readings were, many of them, derived from the recitation of actors. When, however, we consider that actors are more apt to alter texts for theatrical purposes, or to corrupt them from mere carelessness, than to preserve them pure, without having any peculiar inducement to do so, we can scarcely expect much from their vague recollections. It is now, I believe, generally agreed that our old copies were derived from prompters' books, an impure source, no doubt, but still the only source from which the actors themselves must have sipped up whatever they could have imbibed of the poet's genuine text. Their parts, hastily written out, and got by heart with just enough exactness to be spouted on a stage with the assistance of a prompter, would have been subject to all sorts of variations and corruptions every time they were repeated, and even from the first could never have been depended upon to decide minute differences, such as we meet with in comparing the readings of the Old Corrector with those of the old copies. Surely the old copies, however carelessly printed, must have been more correct than the scraps and orts dropped from mouthing players. When I speak of old copies, I do not mean evidently surreptitious editions, such as the quarto 1603 of Hamlet, or the Chronicle History of Henry the Fifth, but those which seem to have proceeded in a more regular way from the company to which Shakespeare, as far as we know, always belonged. Surreptitious and imperfect copies may have been obtained by short-hand; but who in his senses would have resorted to such an objectionable method, unless from necessity? what thief ever cut his own pocket? I cannot, therefore, but consider as erroneous, the notion that Shakespeare's plays, as printed in the first folio, had ever passed through the corrupting process of short-hand. Corruptions, no doubt, arose in his works, as in those of his contemporaries, from the vowels being confounded with one another; but this confusion, I suspect, proceeded not from the use of short-hand, but from most of the vowels being near neighbours in the printer's lower case. The consequence of this is pointed out in Zachary Jackson's preface.

It is no easy matter to determine from internal evidence alone whether a genuine reading was attained by conjecture or authority: conjecture can lead us to genuine readings, and no manuscript or old copy can do more. But when we meet with a number of apparently genuine readings mixed up with a multitude of palpable sophistications, we are, perhaps, warranted in judging of the former by the company they are found in, and in setting down both good and bad as the results of conjecture. This is the case with the readings of the Old Corrector. We know, too, for certain, that many of the best of them occurred to Rowc, Pope, and others, all of whom proceeded by conjecture; why might not, therefore, earlier correctors have arrived at the same results by the same means? I have observed, however, that some of the worst readings, some that are too nonsensical to be sophistications (for sophistications, however awkward, are rarely unintelligible) may at least be converted into sense by a moderate application of conjecture. Thus in King John, v. 7, nothing can be more absurd than the reading,—

> "Death, having prey'd upon the outward parts,
> Leaves them *unvisited;*"

as if death could prey on parts without visiting them; but if we read "*ill*-visited," the passage becomes at least intelligible. In Winter's Tale, iii. 2, the reading,—

> "——————— Do not receive affliction
> At *repetition*, I beseech you,"

is not intelligible. It certainly cannot admit of Mr. Collier's explanation (Notes and Emendations, p. 189), "Do not allow *my repetition* of the fatal results of your jealousy to afflict you." The folio reads, "At *my petition*," which is scarcely more intelligible than the correction. By the way, if we attentively examine these two readings, we shall see that Mr. Collier has jumbled them together, borrowing *my* from one, and *repetition* from the other, to make up the explanation which I have just quoted. According to Mr. Collier, "there can be no doubt that *at repetition* is the true language of the poet." If, however, we compare All's Well, &c. v. 3,—

"We're reconcil'd, and the first view shall kill
All *repetition*,"

(where Johnson justly interprets *repetition* by *recollection of the past*); Massinger, Guardian, v. 1, l. 7,—

"——————— *revive* not
A sorrow long since dead;"

and Witch of Edmonton, v. 2, Gifford's Ford, vol. ii. p. 552,—

"You will *revive affliction almost kill'd*
With my continual sorrow;"

we may be led to suspect that "the true language of the poet" was,—

"————— do not *revive* affliction
By repetition, I beseech you,"

and that Massinger and the authors of the Witch of Edmonton imitated this passage as well as that in All's Well &c. In the last speech of Winter's Tale, iv. all editions read, "a double occasion —— which, who knows how that may turn *back* to my advancement?" I agree with Mr. Collier that this is nonsense, though formerly he, as well as all other editors, thought it so clear as to need no explanation. I do not, however, see how the matter is much mended by merely turning *back* into *luck;* and though Mr. Collier tells us that "to *turn luck* is a very common and intelligible expression," I should say that it is rather ambiguous than intelligible. Possibly Shakespeare may have written, "a double occasion —— which who knows *but luck* may turn to my advancement?" At any rate it is better English to say that fortune turns an opportunity, than that an opportunity turns fortune, to a man's advancement.

In each of these cases (not to mention others) it appears to me that the Old Corrector, in the midst of the nonsense which he has set down, but which he could not possibly have understood, has preserved a word which may have come from Shakespeare's pen. If many similar instances should be detected, it would lead us to suspect that he might have had access to authorities materially differing from those which have come down to us. We might also reasonably infer from such cases that he did not always understand the readings with which he crowded the margin of his folio. But to determine this, and fifty other doubtful points, it is requisite that his folio should be thoroughly and searchingly studied by an unprejudiced and impartial person. At present, all that we know of the Old Corrector amounts to little; nine tenths of what we have been told of him cannot pass for more than supposition and surmise. In this state of things, the only safe way of using his readings is to treat them as conjectures. By this phrase, I do not mean that they should be treated as conjectures are too often treated by modern critics. They should be treated fairly and dispassionately; their merits should be taken into account as well as their defects; they should not be hastily condemned for frivolous or unfounded reasons. But as long as the present feeling against conjecture continues, an emendation will rarely be allowed a fair trial, and while editors continue to cling to old copies, they will be irresistibly tempted to defend their corruptions by strained and unwarrantable interpretations. At present a conjecture

"Tarda venit, seris factura nepotibus umbram;"

whatever may be its excellence, it will be in luck if at the end of a century it chances to meet with general approval.

If I am not misled by my regard for Walker's memory, and the reverence which I have always felt for his commanding abilities, he will be found to have followed a middle course in criticism, equally removed from the rashness of the earlier editors, and from the overstrained caution of their successors. I should say that not merely his principles are correct, but that he has applied them correctly. Good principles are worth little, unless we are prepared to act on them, and have ability to act on them properly. As far as mere principles are concerned, there is not much to choose between Hanmer, the most licentious of the earlier editors, and Mr. Halliwell, perhaps the most scrupulous of modern ones. "A too rigid adherence," says the latter, "to the original text, on the one hand, and an undue facility in admitting variations from it, on the other, are errors easily incurred, and beyond the ability of any editor, however sound may be the principles on which his text is formed, entirely to avoid; but a determination to adhere to the phraseology of the earliest editions, whenever the idiom is clearly established to be genuine, and a desire to accept the best emendations in cases where the old readings are corrupt and unmeaning, are, it is sincerely believed, the best means of creating a text, that shall for the most part be accepted as permanent." Hanmer is equally edifying. "This," says he, "the reader is desired to bear in mind, that, as the corruptions are more numerous, and of a grosser kind than can well be conceived but by those who have looked nearly into them, so in the correcting them this rule hath been most strictly observed, not to give a loose to fancy, or indulge a licencious spirit of criticism, as if it were fit for anyone to presume to judge what Shakespeare ought to have written, instead of endeavouring to discover truly and retrieve what he did write: and so great caution hath been used in this respect, that no alterations have been made, but what the sense necessarily required, what the measure of the verse often helped to point out, and what the similitude of words in the false reading and in the true, appeared very well to justify." How far these eminent editors have practised what they profess, may be easily ascertained by comparing with the old copies the handsome quartos of the one, and the magnificent folios of the other. It is remarkable, however, that Mr. Halliwell speaks merely of accepting emendations; he says nothing of proposing them. Surely it is the duty of an editor, who founds his text on the old copies, to ascertain himself on what he is building; to keep his eyes open; to look out for faults, and, when they are found, himself to apply the remedy. Now this is what Walker has done in the present work. He has pointed out innumerable blunders not merely in the first folio of Shakespeare, but in other old books; nor has he noticed individual blunders only, but also whole classes of blunders; and having ascertained the disease, he has not shrunk from attempting to cure it. Nor has he confined himself to looking out for faults. He has also noticed various peculiarities of phraseology, and has not unfrequently defended passages which had been attacked without cause. Throughout his work, he has displayed the results of an exact system of study combined with profound critical sagacity, and in all his steps we may observe the influence of perfect candour and undeviating impartiality. His researches are so extensive, his inquiries so skilfully conducted, and his opinions so powerfully supported, that, whenever his works are studied thoroughly, we may look for a general revolution in the character of Shakespearian criticism. His volumes certainly contain materials for a completely new text of Shakespeare.

Walker's library was scanty, and many of his quotations are made from modern editions; consequently, the modern printers may have been guilty of some of the blunders which he has noticed. Several of these, however, I have been able to trace to the old copies. With regard to Shakespeare, Walker possessed the reprint of the first folio, and had evidently studied it with great assiduity. I suspect he knew little of the quartos, perhaps no more than what he picked up from occasional inspection of the Variorum of 1821. He could scarcely have been acquainted with Steevens's reprint of them; otherwise he would certainly have referred to it occasionally: as it is, he never once mentions it. This ignorance of the quartos is not of so much consequence as might be supposed, for it only affects some of the plays; and even in several of these the folio, perhaps, gives the better text. Walker, moreover, did not require the assistance of the quartos to enable him to detect the glaring faults of the folio. His defective knowledge, however, of the quartos has now and then led him to employ conjecture in removing the palpable errors of the folio, when the corresponding quarto affords the genuine reading. The quartos, also, are not merely of service in settling certain readings in certain plays. As in some plays the folio was evidently printed from them, it has not merely all the defects of a reimpression, but, as the original copy is still in existence, we can prove and bring home to the folio its various faults. Hence we may form an opinion, how far it is to be trusted in those plays of which it is the first impression. If Messrs. Jaggard and Blount could not print correctly from printed books, we may judge to what an extent they would have been likely to blunder in printing from manuscripts. The facility of comparing different authorities enables us occasionally not merely to remove blunders, but to detect sophistications, those rocks under water,

> "Traitors ensteep'd to clog the guiltless keel"

of the unsuspecting editor. This would have been a task worthy of Walker's highest powers. It has not, however, particularly attracted the attention of the commentators, except in regard to the second folio, in which numerous sophistications have been pointed out, principally by Malone. A remarkable one occurs in the later quartos of Hamlet, iv. 7,—"As *liking not* his voyage," where the quarto, 1604, reads, *the king at*, and the folio, *checking at*. That the last is the genuine reading is quite certain, for it is only great poets that can soar to lively and appropriate metaphors; sophisticators can give us the naked sense that the context requires, but nothing more, and this is just what the later quartos give us in this passage. Several sophistications of the later quartos and of the first folio have been noticed by Malone; one is so curious that I may be allowed to speak of it here, particularly as no editor, I believe, has drawn from it the inferences that it naturally suggests. In 1 King Henry IV., v. 3, the early quartos read,—

> "I was not born *a yielder*, thou proud Scot."

That of 1613 has,—

> "I was not born *to yield*, thou proud Scot."

The omission of the final *r* is a common typographical error in the old copies; it forms the subject of Walker's Article lxi., and to his examples I may add one from Verstegan's Restitution of Decayed Intelligence, 1628, Epistle to the English Nation, l. 9, "the courteous *Reade*," for "the courteous *reader*." *A* and *to*, however, are not readily confounded; here we have not a printer's blunder, but a corrector's sophistication for the sake of making sense. We may here see the origin of those defective verses, which are such favourites with some modern editors, but which the editor of the second folio corrects whenever he can. The editor of the first folio, however, saved his successor the trouble of correcting this verse, by himself unscrupulously altering *proud* to *haughty*, thus palming upon posterity, for Shakespeare's genuine text, a reading made up of one typographical error and two sophistications. For my own part, I believe that Shakespeare was incapable of perpetrating the wretched apologies for verse, which require "the retardation of the syllables," and similar editorial machinations to help their lameness. Though, however, I suspect that both these editors, who must have been contemporaries of Shakespeare, understood his versification much better than most modern editors, I, of course, cannot approve the rash and blundering manner in which they attempted to remove the corruptions which they had detected. Not that the first or second folio of Shakespeare is worse in this respect than other old copies. The change of *proud* into *haughty* is a trifle to an outrageous sophistication that appears in the second edition of the Maid's Tragedy, v. 2. In this passage the first edition reads,—

> "So, if he raile me not from my *resolution*
> As I believe *I* shall not, I shall fit him."

In the next edition, instead of the second line, we find the words, "I shall be strong enough;" a sophistication which runs, I believe, through all subsequent editions, ancient and modern. No doubt the original reading is slightly corrupt, but the cure is obvious. We should read,—

> "So if he rail me not from my *resolve*,
> As I believe *he* shall not, I shall fit him."

The corruption in the second line resembles that in Cymbeline, iv. 2, fol. p. 388, col. 2,—

> "*Thou* diuine Nature; *thou* thy selfe *thou* blazon'st" &c.,

where Pope's substitution of *how* for the second *thou* has been received by universal consent. In Pericles, iii. 2, the first edition has the following defective line,—

> "Such strong renown as time shall never."

where Mr. Dyce cures both the sense and metre by adding *raze*, no doubt the genuine word. The other old copies have the palpable sophistication, "as *never shall decay*." In the Maid's Tragedy, ii. 2, I must confess, I think Theobald was right in altering the corrupt reading of the original edition, "Be *teares* of my story," to "Be *teachers* of my story." The reading of the subsequent old copies,

"Tell that I am forsaken," seems to me another cool sophistication, the hint of which was given by a subsequent passage,

> "It is the lady's pleasure we be thus
> In grief she is forsaken."

With these and similar sophistications before my eyes, I must utterly dissent from Mr. Halliwell's notion (see his pamphlet on *Smothers her with Painting*, page 4), that old correctors are more likely to be right than modern ones. Old readings deserve peculiar regard only when they seem to be derived from some now lost authority. If we once admit that they are mere conjectures, we give up their only claim to more than ordinary notice. A good modern critic, well versed in Shakespeare's language, would be more likely than one of the poet's contemporaries to correct his text with success, because conjectural criticism has now been cultivated for more than two centuries longer, it has been reduced to a consistent system, and its principles are well understood. What critic of the present day would dream of altering "As I believe I shall not, I shall fit him," into "I shall be strong enough"?—who would presume to propose any conjecture without being able to show with some probability how the assumed corruption was derived from the proposed new reading?

I have ventured on these observations from thinking it not improbable that readers, who are accustomed to the system of recent editors, may imagine that Walker has occasionally gone too far in applying conjecture to remove the corruptions of the old copies. If, however, they carefully peruse his volumes, and strictly examine the grounds on which he has founded his opinions, I trust that their scruples on this point will gradually disappear. We should remember that it is only where our authorities are defective that it is requisite to resort to conjecture. In the criticism of the New Testament, for instance, where scholars are as much bewildered as assisted by the multitude of manuscripts, conjecture is unnecessary; one authority supplies the defects of another; the only difficulty is to select with judgment. Now, in Shakespearian criticism we have the reverse of all this. The first folio is not merely our best, but our only authority for more than half the plays; in the rest it is frequently derived from the latest and worst of a series of quartos, of which even the earliest and best, when it comes to be examined, too often turns out to be only comparatively correct. These are the foundations on which an editor of Shakespeare has to build; these are the guides whom too many critics are willing blindly to trust, rather than weigh probabilities fairly and impartially, and act according to the result. Some editors not merely leave corruptions in the text, but snatch at every shadow of a pretext to defend them as genuine readings; the more intelligent admit in their notes that this or that conjecture was probably what Shakespeare wrote, and yet with strange inconsistency leave in the text the very corruptions they condemn in their annotations. This is not the manner in which people proceed in other matters; it is only in Shakespearian criticism that they toil to do nothing, and take the trouble to cultivate knowledge without desiring that it should produce a crop of acts and deeds.

It is far from my wish that the reader should take my word only for the defects of the folio. Let him turn to the preface of Mr. Dyce, who has lately given us the best text that has yet appeared of Shakespeare, and peruse the formidable list of delinquencies, far too long to insert here, which that accomplished critic has attributed to Heminge and Condell; let him turn to Mr. Hunter's testimonial, which Mr. Dyce has sanctioned by his high authority: "Perhaps in the whole annals of English typography there is no record of any book of any extent and any reputation being dismissed from the press with less care and attention than the first folio;" let him turn to Mr. Grant White's *Shakespeare's Scholar*, p. 6, and he will find that critic, who is most prejudiced in favour of Heminge and Condell, lamenting that "their labour of love," "this precious folio, is one of the worst printed books that ever issued from the press." After these testimonials, what shall we think of the anonymous critic, who reviewed the Old Corrector in *Blackwood's Magazine*, 1853, and came to the curious conclusion, "that the text of no author in the world is so immaculate as that of our great national poet, or stands in less need of emendation, or departs so little from the words of the original composer"! Surely such a critic is only worthy to associate with "the kinde Life-rend'ring *Politician*," who exercises his philanthropy in the Hamlet of the first folio, and to pass his days on

> " ———————— the dreadfull *Sonnet* of the Cliffe,
> That beetles o're his base"

in a column of the same immaculate edition.

With regard to the text of Shakespeare, the best critics have pronounced that our authorities are defective; it is in exact proportion to this defect that it is our duty to resort to conjecture. That we cannot do altogether without it, is admitted by every editor, even by those who are most disposed to extol the old copies with preposterous panegyrics. But it goes against the grain with them; they are willing to submit to any inconvenience, they eagerly snatch at at any trifling excuse, rather than frankly adopt the only available remedy. The professors of other arts are frequently exposed to serious risks, but they are willing to confront them from a reasonable hope of success. A physician would think it disgraceful to throw up a doubtful case, and let the patient perish without an effort to save him, because he was not absolutely certain of the nature of the disease. Generals and statesmen exercise their respective arts in a cloud of uncertainties, though they are well aware that not merely their own reputations, but the fates of armies and empires depend on their decisions. These men are not afraid of acting on probabilities. It is only those whose errors cannot be irretrievable, those who deal in such mighty matters as words, and syllables, and letters, and half-letters, that shrink from responsibility, and tremble at the remotest chance of a mistake. "*Dum omnia timent, nihil conantur.*" They sit with their hands before them, while the grossest corruptions remain in the text.

But we should greatly deceive ourselves if we imagined that even a liberal use of conjecture involved neglect of the old copies. On the contrary, it is on the old copies that conjectures must be founded; it is their errors that the critic is required to correct; those errors must be detected before they can be removed, and that can only be done by narrowly examining the text that contains them. Modern critics appear to pay too little attention to the indirect testimony of the old copies, or, in other words, to the testimony of the context. They seem to shrink from comparing a suspicious word or phrase with the clear, consistent passage that accompanies and at the same time condemns it. Not such was the practise of Walker. The words, "see context," are constantly recurring from the beginning to the end of his work. In perusing his notes, we meet with repeated proofs of the close attention with which he had studied the only old copy of Shakespeare that he possessed, the reprint of the first folio, and of the exactness with which he had examined its peculiarities. It will be observed, that he not unfrequently agrees with the earlier editors, as well as with Mr. Collier's Old Corrector, but we never find in his notes the strange mixture of probable truth and palpable error, of apparent skill and outrageous blundering, which may be observed occasionally in the former, but which is a marked characteristic of the latter. I, of course, do not maintain that all his emendations are right; my notes, I think, will show that I am not a blind approver of all his opinions; but I may be allowed, I hope, to say how warmly I admire his quickness of observation, his eminent critical sagacity, the extent and accuracy of his knowledge; and, above all, his candour, fairness, and perfect impartiality. I certainly cannot, nor do I desire to, claim for him the merit of that exaggerated caution, which, in fact, is only a duller kind of rashness, the caution that bewitches its victim into shutting his eyes, and opening his mouth, and swallowing anything that an old printer may send him. Walker's caution was of a different kind; it examined both sides of a doubtful question, and was on the watch to detect error in all its shifting disguises. It was this enlarged and enlightened caution that enabled him to wield with full effect the powerful weapon of conjecture, and at the same time restrained him from a rash and wanton resort to it. Every friend of literature must deeply lament that one so eminently gifted with every critical qualification was not spared to complete and publish this important work, that he was not allowed to develope his principles in their ultimate results, and finally to take his place, not merely among the elucidators, but the editors of Shakespeare.

In conclusion, I have to acknowledge the kindness of Mr. Dyce in advising me on several points on which I had occasion to consult him. I should not be doing justice to my own feelings if I did not offer my warmest acknowledgments to Mr. George Crawshay. The considerable expense incurred in publishing this work and the *Versification* has been entirely borne by this gentleman. In the most handsome and liberal manner he has fulfilled his promise to his dying friend, and at the same time conferred a lasting benefit on the literature of his country.

WILLIAM NANSON LETTSOM.

P.S.—At vol. iii. p. 80 of this work, I ought to have stated that Mr. Grant White (*Shakespeare's Scholar*, p. 274) has erroneously attributed Walker's conjecture (*infinite cunning* for *insuite coming*) to Mr. Thomas Walker, the author of the Original.

In editing these volumes, I have occasionally added some references, and altered a few others, so that here and there an edition may be referred to that has been published since the 15th of October, 1846, the date of Walker's death.

W. N. L.

SHAKESPEARE.

In the subsequent quotations, the act and scene of the play are indicated respectively by Roman letters and numerals; *e.g.* Macbeth, i. 4; Hamlet, iii. 2. The abbreviation *fol.* signifies the first folio edition of the plays, published in 1623; but the extracts are made from a reprint of that edition, given to the public by Messrs. Vernor and Hood in 1808. *S. V.* refers to a treatise of mine entitled "Shakespeare's Versification and its Apparent Irregularities Explained, &c." *Var.* is Boswell's Variorum edition of Shakespeare, in 21 volumes, 1821, except when any other Variorum edition is specified.

I.

Passages of Shakespeare in which verse has been mistaken for prose, and *vice versa*.

As You Like It, iii. 2; so arrange,[1]—

"*Jacques.* I thank you for your company; but, good faith,
I had as lief have been myself alone.
Orlando. And so had I; but yet, for fashion sake,
I thank you too for your society.
Jacques. God b' wi' you; let's meet as little as we can.
Orlando. I do desire we may be better strangers."

For *God b' wi' you*, see S. V. art. xliv.

---

[1] This passage is printed as verse in the first folio.—*Ed.*

2 K. H. IV. iv. 3,—

> "My lord, 'beseech [for *I beseech*] you, give me leave to go
> Through Glostershire: and, when you come to court,
> Stand my good lord, 'pray, in your good report."

A late writer has anticipated me in remarking, that the list of invitations in Romeo and Juliet, i. 2, is in verse; in l. 7, he has properly supplied the deficient syllable,—

> "My fair niece Rosaline, *and* Livia."

The writer in question, if I recollect right, is Mr. Courtenay. In l. 2, I suspect that for *Anselme* we ought to read *Anselmo;* as in T. N. ii. 4, *Feste* the jester ought perhaps to be *Festo*.

Much Ado, &c. i. 1,—

> "I shall see thee, ere I die, look pale with love."

The expression seems poetical; I suspect that we have here a line of verse, and that we ought to read *'Shall* or perhaps *I'll;* see S. V. art. xlviii.

Ib. 3,—

> "Yea, but you must not make full show of this,
> Till you may do 't without *controlement:*
> You have, of late, stood out against your brother,
> And he hath ta'en you newly into'*s* grace;
> Where '*tis* impossible you should take root,
> But by *th'* fair weather that you make yourself:
> [ ] 'tis needful that you frame the season
> For your own harvest."

In l. 1, I have expunged *the* before *full show* as injurious even to the sense. *Controlment* is also written *controlement*, K. John, i. 1, fol. Histories, p. 1, col. 1,—

> "Controlement for controlement: so answer France."

It is also used as a quadrisyllable. Copy of alexandrines

in Hazlewood's collection of "Critical Essays," vol. ii. p. 277,—

"Oh, that I had mine olde wittes at commandement;
I knowe, what I coude say without controlement."

See S. V. art. xiv. In l. 5, the common editions have "take *true* root," which perhaps is right; *true* may have been absorbed by *take*. The fol. omits *true;* [the quarto inserts it.—*Ed.*] This metrical use of *impossible*, *terrible*, and the like, is (as is well known) very common in the Elizabethan poets. It occurs even in Chapman's Iliad, where it is very remarkable;

xiii. Taylor, vol. ii. p. 23, l. 17,—

"—————————— had not Polydamas
Thus spake to Hector: Hector still, impossible 'tis
to pass [point: Hector, still impossible, &c.]
Good counsel upon you."

Penult. perhaps "*Therefore* 'tis needful, &c." (As regards the metaphor—a proverbial expression, as I conjecture—compare 2 K. H. VI. v. 1,—

"Scarce can I speak, my choler is so great.
. . . .
But I must make fair weather yet awhile,
Till Henry be more weak, and I more strong."

Massinger, A Very Woman, iv. *ad fin.;*
Cuculo is speaking of Almira's displeasure,—

"Here's a new trick of state; this shews foul weather;
But let her make it when she please, I'll gain by it [by 't]."

Spenser, F. Q., B. iv. C. ii. St. xxix. where Sir Paridell and Sir Blandamour are reconciled to each other,—

"——— of all old dislikes they made faire weather.")

Much Ado, &c. v. 1,—

"In a false quarrel there is no true valour.
I came to seek you both."

Ib. in the midst of verse; Borachio—replying to Don Pedro's query,—

"But did my brother set thee on to this?"—

says,—

"Yea, and paid me richly for the practise of it."

Qu.,—

"Yea;
And paid me richly for the practise on 't."

K. Lear, i. 4,—

"Come, sir,
I would you would make use of that good wisdom,
Whereof I know y' are fraught; and put away
These dispositions, which of late transform you
From what you rightly are."

(Boswell too—see Var. 1821, notes *in loc.*—has remarked that the above words are printed as verse in the folio.)

. . . .

"Does any here know me?—Why, this is not Lear:
Does Lear walk thus? speak thus? Where are his eyes?
Either his motion weakens, or 's discernings
Are lethargied."

Thus far the ed. 1770, "collated with the ancient and modern editions," which gives the whole of this speech as verse, agrees with me, except only as regards the *'s*. In the remainder we differ, both as to text and metrical arrangement,—

"—————— Sleeping or waking?—Ha!
Sure 'tis not so.
Who is't [omitting *that*] can tell me who I am?—Lear's shadow?—
I would learn that; for by the marks of sov'reignty,

Knowledge and reason, I should be false persuaded
[That] I had daughters."

Most of this is confirmed by the folio, so far at least as the present passage is contained there. It has,—

"Do's any heere know me?
This is not Lear:

. . . .

——————Ha! Waking? 'Tis not so?
Who is it that can tell me who I am?
Foole. Lear's shadow."

(I have omitted to notice several differences which do not affect the metre.) The passage in the folio ends with "Lear's shadow." Knight gives it in a great measure correctly.[2]

All's Well, &c. ii. 2,—

"I play the noble housewife with the time
To entertain '*t* so merrily with a fool.

. . . .

Most fruitfully; I'm there before my legs.
Countess. Haste you again."

---

[2] It is evident that, when Walker says this, he can only refer to the metrical arrangement, as he adopts a text principally founded on the quartos, though he had the folio before him, while Mr. Knight blindly follows the latter. It appears to me that just here the quartos give an unsophisticated text, though one disfigured by some palpable blunders, while in the folio we have a text derived from a good original, but sophisticated in a blundering way for the sake of the metre. Mr. Knight seems to have had the sagacity to discern this, though his prejudices stifled the dictates of his natural good sense. I allude to the note where he tells us that several words have been rejected in the folio to render the passage metrical.—*Ed.*

Ib. 3,—

> "These boys are boys of ice, they'll *none of her* :[3]
> Sure they are bastards to the English.
> The French ne'er got 'em."

Vulg. "they 'll none *have her*."—But *quere*, is this a Shakespearian phrase? The other reading I found in a small 1747 edition; perhaps it is a gratuitous alteration, such as are frequent in that edition (*e.g.* As You Like It, iv. 1, —"*make fast* the doors," for "*make* the doors"; T. and C. iii. 3.. "*Oh*, rouse yourself!" for "*Sweet*, rouse yourself!") but I have adopted it, because it agrees with S.'s diction. [For the phrase "*they 'll none of her*," compare] T. and C. ii. 3,—

> "—— —— Go tell him this; and add,
> That, if he over-hold his price so much,
> We 'll none of him; but let him, like an engine
> Not portable, lie under this report:
> Bring action hither, this cannot go to war."

(*Qu.*, "*can't* go"; for the pause is too slight for the additional syllable; see S. V. art. ix. Or is *hither* to be pronounced *here? ib.* art. x. p. 105, *sqq*. The former seems the more probable.) iii. 1: "My niece is horribly in love with a thing you have, sweet queen. *Hel.* She shall have it, my lord, if it be not my lord Paris. *Par.* He? no, she 'll none of him; they two are twain." T. of the S. iv. 3, Petruchio says, speaking of Katherina's gown, "I 'll none of it." T. N. ii. 2,—

> "She took the ring of me!—I 'll none of it."

---

[3] This good emendation is Rowe's. It appears in his, Pope's, Theobald's, and Hanmer's editions. All these, however, give the passage as prose.—*Ed.*

For *English* as a trisyllable, see S. V. art. ii. iii. So K. H. VI. i. last scene,—

"Rescued is Orleans from the English."

(*Male quidam*, "English wolves."[4]) L. L. L. iv. 2,—

"O thou monster Ignorance, how deformed dost thou look!
Hol. Sir, he hath never fed of the dainties that are bid in a
book;" &c.

The latter line is verse in the folio; this, however, would be a doubtful argument; see context in that edition. Compare the other instances in the same metre, pp. 15, 16, below. *Ib.* a little further on, perhaps,—

"*Nath.* *Perge*, good master Holofernes, *perge*, so it shall
please you to abrogate scurrility.
Hol. I will something affect the letter, for it argues facility."

v. 1, *ad fin.* I imagine,—

"*Dull.* I'll make one in a dance, or so; or I will play
On the tabor to the worthies, and let them dance the hay.
Hol. Most dull, honest Dull, to our sport, away."

For this cannot surely have been accidental. (In the last line perhaps we should rather point,—

"Most dull, honest Dull!—to our sport, away.")

So in Green's Tu Quoque, Dodsley, vol. vii. p. 45, arrange,

"Sir, your musick is so good that I must say I like it:
But the bringer so ill welcome, that I could be content to lose it.
If you play'd for money, there't is; if for love, here's none;
If for good will, I thank you, and, when you will, you may be
gone."

Pericles, i. 3, *qu.* (though I doubt much:)—

"Now do I see
He had some reason for 't; for if a king
Bid a man be a villain, he is bound
By the indenture of his oath to be one."

---

[4] One of the sophistications of the 2nd folio.—*Ed.*

K. H. VIII. ii. 2, letter,—

"My lord,—The *horse* your lordship sent *me* for,
With all the care I had, I saw well chosen,
Ridden, and furnish'd: They were young, and handsome,
And *o' th'* best breed *o' th'* North.
When they were ready to set out for London,
A man of my lord cardinal's, by commission,
And main power, took them from me; with this reason,
His master would be serv'd before a subject,
If not before the king: which stopt our mouths, sir."

In the folio, even the words immediately following,—

"I fear he will, indeed: Well, let him have them;
He will have all, I think;"

which have been universally recognized as verse, are printed as prose. In l. 1, where the received text is, "the horses you sent for," *me* seems to be required by the sense as well as by the metre. A. and C. v. 2, is in point,—

"———————————— Proculeius,
What thou hast done, thy master Cæsar knows,
And he hath sent for thee: for the queen,
I'll take her to my guard."

Here also we should read, "And he hath sent *me* for thee." *Horse*, I need not say, is a common form for *horses*. (So by the way it is to be understood K. H. V. iv. 1,—

"Doth rise, and help Hyperion to his horse."

Shakespeare remembered his Ovid.) L. 7, "And main power," &c. This division of an *accentual trochee* (if we may use the phrase) between two separate feet, is so frequent in this play, as to show that it must have been studied. It is a favourite with Chapman and Jonson. For instances of letters in verse see Sackville's Gorboduc, iii. Dodsley, ed. 1825, vol. i. p. 142; Spanish Tragedy,

iii. Dodsley, ed. 1825, vol. iii. p. 139; again, p. 152. Massinger, Great Duke of Florence, iv. 1, Moxon, p. 180, col. 2, a letter in ten-syllable rhyme. Beaumont and Fletcher, Maid in the Mill, i. 2, Moxon, vol. ii. p. 583, col. 2. Bonduca, iii. 2, vol. ii. p. 58, col. 1. The letter in Shirley's Cardinal, iii. 1, Gifford and Dyce, vol. v. p. 312, though printed as prose, is in verse.

The third scene of King Henry VIII. v., supposing it to be all verse, is an entangled skein. I have arranged it as well as I could. I find that the part from "Pray, sir, be patient," to "What should you do," is printed as verse in the folio, though somewhat differently arranged; and likewise in the Var. 1821, except the speech, "I am not Samson," and the following ones. The first speeches are, I think, easy.

"*Porter.* You'll leave your noise
Anon, you rascals: Do you take the court
For Paris-garden? ye rude slaves, leave your gaping.
(*Within.*) Good master porter, I belong to *th'* * larder.
Porter. Belong to *th'** gallows, and be hang'd, you rogue!
Is this a place to roar in?—

(* So, too, the folio.)

Fetch me a dozen crab-tree staves, and strong ones;
These are but switches to 'em.—I'll scratch your heads:
You must be seeing christenings! Do you look
For ale and cakes here, you rude rascals?
Man. Pray, sir,
Be patient; 'tis as much impossible," &c.

(A little below, I would arrange,—

"How got they in, and be hang'd?
Man. Alas, I know not:
How gets the tide in?")

Part at least of the dialogue, from the speech of the Porter's Man beginning "I am not Samson," to the entrance of the Lord Chamberlain, is evidently in verse. I have made some hesitating attempts to restore the metre. Capell, too, has tried his hand at it.

"I shall be with you presently,
Good master puppy.—Keep the door close, sirrah.
Man. What would you have me do?
Porter. What should you do,
But knock them down by th' dozens? Is this Moorfields
To muster in? or have we some strange Indian
With *th'* great tool come to court, &c.

. . . .

——————————————————they need
No other penance: That fire-drake did I hit
Three times *o' th'* head, and three times was his nose
Discharg'd against me: he stands there, like a mortar-piece,
To blow us.

. . . .

I miss'd the meteor once, and hit that woman,
Who cried out 'clubs!' when I might see from far
Some forty *truncheoners** draw to her succour
(* On *truncheoners*, see S. V. art. xliii.)
Which were the hope
O' th' † Strand, where she was quarter'd. They fell on:
I [ ] made good my place: at length they came
To *th'* † broomstaff with me; I defied them still:
(† So too the folio.)
When suddenly a file of boys behind them,
Loose shot, deliver'd such a shower of pebbles,
That I was fain to draw my honour in,
And let them win the work: the devil was
Amongst them, I think, surely.
Porter. These are the youths
That thunder at a playhouse, and [ ] fight
For bitten apples; that no audience, but

The Tribulation of Tower-hill, or
The limbs of Limehouse, their dear *brethren*,
Are able to endure. I've some of them
In *Limbo Patrum*, and there they're like to dance
These three days;
Besides the running banquet of two beadles,
That is to come."

This last speech is at least doubtful; even the preceding one is perplexing. In some parts of the above dialogue I have ventured beyond the lawful limits of an emendator. End of the scene,—

" *Porter.* Make way there
For *th'* princess.
Man. You great fellow, stand close up,
Or I will make your head ache.
Porter. You i' th' camlet,
Get up o' th' rail; I'll pick you o'er the pales else."

Othello, iv. 1,—

"I marry her!—what! a customer![5]
I pr'ythee bear more charity* to my wit,
Don't think it so unwholesome. Ha, ha, ha!"
(* See S. V. art. xl.)

Ib.,—

"I'll not expostulate with her, lest her body
And beauty unprovide my mind again:
This night, Iago.

---

[5] The first folio gives the passage as *verse*, thus,—

"I marry. What? A customer; prythee beare
Some charitie to my wit, do not thinke it
So vnwholesome. Ha, ha, ha."

The quarto 1622, Steevens's reprint, has,—

"I marry her? I prethee beare some charity to my wit,
Doe not thinke it so vnwholesome: ha, ha, ha."

The quarto 1630 seems made up of the two. It reads, according to Steevens, "What a customer? I prethee," &c.—*Ed.*

Iago. Do 't not with poison, strangle her in her bed,
Even the bed she hath contaminated.*

(* Dyce, too—Remarks, p. 246—suspects this speech to be two lines of blank verse.)

Othello. Good, good:
The justice of it pleases; very good.
Iago. And,
For Cassio, let me be his undertaker:
You shall hear more by midnight."

But the latter part is very doubtful. In Julius Cæsar, ii. 3, the paper which Artemidorus presents to Cæsar is, if I mistake not, in verse,—

"Cæsar, beware of Brutus; take heed of Cassius;
Come not near Casca; have an eye to Cinna;
Trust not Trebonius; Mark well Metellus Cimber;
Decius Brutus loves thee not; *th' hast* wrong'd
Caius Ligarius. There 's but one mind
In all these men, and it is bent '*gainst* [for *against*] Cæsar.
If thou be'st not immortal, look about you;
Security gives way to conspiracy.
The mighty Gods defend thee!
Thy lover.
Artemidorus."

(The three last words are *extra metrum.*)

In l. 8, pronounce *secur'ty* according to Shakespeare's almost invariable usage; S. V. art. xl. All's Well, &c. ii. 4, *init.*,—

"*Hel.* My mother greets me kindly: Is she well?
Clo. She is not well; but yet she has her health:
She 's very merry; but yet she is not well:
But, thanks be giv'n, she 's very well, and wants
Nothing i' th' world: but yet she is not well.
Hel. If she be very well, what does she ail,
That she 's not very well?"

Winter's Tale, v. 2, conclusion of the dialogue between the two gentlemen, possibly,—

"Who would be thence, that has the benefit
Of access? every *winking* [for *wink*] of an eye
Some new grace will be born: our absence makes us
Unthrifty to our knowledge: Let 's along."

(Compare Timon, v. 1, for the thought,—

"——————— Nay, let 's seek him:
Then do we sin against our own estate,
When we may profit meet, and come too late.")

King Lear, *init.* *Qu.*,—

"I thought the king had more affected *th'* duke
Of Albany than Cornwall.
Gloster. It did always
Seem so to us: but now, in the division
O' th' kingdom, it appears not which *o' th'* dukes
He values most; for qualities are so pois'd,
That curiosity in neither can make choice
Of either's moiety."

After *moiety*, there is a short pause in the conversation, which is resumed in prose: "Is not this your son, my lord?" *Qualities* is the reading of the folio; the first quartos, according to Johnson (according to the edition of 1770, all the quartos), have *equalities*, which is the received reading. Pronounce *curiosity*, *curious'ty*, S. V. art. xl. Yet *th' duke*, in this place, seems very unlike Shakespeare; and *equalities* is perhaps more in place than *qualities*. (*Qualities*, as *e.g.* All 's Well, &c. i. 3,—

"Fortune, she said, was no goddess, &c.—Love no god, that would not extend his might, only where qualities were level.")

Lear, iv. 1, after—

"Life would not yield to age.

Old Man. O my good lord,
I have been your tenant, and your father's tenant,
These fourscore years."

Pericles, iii. 1. *Qu.*,—

"Slack th' bolins there; thou wilt not, wilt thou?—Blow
And split thyself!
2nd Sailor. But sea-room, an the brine
And cloudy billow kiss the moon, I care not.
1st Sailor. Sir,
Your queen must overboard; the sea works high,
The wind is loud, and will not lie, till *th'* ship
Be clear'd *o' th'* dead.
Pericles. *That is* your superstition.
1st Sailor. Pardon us, sir; with us at sea it still
Hath been observ'd; and we
Are strong in custom (*see* Dyce, Remarks, p. 265); therefore, briefly, yield her;
For she must o'erboard straight.
. . . .
Sir, *we've* a chest beneath the hatches, caulk'd
And bitumed ready."

1 K. H. IV. ii. 2,—

"Come, neighbour,
The boy shall lead our horses down the hill;
We'll walk afoot awhile, and ease our legs.
Thieves. Stand.
Travellers. Jesu bless us!
Falstaff. Strike; down with 'em; cut
The villains' throats: Ah! whoreson caterpillars!
Bacon-fed knaves! they hate us youth: down with 'em;
Fleece 'em.
Trav. O, we're undone, both we and ours, for ever!
Falstaff. Hang ye, gorbellied knaves! Are ye undone?
No, ye fat chuffs;
I would your stores were here!—On, bacons, on!

What, [ye] knaves?
Young men must live: You are grand-jurors, are ye?
We'll jure ye, 'faith!" [for *i' faith.*]

Tempest i. 1. *Qu.*,—

"Where is the master, boatswain?
Boatswain. Do you not hear him?
You mar our labour; keep your cabins; you do
Assist the storm.
Gonzalo. Nay, good, be patient.
Boats. When the sea is: Hence!
What care these roarers for the name of king?
To cabin; silence: trouble us not.
Gonz. Good; yet remember whom thou hast aboard."

In the folio, *keep*, printed with a capital, begins a line, as if to indicate that the passage was verse, though the editors had mistaken the arrangement.—*Ib.*,—

"A plague
Upon this howling! they are louder than
The weather, or our office:—Yet again!
What do you here? Shall we give o'er, or drown?
Have you a mind to sink?"

Comedy of Errors, iii. 2,—

"And, I think,
If my breast had not been made of faith, and my heart of steel,
She had transformed me to a curtail dog, and made me turn i' th' wheel."

And so Knight; except that with him *And, I think*, forms part of the first line; which renders it over-measure, ὡς ἐμοίγε δοκεῖ. (And for the same reason, iii. 1,—

"If thou had'st been Dromio to-day in my place,
Thou would'st have chang'd thy face for a name, or thy name for an ass;"

I would write *Thou'ldst*. For the metre is not exactly

the same as that which occurs so frequently in L. L. L.) We have thus an easier transition to the blank verse which follows. Hamlet, v. 2, I imagine,—

"The king, and queen, and all are coming down.
Hamlet. In happy time.
Lord. The queen desires you use
Some gentle entertainment to Laertes,
Before you fall to play.
Hamlet. She well instructs me."

M. of V. i. 2, *ad fin.*,—

"Come, Nerissa.—Sirrah, go before:
Whiles we shut the gate upon one wooer, another knocks at the door."

And so Knight. T. of the S. iii. 2,—

"What then?
Bion. He is coming.
Bapt. When will he be here?
Bion. When he stands where I am, and sees you there."

As You Like It, ii. 4,—

"Ay,
Be so, good Touchstone:—Look you, who comes here;
A young man, and an old, in solemn talk."

This, too, serves as a stepping-stone from the prose dialogue preceding to the conversation in verse between Corin and Silvius, iv. 3; the second speech is printed as verse in the folio; which, coupled with its being followed by a dialogue, also in verse, inclines me to think that Shakespeare meant it as such,—

"I warrant you, with pure love and troubled brain
He hath ta'en his bow and arrows, and '*s* gone forth
To—sleep: Look, who comes here."

Warrant, *warr'nt*, as usual; S. V. art. iv. p. 65.

All 's Well, &c. iii. 5, perhaps,—

"That jack-an-apes with scarfs: Why is he melancholy?
Hel. Perchance he 's hurt i' th' battle.
Par. Lose our drum!
Well.
Mar. He's shrewdly vex'd at something: Look, he' has spied us."

Twelfth Night, iv. 1, perhaps,—

"Come, sir,
I will not let you go. Come, my young soldier,
Put up your iron: you are well flesh'd; come on."

Followed by verse. (2 K. H. VI. ii. 1. I cannot exactly arrange this,—

"Born blind, an 't please your grace.
Wife. Ay, indeed, was he.
Suffolk. What woman 's this?
Wife. His wife,
An't like your worship.
Gloster. Hadst thou been his mother,
Thou couldst have better told.
K. Henry. Where wert thou born?
Simpcox. At Berwick," &c.

The dialogue proceeds in verse. The arrangement, *Thou couldst have better told,* seems clearly to indicate verse.) T. N. i. 5,—

"I know not, madam; 'tis a fair young man,
And well attended.
Olivia. Who of my people hold him in delay?
Maria. Sir Toby, madam, your uncle.
Olivia. Fetch him off, *pray;* he speaks
Nothing but madman; fie on him! Go you,
Malvolio; if it be a suit from *th'* duke,
I'm sick, or not at home;
What you will to dismiss it."

Yet the latter part can hardly be right; the verse and the prose seem to be unnaturally blended.

iii. 1,—

> "Most excellent-accomplish'd lady, th' heavens
> Rain odours on you!
> . . . .
> My matter hath no voice, lady, but to
> Your own most pregnant and vouchsafed ear."

M. for M. iii. 2, apparently,—

> "Ever your fresh whore, and your powder'd bawd;
> An unshunn'd consequence: it must be so."

As You Like It, ii. 6, *init. Qu.*,—

> "Dear master, I can go no further: O,
> I die, *I die* for food. Here lie I down
> And measure out my grave. Farewell, kind master!"

The folio prints it as verse in a scrambling sort of way. I have only newly arranged it.

A. and C. i. 2, near the beginning, perhaps,—

> "O, that I knew this husband, which, you say,
> Must change his horns with garlands!"

Ib.,—

> "*There is* a palm presages chastity,
> If nothing else.
> *Charm.* Even as th' o'erflowing Nilus
> Presages famine.
> *Iras.* Go, you wild bedfellow,
> You cannot soothsay."

Nilus surely indicates verse. All 's Well, &c. iv. 3, *Qu.*,—

> "That shall you, and take leave of all your friends.
> . . . .
> "2 *Lord.* Captain,
> What greeting will you to my lord Lafeu?
> I am for France."

i. 3, near the beginning, possibly verse,—

"———————— the complaints
I' have heard of you, I do not all believe;
It is [for '*tis*] my slowness that I do not: for
I know you lack not folly to commit them,
And have ability enough to make
Such knaveries yours."

Hamlet, ii. 2, perhaps,—

"Why, then 'tis none to you; for there is nothing
Either [S. V. art. x.] good or bad, but thinking makes it so:
To me it is a prison."

(The appearance of verse, however, is sometimes deceptive. The first part of the treaty of peace, as read by Gloster, 2 K. H. VI. i. 1, resolves itself without much difficulty into tolerable verse; yet it certainly was never meant for such,—

"It is agreed between the French king Charles,
And William de la Poole, Marquis of Suffolk,
Embassador for Henry king of England,
That the said Henry shall espouse the lady
Margaret, daughter unto Regnier, king
Of Naples, *Sicil*, and Jerusalem;
And crown her queen of England on the thirtieth
Of May [the] next ensuing. Item,—that
The dutchy Anjou and the county Maine
Shall be released and deliver'd to
The king her father."

Sicil for *Sicilia*, as a little above,—

"In presence of the kings of France and Sicil."

I have also expunged *of* before *Anjou* and *Maine*. The last article—though substantially the same—is differently expressed in the Cardinal's supplementary recital, which is palpable prose. A transition from verse to prose under such circumstances cannot possibly have been intended, even by the author of 2 and 3 K. H. VI.)

On the other hand, in a few passages of Shakespeare, prose has been mistaken for verse, This, however, is very rare. Coriolanus, ii. 1,—

"These are the ushers of Marcius: before him
He carries noise, and behind him he leaves tears."

This has also been corrected by Knight and Dyce, Remarks, p. 160. Hamlet, iv. 6, *init.* prose surely,—

"What are they that would speak with me?
Attendant. Sailors, sir;
They say, they have letters for you.
Hor. Let them come in:
I do not know from what part of the world
I should be greeted, if not from lord Hamlet."

Taming of the Shrew, ii. 1,—

"Saving your tale, Petruchio, I pray,
Let us, that are poor petitioners, speak too:
Baccare! you are marvellous forward."

(For *I pray*, qu. *pray.*) See context.
[The folio gives this speech as prose.—*Ed.*]
iv. 2,—

"Quick proceeders, marry! now tell me, I pray,
You that durst swear that your mistress Bianca
Lov'd none in the world so well as Lucentio."

(Point: *Lucentio,*—) The folio, too, gives this speech as prose [or rather begins the second line with a small letter.—*Ed.*]; this, however, of itself would prove nothing. 1 K. H. IV. iii. 3. "Go bear this letter"—to "in the afternoon." 1 K. H. VI. iii. 1,—

"1 *Servant.* Content: I'll to the surgeon's.
2 *S.* And so will I.
3 *S.* And I will see what physic the tavern affords."

Romeo and Juliet, ii. 5,—

"Your love says [*insert comma*] like an honest gentleman,
And a courteous, and a kind, and a handsome,
And, I warrant, a virtuous :—Where is your mother?"

The speech following proves nothing. Tempest, v. 1, towards the end of the play,—

"Will money buy them?
Ant. Very like, one of them
Is a plain fish, and, no doubt, marketable."

I do not feel quite certain that Antonio's speech ought not to be printed as prose.

II.

Passages of Shakespeare in which a compound epithet or participle (or a double substantive) has been resolved into two simple epithets, or an adverb and an epithet, &c.

K. R. II. iii. 2,—

"As a long-parted mother with her child
Plays fondly with her tears, and smiles in meeting,
[*dele* comma after *tears.*]
So weeping, smiling, greet I thee, my earth,
And do thee homage with my royal hands."

Surely Shakespeare wrote, *more suo*, *weeping-smiling*;—an attempt to embody in a word the same complex image, which Homer, according to the genius of his language, expressed by δακρύοεν γελάσασα. (Compare the Greek κλαυσιγέλως· Xen. Helen. vii. 2, 9, *ad fin.* "πάντας δὲ τοὺς παρόντας τότε γε τῷ ὄντι κλαυσιγέλως εἶχεν." Note in Daniel,

Civil Wars, B. vi. St. lxxxviii. the hyphen, "toucht with sorrowing-joy." K. H. VIII. iii. 1,—

"———— O, good my lord, no Latin:
I am not such a truant since my coming,
As not to know the language I have liv'd in:
A strange tongue makes my cause more strange, suspicious:
Pray speak in English."

It is impossible that Shakespeare should have perpetrated such an awkwardness. Read *strange-suspicious.*

Compare the similar flatness in the passages next quoted, as well in some others emended elsewhere. King John, iii. 3,—

"Or if that surly spirit, melancholy,
Had bak'd thy blood, and made it heavy, thick,
Whick else runs tickling up and down the veins," &c.

Heavy-thick. Winter Tale, ii. 1,—

"———————— be but about
To say, 'She is a goodly lady,' and
The justice of your hearts will thereto add,
''Tis pity she 's not honest, honourable.' "

Honest-honourable; i.e. (if I mistake not) not merely *honourable,* by reason of her birth, dignity, and grace of person and mind,*—but likewise *honest, i.e.* virtuous;—honourable with honesty.

(* All 's Well, &c. ii. 3,—

"———— She is young, wise, fair;
In these to nature she 's immediate heir,
And these breed honour.")

Compare K. H. VIII. i. 1, not far from the beginning,—

"As I belong to worship, and affect
In honour honesty;"

and Othello, v. 2,

"But why should honour outlive honesty?"

(Each of these words by the way—*honour* and *honesty*—was at times used in both meanings. Cymbeline, iv. 2,—

"—————— He said, he was
Dishonestly afflicted, but yet honest."

And the sentiment quoted above from K. H. VIII. is thus expressed in Cymbeline, v. 5,—

"Give answer to this boy, and do it freely;
Or, by our greatness, and the grace of it,
Which is our honour, bitter torture shall
Winnow the truth from falsehood."

Cyril Tourneur, Revenger's Tragedy, ii. 1, Dodsley's Old Plays, Collier's ed. vol. iv. p. 306,—

"—————— most constant sister,
In this thou hast right honourable shown,
Many are call'd by their honour, that have none.")

Julius Cæsar, i. 3,—

"And the complexion of the element
Is favour'd like the work we have in hand,
Most bloody, fiery, and most terrible."

Read "Most *bloody-fiery*, and," &c. *αἱμόφλοξ*, as a Greek tragedian might have expressed it, or, in Latin poetical language, *sanguineum ardens;* covered over with fiery meteors of a blood-red colour.

Merchant of Venice, iii. 4,—

"As I have ever found thee honest, true,
So let me find thee still."

Honest-true.

Love's Labour 's Lost, v. 2,—

"—————— to wail friends lost
Is not by much so wholesome, profitable,
As to rejoice at friends but newly found."

Wholesome-profitable.

(The folio—if any such evidence were needed—has *honest true, wholesome profitable.*) Winter's Tale, v. i,—

"———— Most dearly welcome!
And your fair princess, goddess!"

Princess-goddess.

In the passages which follow, the received reading is faulty in various ways; sometimes in the same manner as in the last seven passages (excepting, by the way, that from Julius Cæsar, which belongs to a different head), and sometimes in other ways. In many cases, an un-Shakespearian tameness has been held sufficient to convict a passage of corruption.

Romeo and Juliet, i. 1 (I give the passages as I suppose they ought to be corrected),—

"And made Verona's ancient citizens
Cast by their grave-beseeming ornaments;"

beseeming gravity, σεμνοπρεπεῖς. (Compare Hamlet, iv. 7,

"———— for youth no less becomes
The light and careless livery that it wears,
Than settled age his sables, and his weeds,
Importing health and graveness.")

And so perhaps Spenser, F. Q. vi. v. xxxvi,—

"———— he toward them did pace,
With staged steps and grave-beseeming grace;"

though here I am not quite certain.

Merry Wives of Windsor, ii. 1 (if, indeed, this is not too obvious),—"Let 's be revenged on him; let 's appoint him a meeting; give him a show of comfort in his suit, and lead him on with a fine-baited delay, till he hath pawned his horses to mine host of the Garter." Much Ado,

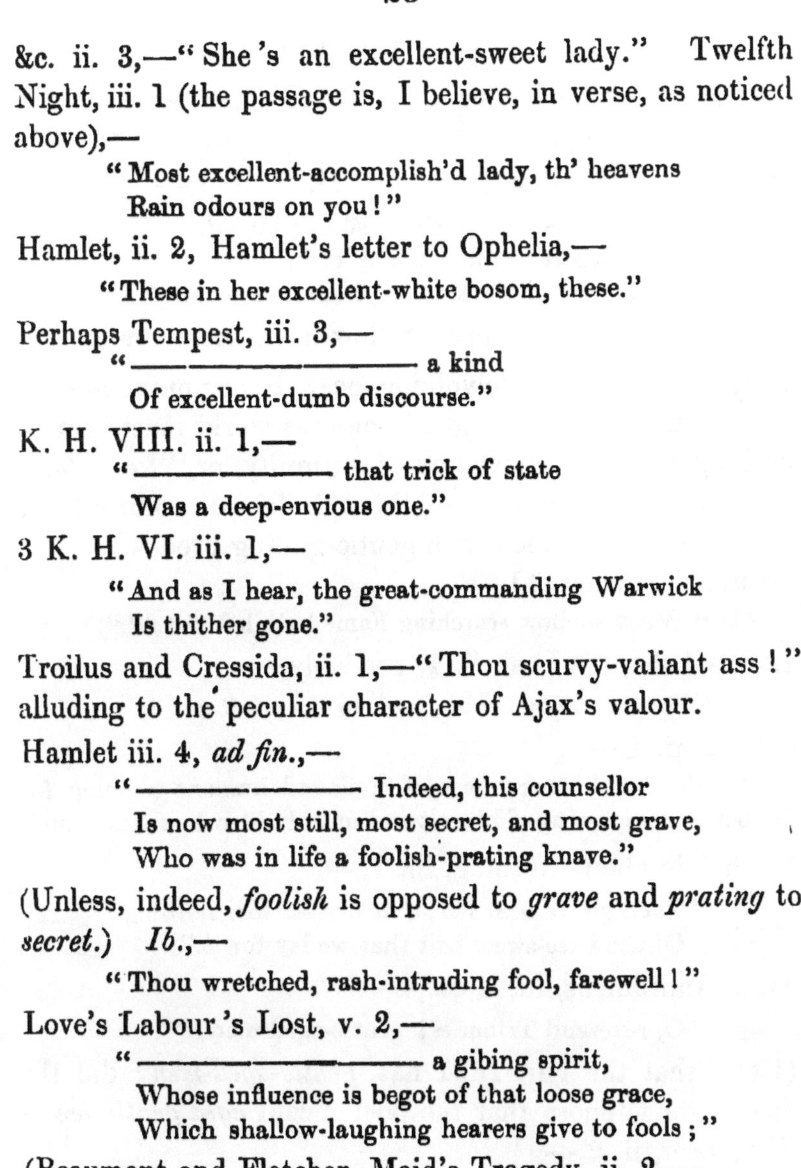

&c. ii. 3,—"She 's an excellent-sweet lady." Twelfth Night, iii. 1 (the passage is, I believe, in verse, as noticed above),—

> "Most excellent-accomplish'd lady, th' heavens
> Rain odours on you!"

Hamlet, ii. 2, Hamlet's letter to Ophelia,—

> "These in her excellent-white bosom, these."

Perhaps Tempest, iii. 3,—

> "—————————— a kind
> Of excellent-dumb discourse."

K. H. VIII. ii. 1,—

> "—————— that trick of state
> Was a deep-envious one."

3 K. H. VI. iii. 1,—

> "And as I hear, the great-commanding Warwick
> Is thither gone."

Troilus and Cressida, ii. 1,—"Thou scurvy-valiant ass!" alluding to the peculiar character of Ajax's valour.

Hamlet iii. 4, *ad fin.*,—

> "—————— Indeed, this counsellor
> Is now most still, most secret, and most grave,
> Who was in life a foolish-prating knave."

(Unless, indeed, *foolish* is opposed to *grave* and *prating* to *secret.*) *Ib.*,—

> "Thou wretched, rash-intruding fool, farewell!"

Love's Labour 's Lost, v. 2,—

> "—————————— a gibing spirit,
> Whose influence is begot of that loose grace,
> Which shallow-laughing hearers give to fools;"

(Beaumont and Fletcher, Maid's Tragedy, ii. 2,—

> "—————— in this place work a quicksand,
> And over it a shallow smiling water,
> And his ship ploughing it; and then a Fear."

Perhaps *shallow-smiling*, but I doubt.)

And in like manner King Richard III. iv. 4,—

> "Relenting fool, and shallow-changing woman!"

ταχυμεταβόλος, and so folio. K. H. V. ii. 4,—

> "———————— she is so idly king'd,
> Her sceptre so fantastically borne
> By a vain, giddy, shallow, humorous youth," &c.

Perhaps *shallow-humorous*, shallow in his humours.

Drayton, Preface to Polyolbion, near the beginning:—"in such a season, when the idle humorous world must hear of nothing that either savours of antiquity, or," &c. *Idle-humorous. Ib.*,—write:—"through delicate-embroidered meadows, often veined with gentle-gliding brooks."

(Milton's Arcades, 41,—

> "What shallow-searching Fame hath left untold.")

Love's Labour 's Lost, ii. 1, probably,—

> "Some merry-mocking lord, belike; is 't so?"

Othello, ii. 1,—

> "putting on the mere form of civil and humane seeming for the better compassing of his salt and most hidden-loose affection."

Much Ado about Nothing, iii. 1,—

> "Then go we near her, that her ear lose nothing
> Of the false-sweet bait that we lay for it."

Titus Andronicus, iii. 1, *qu.*,—

> "O, reverend Tribunes! gentle-aged men!"

(I find that the Var. 1821 has, *gentle-aged-men;* did the emendator suppose that the poet meant *aged gentlemen?*)

King Lear, ii. 2,—

> "These kind of knaves I know, which in this plainness
> Harbour more craft and more corrupter ends
> Than twenty silly-ducking observants."

And so the folio. Perhaps, also, a little below, "You stubborn-ancient knave." Compare "gentle-aged," &c. King Henry VIII. ii. 1,—

> "———————— the last hour
> Of my long-weary life is come upon me."

(In Spenser, Prothalamion, 6, perhaps, "my long-fruitlesse stay.") M.N.D. i. 1 (if, indeed, this be not too obvious),—

> "Thrice blessed they, that master so their blood
> To undergo such maiden pilgrimage:
> But earthlier-happy is the rose distill'd," &c.

i.e. more earthly-happy. 1 King Henry VI. iv. 7,—

> "Here is a silly-stately style indeed!"

3 King Henry VI. ii. 5, Henry's first soliloquy,—

> "Than doth a rich-embroider'd canopy," &c.

6,—

> "Now death shall stop his dismal-threatening sound."

iv. 8,—

> "Cold-biting winter mars our hop'd-for hay."

King Henry VIII. iii. 2,—

> "I know you have a gentle-noble temper,
> A soul as even as a calm:"

ἡσυχογενναῖον, if I may coin a somewhat uncouth compound.

Merchant of Venice, iv. 1,—

> "Thou 'lt show thy mercy and remorse, more strange
> Than is thy strange-apparent cruelty."

Comedy of Errors, iii. 2, I think,—

> "Teach me, dear creature, how to think and speak;
> Lay open to my earthy-gross conceit,
> Smother'd in errors, feeble, shallow, weak,
> The folded meaning of your words' deceit."

K. John, ii. 2, I think,—

"Cry havock, kings! back to the stained field,
You equal-potent, fiery-kindled spirits."

ἰσοκρατεῖς.[6] (I believe I am wrong. L. L. L. v. 2.,—"So *portent-like* will I o'ersway his state, That he shall be my fool, and I his fate." What has *portent* to do here? *Potent-like.*)

King Richard II. iii. 2,—

"Not all the water in the rough-rude sea
Can wash the balm from an anointed king."

(Did Beaumont and Fletcher intend a parody, Noble Gentleman, v. i.? Moxon, vol. ii. p. 279, col. 1,—

"Not all the water in the river Seine
Can wash the blood out of these princely veins.")

Compare Comedy of Errors, v. 1,—

"She never reprehended him but mildly,
When he demean'd himself rough-rude, and wildly."

K. R. II. iii. 4,—

"——————————how dares
Thy harsh-rude tongue sound this unpleasing news?"

---

[6] This is the only passage in which Shakespeare uses *potent* as a substantive. This is suspicious (even though the folio prints the word with a capital), and throws suspicion on the conjecture *potent-like* in L. L. L., which was proposed long ago by Mr. Singer. On the other hand, Shakespeare, I believe, always accents *portent* on the last syllable; this seems fatal to Hanmer's conjecture *portent-like.* The old copies read *perttaunt* and *pertaunt* in L. L. L. Mr. Collier's old Corrector reads *equal potent, fire-ykindled,* in K. John, and *potently* in L. L. L. He probably intended to write *equal-potent.* The prefix *y* is not, I fancy, used seriously in the undoubted plays of Shakespeare. Walker's MS. has *equal-potents,* no doubt a slip of the pen.—*Ed.*

Sonnet xxxii. possibly,—

"These poor-rude lines of thy deceased lover."

Othello, ii. 1, conclusion of Iago's speech, "Lay thy finger," &c.—"A pestilent-complete knave;" see context. Compare "excellent-accomplish'd," above.—*Ib.* Iago's concluding soliloquy,—

"The Moor, howbeit that I endure him not,
Is of a constant, loving, noble nature."

I think Shakespeare wrote *constant-loving;* inasmuch as Othello's nature, with all its aptitude for true, manly affection, could hardly be described as, emphatically, a *loving* nature. Two G. of Verona, iii. 2, near the end,—

"——————————— the night's dead silence
Will well become such sweet-complaining grievance."

iv. 4,—

"I am my master's true-confirmed love."

Julius Cæsar, v. 5,—

"All the conspirators, save only he,
Did what they did in envy of great Cæsar;
He only, in a general-honest thought,
And common good to all, made one of them."

κοινοφελεῖ διανοίᾳ, as Æschylus would say; Eumen, 940, Scholefield.

(*General-honest* occurs in a different sense in Tourneur, Revenger's [*Revengers'?*] Tragedy, i. 1, Dodsley, iv. 290; for here also the hyphen ought to be inserted,—

"A rape! why, 'tis the very core of lust,
Double adultery.
Junior. So, sir.
Second Judge. And, which was worse,
Committed on the lord Antonio's wife,
That general-honest lady."

Generally honoured; see a little below,—

"That lady's fame has spread such a fair wing
Over all Italy," &c.)

All's Well that Ends Well, i. 1,—

"—————————— a world
Of pretty fond-adoptious christendoms,
That blinking Cupid gossips."

i.e., bestowed through fondness. See context. (Note M. W. of W. ii. 2, near the end:—"I shall not only receive this villainous wrong, but stand under the adoption of abominable terms, and by him that does me this wrong.")

Titus Andronicus, i. 2,—

"Dead, if you will, but not to be his wife,
That is another's lawful-promis'd love."

ii. 4,—

"O brother help me with thy fainting hand
. . . .
Out of this fell-devouring receptacle."

v. 2,—

"———— ———— we worldly men
Have miserable mad-mistaking eyes."

i.e., mistaking through madness.

v. 3,—

"—————— as erst our ancestor,
When with his solemn tongue he did discourse
To love-sick Dido's sad-attending ear
The story of that baleful-burning night,
When subtle Greeks surpris'd King Priam's Troy."

Ib.,—

"To be adjudg'd some direful-slaughtering death."

Cymbeline, iii. 5, perhaps,—

> "Come hither; ah, you precious pandar-villain!
> Where is thy lady?"

The reading in the edition of 1821, which seems more probable, is,—

> "——— ah you precious pandar! Villain,
> Where is thy lady?"

Not, at any rate, "pandar, villain." Timon of Athens, iv. 3,—

> "Is not thy kindness subtle-covetous?"

v. 2,—

> "——————————— they confess
> Toward thee forgetfulness too general-gross."

vulg. "general, gross;" fol. "general gross."
Sonnet xliii.,—"Thy fair-imperfect shade;" see context.
3 King Henry VI. v. 1,—

> "———Why, trow'st thou, Warwick,
> That Clarence is so harsh, so blunt-unnatural,
> To bend the fatal instruments of war
> Against his brother, and his lawful king?"

But this I somewhat doubt. 1 King Henry IV. v. 2, *init.* I think,—

> "O, no, my nephew must not know, Sir Richard,
> The liberal-kind offer of the king."

Venus and Adonis, St. clxxx.,—

> "The flowers are sweet, their colours fresh and trim,
> But true-sweet beauty liv'd and died with him."

And so Moxon has printed it. So *true-confirmed*, above.

(Ford, Love's Sacrifice, iii. 2.—Moxon, p. 88, col. 1,—

> "Then let me cast myself beneath thy feet,
> True, virtuous lord." Read *true-virtuous*.)

Two Gentlemen of Verona, i. 2,—

"Please you repeat their names, I'll show my mind,
According to my shallow-simple skill."

Compare *rough-rude*, *wholesome-profitable*, *savage-wild*, (Romeo and Juliet, v. 3.) And so, I think, in Nash and Marlowe's Dido, ii. (Dyce, vol. ii. p. 389.)

"Yet he undaunted took his father's flag,
And dipt it in the old king's chill-cold blood."

Measure for Measure, iii. 2. I suspect: "It was a mad-fantastical trick of him to steal from the state," &c. Compare *high-fantastical*, Twelfth Night, near the beginning; and the like. King John, iii. 1,—

"Then arm thy constant and thy nobler parts
Against these giddy-loose suggestions."

King Richard III. i. 3,—

"How now, my hardy stout-resolved mates,
Are you now going to dispatch this thing?"

Shakespeare very rarely strings together three epithets without an *and*. King Richard II. iv. 1,—

"*North.* My lord,—
K. Rich. No lord of thine, thou haught-insulting man," &c.

Vulg. *haught, insulting.* And so Knight, in spite of his fidelity to the folio, which here inserts the hyphen. 1 King Henry VI. i. 2,—

"Now am I like that proud-insulting ship,
Which Cæsar and his fortune bare at once."

In Merchant of Venice, ii. 8,—

"I never heard a passion so confus'd,
So strange, outrageous, and so variable
As the dog Jew did utter in the streets;"

read undoubtedly *strange-outrageous*; οὕτως ἀτόπως ἔκθυμον. The awkwardness in the common reading is the same as in Julius Cæsar, i. 3, "Most bloody-fiery, and most terrible," above quoted. Taming of the Shrew, iv. 3,—" A gown—with a small compassed cape." Read *small-compassed;* see Stubbs ap. Var. Shak. *in loc.* Twelfth Night, v. 1, I think,—

"If nothing lets to make us happy both,
But this my masculine-usurp'd attire."

A contorted phrase, perhaps, but Shakespearian.
King Richard II. ii. 1,—

"Whose manners still our tardy apish nation
Limps after in base imitation."

Qu., tardy-apish; tardy in mimicry: limping in its very imitation. 1 K. H. VI. v. 4, near the beginning, read,—

"Must I behold thy timeless-cruel death?"

2 K. H. VI. iii. 2,—

"The pretty-vaulting sea refused to drown me."

King Richard III. iii. 5, perhaps,—

"——— his apparent-open guilt omitted."

Timon of Athens iv. 3, *init.*,—

"O blessed-breeding sun!"

ὀλβιότροφε. Cymbeline, iii. 4,—

"True-honest men being heard, like false Æneas,
Were in his time thought false."

Ib. perhaps,—

"————— nor no more ado
With that harsh, noble-simple, [ ] nothing,
That Cloten," &c.

But I suspect that Shakespeare wrote,—

"With that harsh, noble, simple, nothing, Cloten,[7]
That Cloten," &c.;

[7] So Capell and Steevens. The Old Corrector inserts *empty* before *nothing.—Ed.*

the final word of the line having dropt out, by a not very unfrequent accident. 'Επέχω. 1 K. H. VI. iii. 1, l. 1,—

"Com'st thou with deep-premeditated lines," &c.

Passionate Pilgrim, xvi. St. vi.,—

"Serve always with assured trust,
And in thy suit be humble-true."

Venus and Adonis, St. cxi.,—

"The picture of an angry-chafed boar."

Tarquin and Lucrece, St. xxii.,—

"So that, in vent'ring ill, we leave to be
The things we are for that which we expect;
And this ambitious-foul infirmity,
In having much, torments us with defect
Of that we have."

St. cxxxiii., "injurious-shifting Time." cclix., "silly-jeering idiots." Cymbeline, v. 5,—

"———— never master had
A page so kind, so duteous-diligent,
So tender over his occasions, true,
So feat, so nurse-like."

2 King Henry VI. iv. 1,—

"And now the house of York—thrust from the crown
By shameful murder of a guiltless king,
And lofty proud-encroaching tyranny—
Burns with revenging fire."

King John, ii. 2,—

"Commodity, the bias of the world;
The world, who of itself is peised well,
Made to run even, upon even ground;
Till this advantage, this vile-drawing bias,
This sway of motion, this commodity,
Makes it take head," &c.

Ib. perhaps,—

"He is the half part of a blessed man,

———————————

And she a fair-divided excellence," &c. no

iii. 3, *qu.* (and so Monk Mason conjectures),—

"Then, in despite of brooded-watchful day, no
I would into thy bosom pour my thoughts."

Measure for Measure, iii. 1, I believe,—

"This sensible-warm motion to become no
A kneaded clod."

sensibly warm. Hamlet, v. 2,—

"'Tis dangerous when the baser nature comes
Between the pass and fell-incensed points
Of mighty opposites."

(The thought reminds me of Paradise Lost, vi. 307,—

"——— from each side with speed retir'd,
Where erst was thickest fight, th' angelic throng,
And left large field, unsafe within the wind
Of such commotion."

A friend compares Claudian, de Bello Getico, 391,—

"————— graviterque tulere
[Patres Romani],
Urbibus inter se claris de culmine verum
Congressis, aliquid gentes audere minores,
. . . . . . fususque Philippus,
Vilia dum gravibus populis interserit arma,
Prætereunte manu, didicit non esse potentum
Tentandas, mediis quamvis in luctibus, iras.")

Sonnet lxxxii. see context,—

"Thou truly fair wert truly sympathiz'd
In true-plain words by thy true-telling friend."

Tarquin and Lucrece, St. vii.,—

"O rash-false heat, wrapt in repentant cold."

Sonnet cxxvi.,—

"O thou, my lovely boy, who in thy power
Dost hold Time's fickle glass, his sickle, hour;"

write *his sickle-hour;* his hour represented poetically as a sickle. cxxvii., perhaps, "art's false-borrow'd face." cxxxi., "my dear-doting heart." cxxxvii., "things right-true," as I suspect from the context. cxlvii., I think, "th' uncertain-sickly appetite." cliii. surely, "a dateless-lively heat," calorem in æternum vivacem.—(Chapman, *Il.* xx. vol. ii. p. 161, ed. Taylor, Æneas is to be saved "lest the progeny of Dardanus take *date,*" *i.e. end.*) Tarquin and Lucrece, St. iii.,—

"Reckoning his fortune at such high-proud rate."

xcvii., "blind-concealing night." ccxxxix., "the violent-roaring tide." Sonnet lxxxvi. perhaps, "that affable-familiar ghost." Sonnet cxxi.,—

"'Tis better to be vile than vile-esteem'd;"

and so I find Malone quotes it in a note on 1 K. H. VI. i. 4, Var. 1821, vol. xviii. p. 37. Sonnet xxxi.,—

"How many a holy and obsequious tear
Hath dear-religious love stolen from mine eye
As interest of the dead," &c.

i.e., making a religion of its affections. Compare the Lover's Complaint, St. xxxvi.,—

"The accident, which brought me to her eye,
Upon the moment did her force subdue,
And now she would the caged cloister fly:
Religious love put out religion's eye."

Much Ado about Nothing, iv. 1,—

"————————— The wide sea
Hath drops too few to wash her clean again,
And salt too little, that may season give
To her foul-tainted flesh!"

And so read, Tarquin and Lucrece, St. cxlvii.,—

> "The remedy indeed to do me good,
> Is to let forth my foul-defiled blood."

K. Richard III. iv. 4, near the beginning,—

> "A dire induction am I witness to,
> And will to France, hoping the consequence
> Will prove as bitter-black and tragical."

Of this, however, I am doubtful. Two Noble Kinsmen, v. 2 [Dyce, v. 1]; if this scene be Shakespeare's, we should read, I conjecture, near the end—otherwise the line, like that from T. Andr. v. 3, below, seems unnaturally slow,—

> "———— lover never yet made sigh
> Truer than I. O, then, most soft-sweet goddess,
> Give me the victory," &c.

And a few lines below,—

> "Mine innocent-true heart."

5 [Dyce, 3], write,—

> "———— Palamon
> Hath the best-boding chance." [So Knight and Dyce.—*Ed.*]

T. of the Shrew, Induction, 1,—

> "With soft low tongue and lowly courtesy."

(*soft-slow ?*) iv. 3,—

> "Well, come, my Kate; we will unto your father's
> Even in these honest mean habiliments."

Shakespeare's manner, I think, requires *honest-mean*. 4, "and some sufficient-honest witnesses." Winter's Tale, ii. 3,—

> "Look to your babe, my lord; 'tis your's: Jove send her
> A better-guiding spirit!"

Romeo and Juliet, i. 2,—

"——— within her scope of choice
Lies my consent and fair-according voice.
This night I hold an old-accustom'd feast."

1 King Henry IV. i. 1,—

"Upon whose dead corps[8] there was such misuse,
Such beastly, shameless transformation
By those Welshwomen done," &c.

Beastly-shameless, I think. Titus Andronicus, v. 3, towards the end of the play,—

"O, take this warm kiss on thy pale cold lips."

Does not one's ear positively demand *pale-cold?*

Macbeth, v. 3,—

"And with some sweet oblivious antidote," &c.

Sweet-oblivious, I think. Sonnet cxxi.,—

"For why should others' false adulterate eyes
Give salutation to my sportive blood?"

False-adulterate, I think. Lover's Complaint, St. xxv.,—

"And bastards of his foul adulterate heart."

Qu., *foul-adulterate;* as *foul-tainted*, *foul-defiled*, above.

1 King Henry VI. ii. 5,—

"——— as, in his haughty great attempt,
They laboured to plant the rightful heir."

Haughty-great. Hamlet, ii. 2, "this brave-o'erhanging firmament." (By the way, the folio's omission of *firmament* probably originated in the similar commencements, *firmament*, *fretted*.) Tempest, iii. 3,—

"Their manners are more gentle, kind, than of
Our human generation you shall find
Many, nay almost any."

---

[8] See S. V. art. li. Walker, however, if I recollect right, does not quote this example in that article.—*Ed.*

Gentle-kind, as, above, *heavy-thick*, *honest-true*, *wholesome-profitable*, *savage-wild*, R. and J. v. 3,—

"The time and my intents are savage-wild;"

(where I have seen *savage, wild*, even in a modern edition; [9]) and the like. Two Gentlemen of Verona, ii. 4,—

"—————————— love,
Whose [10] high-imperious thoughts have punish'd me, &c."

At least, so I think. 1 K. H. VI. iv. 7, near the end,—

"He speaks with such a proud-commanding spirit."

As *great-commanding*, p. 25; *proud-encroaching*, p. 34; *haught-insulting*, p. 32, &c. Midsummer Night's Dream, towards the end,—

"This palpable-gross play hath well beguil'd
The heavy gait of night."

As "*sensible-warm* motion," p. 35. 2 K. H. VI. iii. near the end,—

"O, beat away the busy-meddling fiend," &c.

The following may be noticed under this head. K. H. V. v. 2, "thy speaking of my tongue, and I thine, most *truly falsely*, must needs be granted to be much at one." Write *truly-falsely*. Compare Much Ado &c., ii. 1, "You could never do him so ill-well, unless you were the very man." Two Gentlemen of Verona, i. 2, towards the end,—

"————— that some whirlwind bear
Unto a ragged, fearful hanging rock."

---

[9] So quarto 1597, Pope, Theobald, Hanmer, Capel, and Collier. Var. 1821, and Knight, insert the hyphen. Quarto 1609, fols., Rowe, and received text, have neither stop nor hyphen. I trust Steevens's reprint for the quartos.—*Ed.*

[10] The context *imperiously* commands us to read *Those* with Johnson. Malone's note, except the first line, is perfectly true, but nothing to the purpose. Mr. Staunton confirms Johnson's conjecture, while he opposes it.—*Ed.*

I think, *fearful-hanging*. K. John, iv. 2, near the end,—

> "—————— my rage was blind,
> And foul imaginary eyes of blood
> Presented thee more hideous than thou art."

Foul-imaginary. (*Presented, i.e., represented.*) v. 7, early in the scene, perhaps,—

> "I am the cygnet to this pale-faint swan."

1 King Henry VI. ii. 4, perhaps,—

> "—————— without all colour
> Of base-insinuating flattery."

2 King Henry VI. iii. 1, write,—

> "A breach that craves a quick-expedient stop."

The same corruption has taken place in many other passages of our old writers. Sidney, Defence of Poesie, ed. 1638,[11] p. 557: "—— though I yield that poesy may not only be abused, but that, being abused, by the reason of his sweet charming force it can do more hurt than any other army [*array*] of words," &c.: *sweet-charming;* exercising a pleasing, not a violent, magic; and so in Tourneur, Atheist's Tragedy, Retrospective, vol. vii. p. 346, write,—

> "—————— an elegant and moving speech,
> Composed of many sweet-persuasive points."

(By the way, in Astrophel and Stella, Sonnet xcix. l. 3,—

> "To lay his then mark, wanting shafts of sight,"

for *mark, wanting*, read *mark-wanting*. Epitaph on Sir

---

[11] This is the ninth edition of the work. Walker elsewhere almost invariably quotes Sidney from a folio belonging to Mr. Derwent Coleridge, which is defective in the title-page, but which, Mr. Dyce has kindly informed me, is a copy of the second edition. This latter volume has Walker's corrections in the margin throughout.—*Ed.*

John Mandeville the traveller, Retrosp. vol. iii. p. 280,—

> "All ye that passe by, on this pillar cast eye,
> This epitaph read if you can:
> 'Twill tell you a tombe once stood in this roome
> Of a brave spirited man:"

brave-spirited; spirited is a mere modernism. Marston, Play of the Malcontent, i. 2, Dyce's Webster, vol. iv. p. 39,—

> "Ferneze, thou art the duchess' favourite,
> Be faithful, private; but 'tis dangerous."

Faithful-private, I imagine; were it in Shakespeare, I should have no doubt. v. 2, Dyce's Webster, vol. iv. p. 122, read, "You were too *boisterous-spleeny*." Webster, White Devil, Dyce, vol. i. p. 50, I imagine, "my strong-commanding art." Ford, Fancies Chaste and Noble, ii. 1, near the beginning, Moxon, p. 127, col. 2,—

> "When we were common, mortal, and a subject,
> As other creatures of Heaven's making are," &c.

Common-mortal. Fame's Memorial, Gifford's ed. vol. ii. p. 601, read, "*just-deserved* praise," and 607, *new-fantastic.* Glapthorne, Albertus Wallenstein, iii. 3,—

> "—————— I love her virtue,
> And have in that as noble, rich a dowry,
> As the addition of estate and blood
> Which you 've acquir'd."

Noble-rich. Middleton, Witch, iii. 1, Dyce, vol. iii. p. 290,—

> "—— —————— for I purpose
> To call this subtle, sinful snare of mine
> An act of force from thee."

Surely *subtle-sinful.* Crashawe, Music's Duel, l. 21, read,—

> "—————————— straightway she
> Carves out her dainty voice as readily
> Into a thousand *sweet-distinguish'd* tones."

And so write in a parallel passage from a song of Carew's,—

"Ask me no more, whither doth haste
The nightingale, when May is past,
For in your *sweet-dividing* throat
She winters and keeps warm her note;"

γλυκύνομος. And in Titus Andronicus, iii. 1, Lavinia's tongue,—

"Is torn from forth that pretty hollow cage,
Where, like a sweet melodious bird, it sung
Sweet-varied notes, enchanting every ear."

So write; so also, Heywood, Robert Earl of Huntingdon, Lamb, vol. ii. p. 254, ed. 1835,—

"The winged quiristers, with divers notes
Sent from their *quaint-recording* pretty throats," &c.

Carew, on the Death of the Duke of Buckingham, Clarke, lxi. p. 80 (the second poem),—

"Safe in the circle of his friends,
Safe in his loyal heart, and ends;
Safe in his native valiant spirit;
By favour safe, and safe by merit," &c.;

native-valiant. Beaumont and Fletcher, Maid's Tragedy, v. 2,—

"——— Thou art a shameless villain;
A thing out of the overcharge of nature
Sent, like a thick cloud, to disperse a plague
Upon weak catching women."

Weak-catching; i.e., easily catching. King and No King, iii. 3, early in the scene, read, "*secret-scorching* fires," if the correction is not too obvious to need pointing out. Scornful Lady, v. 1,—

"——————— Credit me,
We have been both abus'd; not by ourselves,
But by that wilful, scornful piece of hatred,
That much-forgetful lady."

Read, I imagine, *wilful-scornful;* scornful deliberately, and of fore-purpose. Two Noble Kinsmen, iii. 6, Knight's Pictorial Shakespeare, "Doubtful Plays," p. 150, col. 1, write,—

> "What ignorant and *mad-malicious* traitors
> Are you," &c.

Beaumont and Fletcher, Pilgrim, v. 4,—

> "Be constant, good."

Constant-good; persevering in goodness. A little below, I think, "*honest-noble* showers;" and sc. 6,—

> "You had a waiting-woman, one Juletta,
> A pretty desperate thing."

Pretty-desperate. Daniel, Civil Wars, B. ii. St. lxvi. (in the edition of 1623, lxvii.),—

> "——— Isabel, the young afflicted queen,"

I half suspect—but I know not whether it is more than a fancy, "as many fancies there be"—that Daniel wrote *young-afflicted*, after Hom. Odyss. xi. 39,—

> παρθενικαί τ' ἀταλαί, νεοπενθέα θυμὸν ἔχουσαι.

(Not that this was Homer's meaning.)

In Donne, Satire iii. ed. 1633, p. 334,—

> "Graius stays still at home here, and because
> Some preachers, *vile ambitious* bawds, and laws
> Still new like fashions, bids [*bid*] him think that she
> [*i.e.*, that that religion]
> Which dwells with us, is only perfect, he
> Embraceth her," &c.

I had once corrected *vile-ambitious;* but I doubt not it is an erratum for "vile *ambition's* bawds." Shirley and Chapman, Chabot, i. 2, Gifford and Dyce's Shirley, vol. vi. p. 99, l. 3,—

> "——— I beseech you nourish better thoughts,
> Than to imagine that the king's mere grace

Sustains such prejudice by those it honours; [,]
That of necessity we must pervert it
With passionate enemies, and ambitious boundless
Avarice, and every licence," &c.

I think,—"and *ambitions* boundless, Avarice, and," &c. Jonson, Fox, i. 1, Gifford, vol. iii. p. 172,—

"Tear forth the fathers of poor families
Out of their beds, and coffin them alive
In some *kind-clasping* prison."

First Part of Sir John Oldcastle, iv. 3,—

"Do not thou, with thy *kind-respective* tears
Torment thy husband's heart, that bleeds for thee," &c.

i.e., expressive of that regard which springs from natural affection; *respect* in our old writers signifying *regard*, and *kind* being *natural, affectionate.* By the way, in Chapman and Shirley's Play, Chabot, Admiral of France, iii. 2, Gifford and Dyce's Shirley, vol. vi. p. 127,—"yet, notwithstanding all these injustices, this unmatchable, unjust delinquent affecteth to be thought inculpable, and incomparable just;"—we ought evidently to read "unmatchable—(*i.e.*—*bly*) unjust," as below "incomparable-just." So *excellent-white, pestilent-complete*, above. Play of Lust's Dominion, Old English Plays, vol. i. p. 113.

"For base lust of a loathed concubine.
Eleaz. Ha! concubine! who does Prince Philip mean?
Phil. (*To Eleaz.*) Thy wife.—(*To Alv.*) Thy daughter,—base aspiring lords;
Who to buy honour are content to sell
Your names to infamy, your souls to hell."

Base-aspiring. Fletcher, Faithful Shepherdess, v. 3,—

"And like a glorious desperate man, who buys
A poison of much price, by which he dies," &c.

Glorious-desperate; glorious (*ut sæpe*) in the sense of *gloriosus;* ostentatious and costly in his suicide.

Beaumont and Fletcher, Faithful Friends, i. 3, towards the end of the act, write,—

> "———————— in whose each part reigns a world
> Of *strange-attractive* pleasures."

iii. 1, write,—

> "——————— he 's a white-cheek'd boy,
> Whose fearful soul a soldier's frown would fright
> From his *fine-mettled* breast." [So Dyce.—*Ed.*]

Knight of Malta, v. 1,—

> "————————— and can you be
> So cruel, thankless, to destroy his youth
> That sav'd your honour," &c.

Cruel-thankless; see context.

King and No King, ii. 1, I think,—

> "————— I have found in all thy words
> A *strange-disjointed* sorrow."

v. 2, near the end, "a *new-strong* constancy;" if this is not too obvious for notice. Massinger, Bondman, iv. 3, write,—

> "————————— teach your tongue,
> In the first *sweet-articulate* sound it utters,
> To sign my wish'd-for pardon."

L. Digges, Lines prefixed to the folio Shakespeare,—

> "Or till I hear a scene more nobly take
> Than when thy half-sword parleying Romans spake."

Half-sword-parleying, if this correction has not been made already. Chapman, Widow's Tears, v. 1, Dodsley, vol. vi. p. 186,—

> "Do not with *vain-affrighting* conscience
> Betray a life," &c.

Jonson, Elegy, Underwoods lxix. Gifford, vol. viii. p. 409,—

> "No, mistress, no, the *open-merry* man
> Moves like a sprightly river;"

at least so I think; opposed to the man who keeps his mirth to himself. See context. Fairfax's Tasso, B. iii. St. lvi.,—

> "The town is stor'd of troughs and cisterns, made
> To keep fresh water, but the country seems
> Devoid of grass, unfit for ploughmen's trade,
> Not fertile, moist with rivers, wells, and streams."

Perhaps Fairfax wrote *fertile-moist*.[12] B. ix. St. vi. read,—

> "And with huge sums of *false-enticing* gold
> Th' Arabian thieves he sent him forth to hire."

And so B. x. St. lxv.—B. xvi. St. xvii.—In B. xv. St. lix. write,—

> "The nymphs applied their sweet-alluring arts."

B. xix. St. xci.,—

> "And from her lips the words slow, trembling came;"

slow-trembling. Herrick, ed. Clarke, xiii. vol. ii. p. 38,—

> "See here a maukin; there a sheet
> As spotless, pure, as it is neat."

spotless-pure. Lodge, Wounds of Civil War, iii. Dodsley, vol. viii. p. 36, write,—

> "O *false-ambitious* pride in young and old!"

v. p. 80,—

> "Such chances wait upon uncertain fate,
> That where she kisseth once, she quelleth twice;
> Then whoso lives content is happy, wise."

Happy-wise; wise to happiness. (For *quelleth* we should read, I imagine, *killeth*. *Quelleth*, I believe, is sometimes

---

[12] This seems supported by the original,—

> "E di fontane sterile e di rivi."—*Ed.*

used in this sense; so that the one word might easily be written, through an oversight, for the other.) Anonymous Lines addressed to W. Browne, Clarke's Browne, vol. i. p. 19, l. 4,—

"Lest secret, rocky envy, or the source
[wrong; *force*, I imagine.]
Of frothy, but sky-tow'ring arrogance;
Or fleeting, sandy vulgar-censure chance
[*dele* hyphen and comma.]
To leave him shipwreck'd," &c.

We should read *secret-rocky*, and, I think, *fleeting-sandy*. Spenser, Faerie Queen, i. v. xviii., "a *cruell-craftie* crocodile," I imagine. *Ib*. xi. xlix. write,—

"By this the drouping Day-light gan to fade,
And yield his rowme to *sad-succeeding* Night."

xii. xxix., "these *bitter-byting* wordes." ii. iii. xxxi., "*sad-afflicted* Troy." iii. i. lvi., "the *false-instilled* fire." lviii., "her *soft-fetherd* nest." ii. xvii., "her *first-engraffed* payne." iii. xxii., "*big-embodied* [*i.e. big-bodied*] branches." xi. xlv., "the *sweet-consuming* woe." iv. ii. xxxiv., "O most *sacred-happie* spirit." Fairfax, xvi. xxxiv.,—

"This said, the noble infant stood a space
Confused, speechless, senseless, *ill, ashamed;*"

see the lines following; *ill-ashamed;* the old distinction between a good and an evil shame, somewhat differently applied. xiv. vi., "*glorious-shining*." xv. ix., "a *gentle-breathing* air." xi. ix., "*shrift-fathers*." xiii. xlviii., "monsters *foul-misshap'd*." x. lviii., "the *sly-enticing* maid." lxv., "*false-enticing* smiles." Jonson, Every Man in his Humour, ii. 1,—

"———— his course is so irregular,
So loose, affected, and depriv'd of grace," &c.

Loose-affected; licentiously inclin'd. *Ib.*,—

"But rather use the soft persuading way."

Soft-persuading. Chapman, *Il.* ix. Taylor, vol. i. p. 204, l. 22, perhaps,—

"And my life never shall be hir'd with *thankless-desperate* prayers."

xv. vol. ii. p. 60,—

"This said, he hasted to his tent: left there his shafts and bow,
And then his double, double shield did on his shoulders throw," &c.

Papæ! *double-double, i.e. twice double*, or fourfold; v. 479,—

αὐταρ ὅγ' ἀμφ' ὤμοισι σάκος θέτο τετραθέλυμνον.

P. 64, "his *unhappy-hasty* foot." xvi. p. 85,—

"Now, brethren, be it dear to you to fight and succour us,
As ever heretofore ye did, with men first excellent."

Meaning *first-excellent;* for Chapman evidently understands the passage as if it stood (v. 556),—

Αἴαντε, νῦν σφῶϊν ἀμύνεσθαι φίλον εστω,
οἷοί περ πάρος ἦτε, μετ' ἀνδρασιν οἳ καὶ αρείους·

although this would require μετ' ἀνδρῶν. xxi. l. 1, p. 168,

"And now they reach'd the goodly swelling channel of the flood," &c.

goodly-swelling,—

ἀλλ' ὅτε δὴ πόδον ἷξον εὐρρεῖος ποταμοῖο, &c.

Marmyon, Antiquary, iii. 1 (it ought to be 4), Dodsley, vol. x. p. 55,—"A *shrewd-convincing* argument!" · Fairfax, xiv. lxxv.,—"those[13] *deadly-wicked* streams." Carew,

[13] The elegant, and generally most correct edition of 1817 omits *those* by an error of the press, and consequently gives us one of those limping lines, which some editors of Shakespeare admire.—*Ed.*

ed. Clarke, x. *init.* p. 28,—" thou *gentle-whispering* wind." xli. p. 62,—at least so I think,—

> " ——————— and makes the *wild-*
> *Incensed* boar and panther mild."

lxviii. p. 88, l. 1, " thy *just-chastising* hand."
lxxi. p. 95,—

> " In motion, active grace, in rest, a *calm-*
> *Attractive* sweetness, brought both wound and balm
> To every breast ;"

construe,—" active grace in motion, a *calm-* (*i.e. calmly-*) *attractive* sweetness in rest, brought," &c. lxiii. p. 83,— "the *close-shameless* prostitute ;" *secretly shameless.* lviii. l. 3, p. 76, *qu.*, " *musical-sweet* tones." lxxiii. p. 103, perhaps,—

> " Breathing, from her celestial organ, *sweet-*
> *Harmonious* notes."

Fairfax, viii. xxviii., " with *broad-outstretched* hand." Sidney, Arcadia, B. i. p. 33, l. 36, *old-growing, senescentis.* P. 82, l. 28, " *old-aged* oak ;" and Defence of Poesy, p. 497, l. ult., " *Old-aged* experience goeth beyond the *fine-witted* philosopher." B. ii. p. 100, l. 3, " a *brave-counterfeited* scorn." B. iii. p. 282, l. 42, perhaps, " *humble-smiling* reverence." B. v. p. 441, l. 10, " these so *great-important* matters ;" *i.q., so greatly importing.* Defence of Poesy, 515, penult., "a *wry-transformed* traveller," I think. Astrophel and Stella, viii. 521, " his *fine-pointed* dart." xlviii. 535, " thy *sweet-cruel* shot." lxxx., " *Sweet-smelling* lip." lxxxv. perhaps, " whose *weak-confused* brain." cvi., " *False-flattering* hope." (There is no tautology here, as *flatter* was frequently used in a sense somewhat different from its present.) Chapman and Shirley, Chabot, i. 1, Giffard and Dyce, vol. vi. p. 96,—

> "I, seeking this way to confirm myself,
> I undermine the columns that support
> My hopeful, glorious fortune, and at once
> Provoke the tempest, though did drown my envy."

Hopeful-glorious, i.e., hopeful of glory. (Lines 1 and 4 are corrupt; for *I, qu., If;* though this would require further alteration:[14] in l. 4, perhaps, "the tempest *that shall* drown.") Shirley, Lines to the Countess of Ormond, p. 432, "*witty-thriving* garbs," *i.e., prospering through ingenuity.* Chapman, Dedication of his Iliad to Prince Henry, 4th page (not numbered), l. 4, perhaps,—

> "So Truth, with Poesy grac'd, is fairer far,
> More *proper-moving*, chaste, and regular,
> Than when she runs away with untruss'd prose."

Chapman, Iliad, xix. old ed. p. 273,—

> "I (wretched dame) departing hence enforc'd, and dying sad."

Dying-sad; sad even unto death. W. Rowley, A Match at Midnight, Dodsley, vol. vii. p. 339, write,—

> "——— Oh how your talking eyes,
> Those *active-sparkling*, *sweet-discoursing* twins,
> In their *strong-captivating* motion told me
> The story of your heart!"

Harrington, Preface to Ariosto, 8th page:—"—— following their *foolish-ambitious* humours ——." Notes subjoined to B. iv. p. 30, "—— that *pretty-fantastic* verse of Ovid ——." viii. xv., "—— the sage and *friendly-wary* dame."

---

[14] Perhaps a line has been omitted, as, "To pause ere I consent; ill should I thrive, If, seeking this way," &c.—*Ed.*

Milton, Ode upon the Circumcision, l. 3,—

> "First heard by happy watchful shepherds' ear;"

happy-watchful, as *unhappy-hasty*, Chapman, above; (*happy-wise*, Lodge, p. 46, is not perhaps exactly parallel.) Another Shakespeare-like compound occurs in the Poem On the Death of a fair Infant, St. iii. "his *cold-kind* embrace." Many compound epithets are scattered through Milton's early poems; some which, although they are printed without the hyphen, are too obvious to need pointing out; *e.g.*, Vacation Exercise, 2, my *first-endeavouring* tongue;" 33, "the *deep-transported* mind;" On the Death, &c., St. v., "a *low-delved* tomb;" and others, which, for want of the hyphen, are either actually misunderstood, or liable to be so; as On the Death, &c., St. xi.,—

> "Her *false-imagin'd* loss cease to lament."

Vacation Exercise, 98, "*ancient-hallow'd* Dee," ἀρχαιόσεμνος. 100, "*royal-towred* Thame," (not *tower'd;* and so write L'Allegro, 117.) L'Allegro, 34, as I suspect, "the *light-fantastic* toe;" and so in the Masque, 144, "a *light-fantastic* round;" analogous to Shakespeare's *high-fantastical*, T. N. i. 1; *mad-fantastical*, M. for M. iii. 2, and the like. (I quote the Masque by this title, because in the editions of Milton's minor poems which were printed during his lifetime it is simply entitled "A Mask presented at Ludlow Castle," &c. The title *Comus* belongs properly to the poem as altered by Dr. Dalton for the purpose of musical representation.) Il Penseroso, 1, I suspect, "*vain-deluding* joys." 155, "the *high-embowed* roof." And so it is quoted in Sir Egerton Bridges's Life of Milton, and in James Montgomery's Introduction to

Tilt's illustrated edition of Milton, 1843; though in the text of this edition itself it is *high-embowered*, I suppose from an error of the press. (*Embowed*, by the way, is not a different form of *to bow*, but signifies *arched*, *to embow* being formed immediately from *bow*, *curvatura*. Drayton, Muses' Elysium, iii. ed. 1630, p. 35, where Erato is addressed as the patroness of mathematics,—

> "Then, Erato, wise Muse, on thee we call,
> In lines to us that dost demonstrate all,
> Which neatly, *with thy staff and bow*,
> Dost measure and proportion show;"

i.e., *with straight and curved instruments*. *Bough*, by the way, is not unfrequently written *bow* in the Elizabethan writers; *e.g.*, Arcadia, B. iii. p. 374, l. 34, "and thereunder a bower was made of *bowes*;" if not even in Dryden's time. Bacon in his Essay of Building speaks of *embowed windows*, *i.e.*, *oriels*. Harrington's Ariosto, xxxii. xciii.,—

> "Eu'n as we see the sunne obscurd somtime,
> By sudden rising of a mistie clowd,
> Engendred by the vapor breeding [*vapor-breeding*] slime,
> And in the middle region then embowd."

Marginal note:—"For when the vapors ascend as hie as the middle region, straight they grow to haue a great concauitie in them, which makes the wind beare them up," &c. So I think we should understand Spenser, F. Q. iv. xi. xxvi.; otherwise *stooping with bowed back* looks tautological,—

> "And eke he somewhat seemd to stoupe afore
> With bowed backe, by reason of the lode,
> And auncient heavie burden which he bore
> Of that faire citie," &c.

The construction is, *with back bowed by reason of*, &c. Visions of the World's Vanitie, ii.,—

"I saw a bull, as white as driuen snow,
With gilded horns embowed like the moon."

Bowed, in the Masque, 1015,—

"Where the bow'd welkin slow doth bend,"

is another form of *embow'd*.) To return to the subject of compound words, I think, I should write in Drayton's David and Goliah, p. 195, ed. 1630,—

"His [Goliah's] voice was hoarse and hollow, yet so strong
As when you hear the murmuring of a throng
In some *vast-arched* hall."

Masque, 113, "their *nightly-watchful* spheres."
212,—

"————————— attended
By a *strong-siding* champion, Conscience."

321, *sensu postulante*,—

"————— Shepherd, I take thy word,
And trust thy honest-offer'd courtesy."

375,—

"————————— Wisdom's self
Oft seeks to sweet-retired Solitude."

403, I believe, "this *wild-surrounding* waste." 556, "a steam of *rich-distill'd* perfumes." 882, "her *soft-alluring* locks."

1005,—

"Holds his dear Psyche *sweet-entranc'd*."

Lycidas, 139,—

"Throw hither all your *quaint-enamell'd* eyes."

Later Poems. Sonnet xxiii. 1, "my *late-espoused* saint;" if this be not too obvious for notice. (*Ib.* 4, it would be better to print *Death* with a capital, the allusion being evidently to the personified Θάνατος of the Alcestis; and so Dyce has printed it in his Specimens of English Sonnets.)

P. L. vi. 220, perhaps,—

"Millions of *fierce-encountring* Angels fought."

389,—

"Chariot and charioteer lay overturn'd,
And fiery foaming steeds."

(For *charioteer* write *charioter;* see S. V. p, 225.) Should we not write *fiery-foaming*, spumantes ignem? Claudian. de Cons. Olyb. et Prob. 4,—

"Blandius elato surgant temone jugales,
Efflantes roseum frænis spumantibus ignem."

(I do not mean to speak of these as misprints in the early editions of Milton; but simply to observe, that compound epithets appear to me to have been intended, which are not always indicated by a hyphen.)

ix. 351,—

"But God left free the will, for what obeys
Reason, is free, and reason he made right,
But bid her beware [*be ware*], and still erect,
Lest by some fair appearing good surpriz'd
She dictate false, and misinform the will," &c.

Fair-appearing.[15]

---

[15] The first and second editions have *beware* and *fair appearing*. Todd properly writes *be ware* and *fair-appearing*. Some other modern editions vary in the writing.—*Ed.*

Compound epithets are not unknown in Chaucer, Clerkes Tale, v. 8918,—

> "She mighte not adversite endure,
> As coude a *poure-fostred* creature."

Knightes Tale, v. 2550,—

> "Ne no man shal unto his felaw ride,
> But o course, with a ***sharpe-ygrounden*** spere."

Ib. v. 2029, (ὡς ἔμοιγε δοκει·)—

> "And all above depeinted in a tour
> Saw I conquest, sitting in great honour
> With thilke sharpe swerd over his hed
> Yhanging by a *subtil-twined* thred."

Fletcher, &c., Love's Pilgrimage, iii. 2,—

> "——————— Did you see
> How sweetly fearful her pretty self
> Betray'd herself?"

"How *sweetly-fearfully*."

III.

The following are instances of what may, perhaps, be described as an instinctive striving after a natural arrangement of words, inconsistent indeed with modern English grammar, but perfectly authorized by that of the Elizabethan age.

K. R. III. v. 3,—

> "But if I thrive, the gain of my attempt
> The least of you shall share his part thereof."

Or, as it might be expressed in Greek; ἢν δὲ τοὐναντίον

εὐτυχῆ ἡ ἐμὴ πεῖρα, τῶν αποβαινόντων οὐδεὶς ὑμῶν ὃς οὐκ ἂν μετάσχοι. Winter's Tale, iv. 3,—

"—————— O, these I lack,
To make you garlands of, and my sweet friend,
To strew him o'er and o'er."

ὥσθ' ὑμᾶς μὲν στεφανῶσαι, τοῦτον δὲ καὶ πάντα καταστορέσαι. Midsummer Night's Dream, iii. 2,—

"Look, when I vow, I weep; and vows so born,
In their nativity all truth appears."

King Lear, i. 4,—

"—————— No, no, my lord,
This milky gentleness, and course of yours,
Though I condemn it not, yet, under pardon,
You are much more attask'd for want of wisdom," &c.

As you Like It, ii. 3,—

"Know you not, master, to some kind of men
Their graces serve them but as enemies?"

Here too a Greek would find no difficulty. οὐκ οἶσθα, ὅτι ἐνίοις τῶν ἀνθρώπων καὶ τὰ αὐτῶν καλὰ πολέμιά εστιν; One may perhaps compare Sidney, Arcadia, B. iii. p. 323, l. 15, "The general concert of whose mourning performed so the natural tunes of sorrow, that even to them (if any such were) that felt not the loss, yet others' grief taught them grief——." And B. v. p. 447, ult., "For as to Gynecia, a lady known of great estate, and greatly esteemed, the more miserable representation was made of her sudden ruin, the more men's hearts were forced to bewail such an evident witness of weak humanity; so to these men, not regarded because unknown, but rather (besides the detestation of their fact) hated as strangers, the more they should have fallen down in an abject semblance, the more instead of compassion they should have gotten contempt."

Tarquin and Lucrece, St. ccxl.,—

> "————————let it then suffice
> To drown one woe, one pair of weeping eyes."

King Lear, ii..towards the end,—

> "—————— O sir, to wilful men,
> The injuries that they themselves procure,
> Must be their schoolmasters."

Massinger, Bondman, iii. 3, Moxon, p. 86, col. 2,—

> "—————— else it could not be,
> Now miserable I, to please whose palate
> The elements were ransack'd, yet complain'd
> Of nature, as not liberal enough
> In her provision of rarities
> To soothe my taste, and pamper my proud flesh,
> Should wish in vain for bread."

Bacon, Essay of Marriage and Single Life, early in the Essay: "Some there are, who, though they lead a single life, yet their thoughts do end with themselves, and account future time impertinences." Essay of Cunning, last paragraph: "—— therefore you shall see them find out pretty looses in the conclusion, but are noways able to examine or debate matters——." Chapman, Preface to his *Iliad*, 1st page (the pages are not numbered): "To the only shadow of whose [Poesy's] worth yet, I entitle not the bold rhymes of every apish and impudent braggart (though he dares assume any thing); and shall but chatter on molehills (far under the hill of the Muses) when their fortunat'st self-love and ambition hath advanced them highest." That is, "and *they* (or *such*) shall but chatter," &c. *Il.* v. p. 81, fol., if this is exactly in point; (Mars)

"——— had newly slain the mighty Periphas,
Renown'd son to Ochesius; and far the strongest was
Of all th' Ætolians."

vii. p. 100, fol. (Ajax)

"March'd like the hugely figur'd Mars, when angry Jupiter,
With strength on people proud of strength sends him forth to infer [Lat. *inferre*] .
Wrathful contention; and comes on with presence full of fear:
So th' Argive rampire, Telamon, did 'twixt the hosts appear."

Sackville and Norton, Gorboduc, v. near the end,—

"But now, O happy man, whom speedy death
Deprives of life, ne is enforced to see
These hugy mischiefs," &c.

Spenser, Ruins of Time, v. 520,—

"Then did I see a pleasant Paradise,
Full of sweet flowers and daintiest delights,
Such as on earth man could not more devise
With pleasures choice to feed his cheerful sprights."

Hamlet, i 4,—

"That thou ——————————.
Revisit'st thus the glimpses of the moon,
Making night hideous; and we fools of nature,
So horridly to shake our dispositions," &c.[16]

All's Well, &c. iv. 3,—"to belie him, I will not;—and more of his soldiership I know not," &c. As Beaumont and Fletcher, King and No King, v. 4,—

"—————— this our queen
Desir'd to bring an heir, but yet her husband,

---

[16] Walker evidently connects *we fools* with *that*, not (as Malone does) with *making*.—*Ed.*

She thought, was past it; and to be dishonest,
I think, she would not."

Can the following passage be classed with the above? King Henry VIII. v. 1,—

"I swear he is true-hearted; and a soul
None better in my kingdom."

The construction seems to be the same as in the following passages from Elizabethan poets. Greene, Looking-Glass for London, &c. Dyce, vol. i. p. 111,—

"I and thou in truth are one,
Fairer thou, I fairer none:"

(Have I copied this right?[17] or should it be "*Fairest* thou"?)

Dekker, Old Fortunatus, Lamb, ed. 1835, vol. i. p. 65,—

"The glist'ring beams which do abroad appear
In other heavens, fire is not half so clear."

B. and F., Night Walker, i. 2, Moxon, vol. ii. p. 663, col. 2,—

"An impudence, no brass was ever tougher."

Drayton, Moses, B. iii. ed. 1630, p. 180,—

"He whom the whole world hath but such another."

(This is rather perhaps an outrageous Draytonism for "He *than* whom," &c.) Ford and Dekker, Sun's Darling, iii. 3, p. 177, col. 2, Moxon,—

"I feared thine eyes should have beheld a face,
The moon has not a clearer: this! a dowdy."

---

[17] Yes; but the context seems to require *Fairest.* This play is very corrupt. At p. 113, "suits Spenori" is printed seemingly for "sumd his pennons," and three lines are given to Rasni which are the undoubted property of his wife.—*Ed.*

(Write, "*this'*, [or *this's*] a dowdy.") Burns, Fair Lesley,—

> "Return again, fair Lesley,
> Return to Caledonie!
> That we may say, we hae a lass
> There's nane again sae bonny."

Something like this is the construction, M. of V. iv. 1, if I understand it rightly,—

> "—————————— I have a daughter,[18]
> Would any of the stock of Barrabas
> Had been her husband, rather than a Christian!"

Fuimus Troes, iii. 6, Dodsley, vol. vii. p. 422,—

> "Night having drawn the curtain, down I lie
> By one, for worse Saturnius left the sky."

Wilkins, Miseries of Enforced Marriage, i. *ib.* vol. v. p. 17,—

> "—————————— Indeed he is one,
> All emulate his virtues, hate him none."

Vision of Piers Ploughman, l. 892, Wright's ed. 1844, p. 28,—

> "Y-corouned with a coroune,
> The kyng hath noon bettre."

Browne, Britannia's Pastorals, B. i. Song ii. Clarke, vol. i. p. 69,—

> "The drops within a cistern fell of stone;
> Which, fram'd by nature, art had never one
> Half part so curious."

---

[18] The semicolon, which follows *daughter* in most modern editions, is not, I believe, authorized by any old copy. The folios, except the fourth, have not even a comma.—*Ed.*

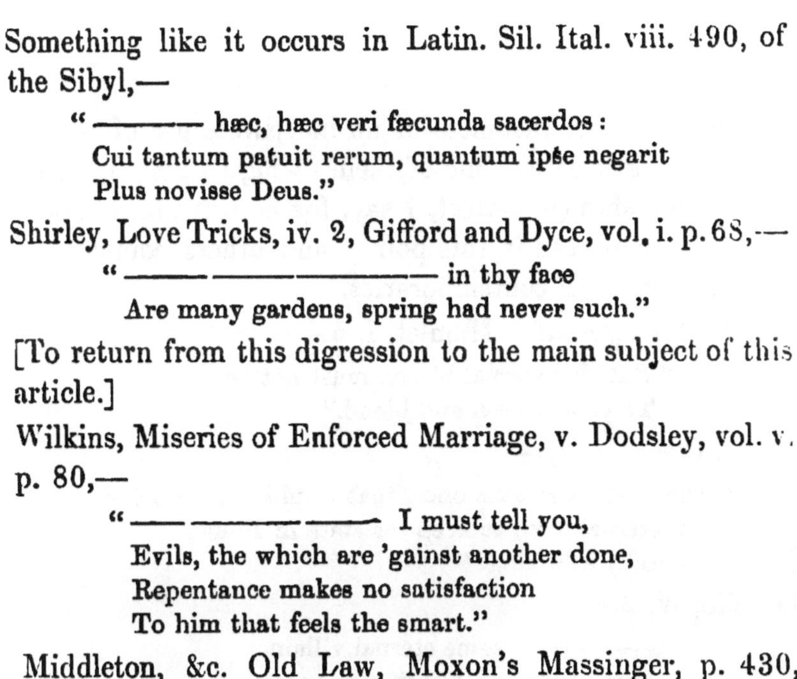

Something like it occurs in Latin. Sil. Ital. viii. 490, of the Sibyl,—

> "——— hæc, hæc veri fæcunda sacerdos :
> Cui tantum patuit rerum, quantum ipse negarit
> Plus novisse Deus."

Shirley, Love Tricks, iv. 2, Gifford and Dyce, vol. i. p. 68,—

> "——————— in thy face
> Are many gardens, spring had never such."

[To return from this digression to the main subject of this article.]

Wilkins, Miseries of Enforced Marriage, v. Dodsley, vol. v. p. 80,—

> "——————— I must tell you,
> Evils, the which are 'gainst another done,
> Repentance makes no satisfaction
> To him that feels the smart."

Middleton, &c. Old Law, Moxon's Massinger, p. 430, col. 2; perhaps it would be better to insert a comma after *strike*,—

> "He you shall strike your stroke shall be profound,
> And yet your foe not guess who gave the wound."

The following in Daniel seems not to belong to the present head, but to be an imitation of the Latin construction; Civil Wars, B. iv. St. vii.,—

> "——————— (she) disdain'd
> To have it thought, she would but hear that wrong
> Mov'd to her, of her lord and husband dead,
> To have his murderer's race enjoy his bed."

Compare Bunyan, Holy War, ed. 1791, p. 217,—"The proposals therefore, which now at last you have sent us, since we saw them, we have done little else, but highly approved and admired them."

IV.

The following are instances of an inaccurate use of words in Shakespeare, some of them owing to his imperfect scholarship (imperfect, I say, for he was not an *ignorant* man even in this point), and others common to him with his contemporaries.

Eternal for *infernal*. Hamlet, i. 5,—

> "But this eternal blazon must not be
> To ears of flesh and blood."

Julius Cæsar, i. 2,—

> "There was a Brutus once, that would have brook'd
> Th' eternal devil to keep his state in Rome,
> As easily as a king."

Othello, iv. 2,—

> "———— some eternal villain,
> Some busy and insinuating rogue,
> Some cogging, cozening slave."

And this, I think, is its meaning, Hamlet, v. 2,—

> "———— O proud Death!
> What feast is toward in thine eternal cell,
> That thou so many princes at a shot
> So bloodily hast struck?"

This seems to be still in use among the common people. In two tales of Allan Cunningham's (Ollier's Miscellany, and London Magazine) I observe the exclamation, "Eternal villain!" I need scarcely notice the Yankee '*tarnal*.

Exorcist and *exorciser* for magician. All's Well, &c. v. 3, towards the end of the play,—

> ———— "Is there no éxorcist
> Beguiles the truer office of mine eyes?
> Is't real that I see?"

Dirge in Cymbeline, iv. 2,—

> "No exorciser harm thee!"

Triple for *third.* All 's Well, &c. ii. 1,—

> "—————————— as a triple eye,
> Safer than mine own two, more dear."

A. and C. i. 1,—

> "Take but good note, and you shall see in him
> The triple pillar of the world transform'd
> Into a strumpet's fool."

(I have no doubt, by the way, that Shakespeare wrote, as some suggest, "a strumpet's *stool;*" I believe that *pillar* requires it. I borrow this emendation from the Var. Notes.[19]) Somewhat otherwise Chapman, Odyss. iv. p. 49,—

> "———————— banish'd by the doom
> Of fate, and erring as I had no home.
> And, now I have and use it, not to take
> Th' entire delight it offers; but to make
> Continual wishes, that a triple part
> Of all it holds, were wanting, so my heart
> Were eas'd of sorrows (taken for their deaths
> That fell at Troy) by their revived breaths."

v. 97 (Chapman has not rendered it exactly),—

> *ὧν ὄφελον τριτάτην περ ἔχων ἐν δώμασι μοῖραν*
> *ναίειν οἱ δ' ἄνδρες σόοι ἔμμεναι, οἳ τοτ' ὄλοντο*
> Τροίη ἐν ἐυρείη ἕκὰς Ἄργεος ἱπποβότοιο.

Imperious and *judicious* for *imperial* and *judicial, e.g.*:— Troilus and Cressida, iv. 5,—"most *imperious* Agamem-

---

[19] I do not find this emendation noted in Var. 1821. It is the property of Warburton. It appears to me very doubtful, even if there is no allusion to the custom of keeping fools in brothels, for which see Johnson's note on Timon of Athens, ii. 2, and Douce's Illustrations, vol. ii. p. 73.—*Ed.*

non." Sidney, Arcadia, B. iii. p. 307, l. 38,—"Yet if there be that imperious power in the soul, as it can deliver knowledge to another, without bodily organs; so vehement were the workings of their spirits," &c. B. v. p. 440, l. 8; see context,—"So evil balanced be the extremities of popular minds, and so much natural imperiousness there rests in a well-formed spirit." King Lear, iii. 4,—

> "Judicious punishment! 'twas this flesh begot
> Those pelican daughters."

Drayton, Moses, B. iii. p. 171, ed. 1630, God is described as ordaining on Mount Sinai,—

> "The ceremonial as [*i.e., as well as*] judicious laws."

(*Contra,* Shirley, Wedding, iii. 2, Gifford and Dyce, vol. i. p. 407, *judicially* for *judiciously,*—"Sir, I do love your daughter.—I thought it necessary to acquaint you first, because I would go about the business judicially.")

One may compare *populous* for *popular*, Webster, Appius and Virginia, ii. 1, Dyce, vol. ii. p. 161, and the note. Perhaps *diffused* for *confused* belongs to this class.

M. W. of W. iv. 4,—

> "Let them from forth a saw-pit rush at once
> With some diffused song;"

compare K. Lear and K. H. V., as referred to in the Var. Notes.

Competitor for *colleague*, A. and C. v. 1,—

> "——————— ——— But yet let me lament,
> With tears as sov'reign as the blood of hearts,
> That thou, my brother, my competitor
> In top of all design; my mate in empire,
> Friend and companion in the front of war," &c.

In T. A. i. 1, ult., *competitor* is used in the ordinary sense; but this act is certainly by another hand than Shakespeare's, —if, indeed, Shakespeare wrote one word of the play. He always, as far as I have observed, uses *competitor* in the sense of *colleague*. In T. A. ii. 1, which (if any part of the play) is his, *competitor* is used for *rival*.

Ceremonies for *omens*. Julius Cæsar, ii. 2,—

"Cæsar, I never stood on ceremonies,
Yet now they fright me."

Intermit for *remit*. *Ib.* i. 1,—

"Pray to the gods to intermit the plague
That needs must light on this ingratitude."

This last, however, seems rather to have originated in a slight degree of carelessness.

Temporary for *temporal*. M. for M. v. 1,—

"I know him for a man divine and holy;
Not scurvy, nor a temporary meddler,
As he's reported by this gentleman."

I suspect, however, that *temporary* may be an erratum for *temporal*, *meddler* being pronounced as a trisyllable; see S. V. art. ii. T. N. iii. 4, is curious,—"Why, everything adheres together, that no dram of a scruple, no scruple of a scruple, no obstacle, no incredulous or unsafe circumstance,——What can be said? nothing, that can be, can come between me and the full prospect of my hopes." It may be an erratum for *incredible*; yet I think not.

Important for *importunate*[20]—*shrine* for *image*.

---

[20] For examples of this use of *important*, which Walker seems to have thought it unnecessary to give, see Nares's Glossary. It

Cymbeline, v. 5,—

"—————— for feature, laming
The shrine of Venus, or straight-pight Minerva."

(Was *straight-pight* meant as a translation of *succinctus ?*)

Merchant of Venice, ii. 7,—

"From the four corners of the earth they come,
To kiss this shrine, this mortal breathing saint."

V.

Comedy of Errors, iv. 2,—

"First, he denied you had in him no right."

Malone, *in loc.*, quotes a MS. of 1609,—

"Not that I deny that men should not be good husbands."

But the phrase occurs elsewhere in Shakespeare himself, as indeed Malone has shown by quoting K. R. III. i. 3,—

"You may deny that you were not the cause
Of my lord Hastings' late imprisonment."

Compare Ford and Dekker, Witch of Edmonton, i. 2,—

"Why, canst thou yet deny thou hast no wife?"

---

is perhaps worth mentioning that in one of the examples (C. of E. v. 1—,

"Whom I made lord of me and all I had
At your important letters"),

the second folio gave the absurd misprint *impotent*, and was followed by the third and fourth, the fourth furnishing the additional blunder, *letter* for *letters;* Rowe conjectured "*all-potent*," and Pope finally restored the genuine reading from the first folio.—*Ed.*

Browne, Religio Medici, P. i. Sect. xxxv. ed. 1643, p. 82, ult.,—"Nor truly can I peremptorily deny, that the soul, in this her sublunary estate, is wholly and in all acceptions inorganical, but that, for the performance of her ordinary actions, is required not only a symmetry and proper disposition of organs, but a crasis and temper correspondent to its operations"—a variety of the same idiom.

(One may compare the Greek *ἀρνεῖσθαι*.

Sophocles Antig. 440, ed. Oxon. 1832,—

> φῂς, ἢ καταρνῇ μὴ δεδρακέναι τάδε;
> ANT. καὶ φημὶ δρᾶσαι, κοὐκ ἀπαρνοῦμαι τὸ μή.

Aj. 95, ed. Oxon. 1826,—

> ἔβαψας ἔγχος εὖ πρὸς Ἀργείων στρατῷ;
> AI. κόμπος πάρεστι, κοὐκ ἀπαρνοῦμαι τὸ μή.

And the French idiom, *e.g.*, De Stael, Cons. sur la Révolution Française, t. i. p. 154, ed. 2,—"si donc telle etoit la situation de la France,——qui pourroit nier qu'un changement ne fut nécessaire?") The following passages may be quoted as not irrelevant: Green's Tu Quoque, Dodsley, vol. vii. p. 10,—

> "*Gartred.* What would you crave?
> . . . .
> *Geraldine.* No more, fair creature, than a modest kiss.
> *Gartred.* If I should grant you one, would you refrain,
> On that condition, ne'er to beg again?"

Chaucer, Frankeleines Tale, v. 11791,—

> "—————— I you forbede, on peine of deth,
> That never, while you lasteth life or breth,
> To no wight tell ye this misaventure."

Passionate Pilgrim, Poem ii.,—

> "She silly queen, with more than love's good will,
> Forbad the boy he should not pass those grounds."

Marmyon, Antiquary, iii. 1 (it should be 2), Dodsley, vol. x. p. 48,—"he is one of the most rare and noble-qualified pieces of gentility, that ever did enrich our climate. *Leonardo.* Believe it, sir, 'twere a kind of profanation to make doubt of the contrary." Sidney, Arcadia, B. iv. p. 420, l. 9,—"Pyrocles, not knowing whether ever after he should be suffered to see his friend, and determining there could be no advantage by dissembling a not knowing of him, leapt suddenly," &c. B. v. p. 467, l. 37,—"But herein we must consider, that the laws look how to prevent by due examples, that such things be not done; and not how to salve such things when they are done."

VI.

Measure for Measure, v. 1,—

"—————— You, lord Escalus,
Sit with my cousin, lend him your kind pains
To *find out this abuse, whence 'tis deriv'd.*"

The construction is the same as in several other passages of Shakespeare. 3 K. H. VI. ii. 1,—

"Dark cloudy death o'ershades his beams of life,
And he nor sees, nor hears us, what we say."

K. Lear, i. 1,—

"———— I know you what you are."

Twelfth Night, i. 2,—

"Conceal me what I am."

M. W. of W. iii. 5, near the end of the act (so understand),—

"Well, I will proclaim myself what I am."

Julius Cæsar, iii. 2, *ad fin.*,—

"Belike they had some notice of the people,
How I had mov'd them."

Merchant of Venice, iv. 1,—

"You hear the learn'd Bellario what he writes."

Winter's Tale, i. 2,—

"———— I am angling now,
Though you perceive me not how I give line."

Hamlet, v. 2,—

"But wilt thou hear me how I did proceed?"

K. Richard II. iii. 3,—

"March on, and mark king Richard how he looks."

Much Ado, &c. v. 2,—

"The god of love,
That sits above,
And knows me, and knows me,
How pitiful I deserve."

2 K. H. IV. iii. 1 (so construe),—

"Then you perceive the body of our kingdom,[21]
How foul it is."

King Richard II. v. 4,—

"Didst thou not mark the king, what words he spake?"

King Henry VIII. iii. 2,—

"The king in this perceives him, how he coasts
And hedges his own way."

Taming of the Shrew, ii. 1,—

"———— I knew you at the first
You were a moveable."

---

[21] Walker follows the folios in putting the comma after *kingdom*, and so Rowe, Pope, Theobald, and Hanmer. I presume it was from inadvertence that later editors, Capell, Malone, Steevens, and even Knight and Collier, put it after *perceive*.—*Ed.*

2 K. Henry VI. iii. 1, near the end,—

> "By this I shall perceive the commons' mind,
> How they affect the house and claim of York."

Contention of the Two Houses, Part I. i. 4, ed. Knight,—

> "And I will stand upon this tower here,
> And hear the spirit what it says to you."

Tomkins, Albumazar, iii. 1, Dodsley, vol. vii. p. 156,—

> "——— ———. I would gladly do it,
> But fear he understands us what we say."

Middleton, Trick to Catch the Old One, ii. 1, Dyce, vol. ii. p. 34,—"I can tell you, thou art known what thou art, son, among the right worshipful, all the twelve companies." A Mad World, my Masters, iv. 2, near the end,—"we are tried what we are."

Harrington's Ariosto, xliii. lxxxi,—

> "Anselmus leaves him busy, and next day
> Cometh to hear him what he hath to say."

Play of Ram Alley, i. Dodsley vol. v. p. 370,—

> "——— ——— you hear her what she says."

So I think Jonson, Apologetical Dialogue subjoined to the Poetaster, ed. Gifford, vol. ii. p. 539,—

> "I pray you, let 's go see him how he looks
> After these libels."

Also Fairfax, ii. xciv.,—

> "No need of me, what I can do or say."

And Sidney, Arcadia, B. iii. p. 267, l. 23,—"when your glass shall accuse you to your face, what a change there is in you."

This too corresponds with the Greek idiom; *e.g.* Il. B. 409, ᾔδεε γὰρ κατὰ θυμὸν ἀδελφεὸν, ὡς ἐπονεῖτο.

— Note Jonson, Induction to Bartholomew Fair, Gifford, vol. iv. p. 369,—"Though it be an ignorance, it is a virtuous and staid ignorance; and next to truth, a confirmed error does well; such a one the author knows where to find him."

VII.

Instances, in which it appears more or less probable that lines have been lost in Shakespeare.

L. L. L. v. 2, the entire passage being in rhyme,—

> "But what, but what, come they to visit us?
> *Boyet.* They do, they do; and are apparell'd thus,—
> Like Muscovites or Russians, as I guess,
> Their purpose is, to parle, to court, to dance:
> And every one his love-feat will advance
> Unto his several mistress."

The want of a rhyme would not of itself prove that a line is lost; for isolated lines sometimes occur in the midst of rhyming couplets: but the words *apparell'd thus* surely require something more like an ἐπεξήγησις than what follows. (Note the distinction between *Muscovites* and *Russians*. Butler, Hudibras, P. i. C. ii. 265, if not meant for burlesque,—

> "He was by birth, some authors write,
> A Russian, some a Muscovite."

—What, as I have elsewhere observed, can *love-feat* mean here? Read "love-*suit*.") So iv. 1, a line may possibly have dropt out before the concluding couplet. This play is remarkably corrupt in the folio.

3 K. H. VI. ii. 6, near the beginning: I suspect a line is lost,—

> "And, now I fall, thy tough commixtures melt;
> And ————————————————
> Impairing Henry strength'ning misproud York,
> The common people swarm like summer flies;" &c.[22]

I find since that in the Contention the passage is written,—

> "And now I die, that tough commixture melts.
> Impairing Henry strengthen'd misproud York:"

In the *first* part of the Contention I have noticed three palpable instances of a line (or more?) having dropt out.

Cymbeline, *init.*,—

> "You do not meet a man but frowns: our bloods
> No more obey the heavens, than our courtiers,
> Still seem as does the king's."

Boswell, Var. 1821,—"This passage means, I think, 'Our bloods, or our constitutions, are not more regulated by the heavens, *by every skyey influence*, than our courtiers apparently are by the looks or disposition of the king: when he frowns, every man frowns.'" This explanation—to say nothing more—is irreconcilable with the words of the passage, which, to admit of it, ought to be "*Not* more obey," &c. But it suggested to me the former part of a conjectural emendation. I suspect that a line is wanting; *e.g.* (to illustrate my meaning),—

> "—————————— our bloods
> *Not* more obey the heavens, than our courtiers

[22] This line, omitted in the folio, was inserted by Theobald from the Second Part of the Contention. Eight lines below, on the other hand, the folio has inserted, to the detriment of the sense, a line apparently concocted from the above,—

("They would not then have sprung like summer flies.")

[Mirror their master's looks: their countenances]
Still seem, as doth the king's."

There are, as it seems to me, several instances in the folio (several, considered collectively, though few compared with the number of lines) of single verses having dropt out; and the folio is the only authority for Cymbeline. The similarity of termination, *courtiers—countenances*, was the cause of the omission. This conjuncture is merely thrown out as a *may-be*. We might also read,—

"—————————— our bloods
Not more obey the heavens, than our courtiers
Still seem, as does the *king*."

For the interpolated *s*, see the article on that point. But this sounds to me un-Shakespearian.

Titus Andronicus ii. 3,—" 'Tis true, the raven," &c. I suspect much that a line (ὁμοιοτέλευτος) has dropt out,—

"'Tis true, the raven doth not hatch a lark,
[Nor the fell lioness bring forth a lamb:]
Yet have I heard (O could I find it now!)
The lion, mov'd with pity, did endure
To have his princely paws par'd all away:
Some say, that ravens foster forlorn children,
The whilst their own birds famish in their nests."

Lambe—larke.

iv. 4,—

"But, Titus, I have touch'd thee to the quick,
Thy life-blood out."

A line is lost, I imagine; something to this effect (not that these were the words),—

"—————— I have touch'd thee to the quick,
[And, through the bodies of thy children, drawn]
Thy life-blood out."

2 King Henry VI. i. 1,—

"Then, York, be still awhile, &c.

. . . .

Till Henry, surfeiting in joys of love
With his new bride, and England's dear-bought queen,
And Humphrey with the peers be fall'n at jars."

Is there not a line wanting between the two last? All's Well, &c. ii. 1, *qu.* (though the want of a rhyme, *alone*, would not prove corruption),—

"———————— grĕat floods have flown
From simple sources, and great seas have dried:
When miracles have by th' greatest been denied,
[ ]
Oft expectation fails, and most oft there
Where most it promises;" &c.

Winter's Tale, iv. 3. Here, I think, a line, or possibly two, have dropt out, which, if preserved, would have obviated the difficulty of construction, which forms the only blot on this most exquisite speech.

"———————— move on, still so, and own
No other function: Each your doing [ ]
————————————————————
So singular in each particular,
Crowns what y' are doing in the present deeds,
That all your acts are queens."

Omissions of the press are, I think, remarkably frequent in this play. Romeo and Juliet, v. 3, see context,—

"We see the ground, whereon these woes do lie:"

surely a line is lost previous to this, rhyming to

"But the true ground of all these piteous woes."

3 K. H. VI. i. 4. The following is a mere conjecture,—

"That face of his the hungry Cannibals
Would not have touch'd [those roses, new in bloom,
The mountain beasts], would not have stain'd with blood."

So that *tigers of Hyrcania* would have something to refer to. "*The* Cannibals," as designating a particular nation; the man-eating Indians specifically. He would not have called the ancient Anthropophagi Cannibals.

Timon of Athens i. 2,—

> "As this pomp shows t' a little oil and root."

Is not something lost after this line?

3 K. H. VI. ii. 5, Henry's soliloquy,—

> "So many *weeks*, ere the poor fools will yean;
> So many *years*, &c.
> So minutes, hours, days, weeks,[23] *months*, and years,
> Past over," &c.

Surely a line must be lost after *yean.*

Pericles, i. 2,—

> "I sought the promise of a glorious beauty,
> From whence an issue I might propagate,
> Are arms to princes, and to subjects joys."

Surely a line has dropt out, somewhat to the following effect,

> "From whence an issue I might propagate
> [Worthy to heir my throne; for kingly boys]
> Are arms to princes, and to subjects joys."

---

[23] *Weeks* was inserted by Rowe, no doubt to correspond with what goes before. He also corrected a blunder of the 3rd and 4th folios, which read *days* for *weeks* in the line but one above. Mr. Collier's old Corrector has altered "So many *years*" to "So many *months*," but this also was done long ago by Rowe, who was followed by every editor down to Capell. The latter restored the reading of the old copies, but with great hesitation. I suspect Rowe was right in both his alterations, as Walker was justified in believing a line to have been lost. We have here eight lines beginning with *So*, seven of them with *So many;* and indeed the whole passage is made up of pitfalls for careless printers.—*Ed.*

(*Arms* seems to be from "Like as the arrows in the hand of a giant, so are the young children."

Measure for Measure, i. 3, near the end. Is not a line lost after *youth ? e.g.*, to substitute my lead for the lost gold of Shakespeare,—

> "———————— In her youth,
> [Her beauty, and her maiden modesty,]
> There is a prone and speechless dialect,
> Such as moves men."

[For two or three instances of omission see the note to King Henry VIII. iii. 2.—*Ed.*]

In some passages part of a line seems to have fallen out. (I do not notice here omissions of single words.)

Coriolanus, v. 5,—

> "———————— and, to this end,
> He bow'd his nature, never known before
> But to be rough, unswayable, and free."

My ear tells me that Shakespeare never could have so concluded a period; neither could he have used *bow'd* thus absolutely. Part of a line has dropt out, somewhat to the following effect,—

> "———————— and to this end,
> He bow'd his nature, never known before
> But to be rough, unswayable and free,
> [To an enforc'd observance.]
> 3 *Con.* Sir, his stoutness,
> When he did stand for consul," &c.

Timon of Athens, i. 2.

Knight has forestalled me in the arrangement of the following lines. Some words, however, have dropt out, which I have endeavoured to restore,—

"Who lives that's not depraved or depraves?
Who dies, that bears not one spurn to their graves
Of their friends gift? [Timon, were I as thou,]
I should fear those, that dance before me now,
Would one day stamp upon me; 'T has been done:
Men shut their doors against a setting sun."

VIII.

'Pray you, *'beseech you*, are frequent in Shakespeare (I remember also *'crave you* in one of his plays, I forget where[24]); and the substitution, in printing, of the longer form for the shorter has destroyed the metre of numerous passages in our old dramatists.

Macbeth, iv. 3,—

"Why in that rawness left you wife and child,
Without leave-taking?—I pray you,
Let not my jealousies be your dishonours," &c.

Write, *metri gratia*, *'Pray you.*

Greene, Friar Bacon and Friar Bungay, Dyce, vol. i. p. 180,

"I pray God I like her as I loved thee."

Read for harmony's sake, *'Pray God*, and pronounce *lovèd.* So also with regard to the forms *'pray*, and *'pray you*, the substitution of the former for the latter will solve the defective numbers of many hundreds of lines in Beaumont and Fletcher. Note by the way *'pray'* and *pray'e*, indicating (like *mon'th*, &c.) the transitional state of the word, in the Little French Lawyer, ap. fol. 1647, p. 64, col. 1,—

"Why do ye speake so lowd? I pray'e goe in
Sweete mistris."

---

[24] Macbeth, iv. 3, "'crave your pardon," where the first folio reads, "*I shall* crave."—*Ed.*

Ib. col. 2,—

> "—————————— Peace, good Madam.
> Stop her mouth, Dinant, it sleeps yet, 'pray' be wary."

And just below,—

> "'Pray' put your light out."

1 K. H. VI. iii. 1, fol. p. 106, col. 1,—

> "Pray' Vnckle Gloster mitigate this strife."

Also *pray y'*; Cartwright, Ordinary, iii. 5, Dodsley, vol. x. p. 227,—

> "Brave sport i'faith.
> *Rimewell.* Pray y', good sir, reconcile them."

The same form occurs iv. 4, pp. 246, 247, and v. 4, p. 258,

> "Pray y', look." [25]

And so write, instead of *pray you*, Cymbeline, iv. 2,—

> "—————————— I am not very sick,
> Since I can reason *of 't*. Pray, trust me here."

Ib.,—

> "Yet bury him as a prince.
> *Gui.* Pray fetch him hither."

Twelfth Night, iv. 1, *ad fin.*,—

> "Nay come, *I prithee*: would thou 'ldst be rul'd by me!
> *Seb.* Madam, I will.
> *Oli.* O say so, and so be!"

Read *I pray*; the other is too rugged for a rhyming couplet. Coriolanus, ii. 3,—

> "What custom wills, in all things should we do't,
> The dust on antique time would lie unswept,
> And mountainous error be too highly heapt

---

[25] So the original edition, 1651, in all these places.—*Ed.*

> For truth to overpeer.—Rather than fool it so,
> Let the high office and the honour go
> To one that would do thus."

The whole speech is in couplets : write therefore, "For truth *t' o'erpeer.*" And so, too, write, Coriolanus, i. 1,—

> "Yet are they passing cowardly. But, 'beseech you,
> What says the other troop?"

for *I beseech you ;* and 2 K. H. VI. ii. 3,—

> "'Beseech your majesty, give me leave to go."

Atque ita passim in vett. poëtis ; e.g., Chapman and Shirley, Chabot, iv. 1, Gifford and Dyce's Shirley, vi. 144,—

> "I beseech your majesty, let all my zeal
> To serve your virtues," &c.

'Beseech.

Compare *'protest.* Ford, Lady's Trial, ii. 1, ed. Gifford, vol. ii. p. 281,—

> "—————————— 'Protest, a fine conceit."

iv. 2, vol. ii. p. 325,—

> "—————————— 'Protest, she eyes me round.

And *trow ;* Much Ado, &c. iii. 4,—" What means the fool, trow?" *ubi vide Var.* M. W. of W. i. 4,—" Who 's there, trow?" (al. *I trow.*[26])

(Beaumont and Fletcher, Wit at Several Weapons, iv. 1,—

> "Does fury make you drunk? know you what you say?"

We should pronounce, I imagine, *know'e.*)

It may be observed in general, that the substitution of the

---

[26] Here the folio reads *I trow ;* in Much Ado, &c., and in Cymbeline, i. 7, *trow*, without the preposition. In these passages the phrase has the same meaning, and apparently answers to the modern *I wonder*. The usual signification of *trow* is *trust, think.*—*Ed.*

fuller forms of words for the abbreviated ones (*e.g.*, *against* for *'gainst*, *alas* for *'las*, *i'faith* for *'faith*, *whatsoe'er* for *whate'er*) is a frequent error in the old editions of our poets.

1 K. Henry VI. v. 1,—

"Marriage, uncle? alas, my years are young."

Surely; "Marrïage, uncle? 'las, my years," &c. (as, *e.g.* 5,—

"Marrïage is a matter of more worth," &c.)

K. Henry VIII. ii. 4, near the beginning,—

"——————— having here
No judge indifferent, nor no more assurance
Of equal friendship and proceeding. Alas, sir,
In what have I offended you?"

And so, I think, Timon of Athens, iv. 2,—

"——————— thy great fortunes
Are made thy chief afflictions. Alas, kind lord!" &c.

Ford, "'Tis Pity She 's a Whore," ii. 6, Moxon, page 33, col. 2,—

"Receive it Annabella.
Ann. Alas, good man!")

Qu. *'Las;* and in Putana's speech just below,—" she said, *'Las* good man!

Marlowe, K. Edward II. Dodsley, vol. ii. p. 392,—

"We'll enter in by *darkness* to Killingworth."

Read *dark*.

Friar Bacon and Friar Bungay, Dyce's Green, vol. i. p. 208,—

"Whatsoe'er betide, I cannot say him nay."

Write *whate'er;* and so correct *metri gratia, passim in*

Greenianis. Chapman and Shirley, Chabot, i. 2, Gifford and Dyce, vol. vi. p. 103,—

"———— ———— is this the consequence
Of an atonement made so *lately* between
The hopeful Montmorency and his lordship?"

Read *late.* i. 1, p.. 90,—

"'Tis brave, I swear.
All. Nay it is worthy your wonder."

Read *worth.* *Ib.* 2, p. 100,—

"Assuring me he never more would offer
To pass [*press*] a suit unjust, which I well know
This is, above all, and have often been urg'd
To give it passage."

Read *oft.*

IX.

E'er for *ever*, *ne'er* for *never* and the like.

Winter's Tale, iv. 3, fol. and vulg.,—

"As you have ever been my father's honour'd [27] friend;"

Write, "As *y' have e'er* been." Indeed the Var. 1813 has "As you have *e'er* been;" but that of 1821, *ever*. *E'er* for *ever*, when used in the sense of *always*,—though much more rare than in its other sense, *unquam*,—occurs now and then in our old poets. I hardly know whether it is needful to produce instances. King John, ii. 1,—

"St. George, that swindg'd the dragon, and e'er since
Sits on his horse' back at mine hostess' door."

---

27 The earlier editors improperly followed the 2nd and succeeding folios in omitting *honour'd.*—*Ed.*

Coriolanus, v. 3,—

"—————————— that kiss
I carried from thee, dear; and my true lip
Hath virgin'd it e'er since."

Twelfth Night, i. 1,—

"And my desires, like fell and cruel hounds,
E'er since pursue me."

Heywood, Fair Maid of the Exchange, sig. B 4, ed. 1625, ap. Dyce, Remarks, p. 76,—

"Men are so captious they'll ever conster [*i.e. construe*] ill."

Write *e'er*. Play of the Country Girl, Retrosp. 2nd Series, vol. ii. p. 21,—

"The contumelious and unmanly darings,
That, to enforce me from the peacefulness
Ere liv'd in my calm bosom, you have most
Uncivilly cast upon me."

E'er, surely. Beaumont and Fletcher, Wit at Several Weapons, iii. 1,—

"Beware a sturdy clown e'er while you live."

Two Noble Kinsmen, v. 3, Knight, Pict. S. p. 164, col. 2,—

"————————— which shows
The one the other. Darkness, which ever was
The dam of Horror," &c.

E'er?

Taylor, Hog hath lost his Pearl, iii. 1, Dodsley, vol. vi. p. 361,—

"If e'er thy tongue did utter pleasing words,
Let it now do so, or hereafter e'er
Be dumb in sorrow."

Henry More on the Soul, P. iii. C. 1, St. 1,—

"The soul's ever durancy I sung before
Ystruck with mighty rage."

For *ever*. Massinger and Dekker, Virgin Martyr, v. i. Moxon, p. 23, col. 1,—

> "―――――― a conscience all stain'd o'er,
> Nay, drown'd and damn'd for ever in Christian gore."

i. 1, p. 1, col. 2,—

> "Abandoning for ever the Christian way."

I notice, even in a poem published in the Gentleman's Magazine, 1735, p. 429, col. 2, l. 343,—

> "――― hateful hatred does for e'er endure,
> And with that hatred, plagues for evermore."

Everlasting. Comedy of Errors, iv. 2,—

> "A devil in an everlasting garment hath him."

As the context is in the ordinary blank verse, I conclude that Shakespeare wrote *e'erlasting;* as in Glapthorne's Hollander, at least if the passage is copied correctly in Retrosp. vol. x. p. 139,—

> "―――――― congeal thy blood
> To an e'erlasting [28] lethargy."

And so perhaps we should write, B. & F., Spanish Curate, ii. 1, the passage being in comic blank verse on the usual model of the twin dramatists,—

> "To have a thin stipend and an everlasting parish,
> Lord, what a torment 'tis!"

And Middleton, Women beware Women, iv. 1, Dyce, vol. iv. p. 603,—

> "But come I to your everlasting parting once,
> Thunder shall seem soft music to that tempest."

"*t'* your *e'er*lasting."

Knight—if it were worth mentioning—has in numerous

[28] The old quarto 1640 has *ere'lasting.—Ed.*

places restored, or left uncorrected, the old corrupt *ever;* *e.g.*, Two Noble Kinsmen *passim.*

So *ne'er* has often been corrupted into *never;* in like manner as we frequently find in old editions *against* for *'gainst*, *alas* for *'las*, *I beseech you* for *'beseech you*, *'pray you* for *'pray*, &c., *metro nolente*, as noticed above; and (more immediately to the point) *over* for *o'er*.

Prologue to K. Henry VIII. (Jonson),—

> "Will leave us never an understanding friend."

K. Henry VIII. v. 2,—

> "Which you shall never have while I live.
> *Chan.* Thus far,
> My most dread sovereign," &c.

Surely *ne'er*. Hamlet, iii. 3,—

> "———————— which when it falls,
> Each small annexment, petty consequence,
> Attends the boist'rous ruin. Never alone
> Did the king sigh, but with a general groan."

This will not do in the heroic couplet.

2 K. Henry IV. i. 1,—

> "———————— for a silken point
> I'll give my barony. Never talk of it."

Measure for Measure, ii. 2,—

> "———————— Most dangerous
> Is that temptation, which doth goad us on
> To sin in loving virtue: never could the strumpet,
> With all her double vigour," &c.

Certainly the metre requires *ne'er*.

Massinger, Duke of Milan, ii. 1, Moxon, p. 57, col. 1,—

> "———————— I preach patience,
> And must endure my fortune.
> 1 *Fid.* I was never yet
> At such a hunt's-up, nor was so rewarded."

Beaumont and Fletcher, Rule a Wife, &c., v. 5, near the end of the play, Moxon, vol. i. p. 366, col. 2,—

> "Thou art a valiant man, and thou shalt never want."

"*ne'er* want,"—the regular Beaumonto-Fletcherian *drag* at the end of the line. In the Demetrius and Enanthe also there are several instances.

In the old editions of the poets, by the way, the contraction of *ever* and *never* is sometimes written *ev'r* and *nev'r*. Tempest, v. 1, fol. p. 17, col. 2,—

> "———————— howsoeu'r you haue
> Beene iustled from your sences."

Othello, ii. 1, p. 317, col. 2,—

> "She that could think, and neu'r disclose her mind."

ii. 3, p. 326, col. 2,—

> "Shall neu'r look backe, neu'r ebbe to humble Love."

4, p. 327, col. 2,—

> "Is not this man iealious?
> *Des.* I neu'r saw this before."

I have a notion that Spenser always does this; but that his editors have altered it. This spelling, however, is in general much less frequent than the other. So I have noticed *ov'r*. Browne, Religio Medici, ed. 1647, P. i. Section 32, verses,—

> "My winters (—'*s*, *is*) ov'r, my drooping spirits sing,
> And every part revives into a Spring."

Sometimes in Harrington's Ariosto; xxix. lxiv.,—

> "Orlando still doth her pursue so fast,
> That needs he must ou'rget her at the last."

xxx. xiv., "he ranged ou'r the cost." lxxvii.,—

> "She red the writing ou'er, five times or six."

By the way, *o'er* is frequently misprinted *over* in our old poets. Massinger, Bondman, iii. 3, Moxon, p. 86, col. 2,—

> "——— I had not been transform'd, and forced
> To play an overgrown ape."

O'ergrown, I rather think, though Massinger's comic metre admits of a wider license than his tragic.

K. Lear, iii. 7,—

> "——————————— It was he
> That made the overture of thy treasons to us;"

qu., *o'erture*.

X.

A interpolated, and sometimes omitted in the 1st folio.

Tempest, iii. 2,—

> "——————————— he himself
> Calls her a nonpareil: I never saw a woman
> But only Sycorax my dam, and she," &c.

Hanmer (*Steevensio teste*) *metri gratia*, "I *ne'er* saw woman." The verse is not irregular (S. V. art. viii. p. 101), but it is inharmonious, I think, and Hanmer's reading seems to be right. *Ever* and *never* are frequently printed by mistake for *e'er* and *ne'er* in the old editions of the poets (see art. ix.); and *a* has in many instances been interpolated in the folio;—I may observe, however, that it scarcely ever occurs in the twelve first comedies. Winter's Tale, v. 1,—

> "Your honour not o'erthrown by your desires,
> I am a friend to them, and you: upon which errand
> I now go toward him;" &c.

Evidently "I'm friend to," &c., and so the folio, which

Knight follows. (The text of this play in the folio—there is no quarto—is printed, by the way, with rather more than usual inaccuracy.) iv. 3,—

> "———————— you were straited
> For a reply; at least, if you make a care
> Of happy holding her."

If you make care. K. John, iv. 2,—

> "Thy hand hath murder'd him: I had a mighty cause
> To wish him dead," &c.

"*I' had* mighty cause."[29] Taming of the Shrew, last scene,—

> "Here is a wonder, if you talk of a wonder.
> *Luc.* And so it is: I wonder what it means."

Dele second *a*. K. Henry VIII. ii. 3,—

> "———————— O now, after
> So many courses of the sun enthron'd,
> Still growing in a majesty and pomp, the which
> To leave 's a thousand times more bitter, than
> 'Tis sweet at first t' acquire; after this process,
> To give her the avaunt!"

Dele a before *majesty;* growing is contracted, like *playing*, *drawing*, *knowing*, &c., *passim;* see S. V. art. xiii. p. 122. Merchant of Venice, v. 1,—

> "———————— now in faith, Gratiano,
> You give your wife too unkind a cause of grief."

"too *únkind* cause;" as *e.g.*, K. Lear, iii. 4,—

> "———— nothing could have subdued nature
> To such a lowness, but his unkind daughters."

2 King Henry VI. iv. 9,—

> "And with a puissant and a mighty power
> Of Gallow glasses," &c.;

---

[29] So in effect Steevens.—*Ed.*

(2 K. H. IV. i. 3, near the beginning,—

"Upon the power and puissance of the king."

Perhaps "*o' th'* king.")

and Hamlet, ii. 2,—

"That lend a tyrannous and a damned light
To their lord's [*lords'*] murder;"[30]

with some other similar passages, may *perhaps* be wrong, but I much doubt it.

Julius Cæsar, v. 1, *qu.*,—

"Look, I draw sword against conspirators;"

vulg., "*a* sword." Macbeth, i. 2,—

"What a haste looks through his eyes! So should he look," &c.

Read, *metri gratia*, "what haste;" and for the same reason, with some editions, read in Othello, iii. 3,—

"Or sue to you, to do[31] peculiar profit
To your own person;"

at least if *a* can be dispensed with here. Cymbeline, iv. 3,—

"A fever, with the absence of her son!
A madness, of which her life's in danger!—Heavens,
How deeply you at once do touch me!"

Wrong surely; the latter *A* originating in the former. And so 1 K. Henry IV. iii. 2,—

"They surfeited with honey, and began
To loathe the taste of sweetness, whereof *a* little
More than a little is by much too much."

---

[30] This is the reading of the quartos; the 1st folio omits the second *a*, and reads also *vilde murthers* for *lords murther*, as the quarto reading is spelt in Steevens's reprint.—*Ed.*

[31] Pope was the first who omitted *a* here, and his example was followed by all the editors of my acquaintance except Mr. Knight and Mr. Collier.—*Ed.*

Taming of the Shrew, i. 2 (Ἄμετρον),—

"O, sir, such *a* life with such a wife, were strange;
But if you have a stomach, to 't a' God's name."

Here, too, the *a* originated in its neighbours. K. H. VIII. ii. 3,—

"——————— Alas, poor lady!
She 's a stranger now again.
Anne. So much the more
Must pity," &c.

Qu., *She 's stranger*, &c.; yet this seems harsh. A. C. v. 2,—

"——————— which thou
So sought'st to hinder.
Within. A way there, a way for Cæsar."

Rather,—

"——————— Way there, way for Cæsar."

Cymbeline, v. 4, *init.*,—

"You shall not now be stol'n, you have locks upon you;
So, graze, as you find pasture.
2 *Gaoler.* Ay, or *a* stomach."

Dele *a*. (The folio, by the way, reads "So graze, as," &c., without a comma after *so;* I think rightly.)

Hamlet, ii. 2,—"O Jephtha, judge of Israel, what a treasure hadst thou! *Pol.* What *a* treasure had he, my lord?" *What treasure*, surely, for grammar's sake.

Othello, iii. 1, *contra metrum;* see S. V. art. lviii.,—

"I humbly thank you for 't. I never knew
A Florentine more kind and honest."

Qu. "I humbly thank you for 't.
I ne'er knew Florentine more kind and honest."

Perhaps we should arrange rather,—

> "I humbly thank you for't; I ne'er knew Florentine
> More kind and honest."

Instances in which this interpolation has taken place in the folio, even according to the commonly received text. Julius Cæsar, ii. 1,—

> "———— and the state of *a* man,
> Like to a little kingdom, suffers then," &c.;

quod restituerunt Eques et Collierius, jure a Dycio reprehensi, *Remarks*, p. 185. T. G. of V. ii. 4,—

> "———— too mean a servant
> To have a look of such a worthy *a* mistress."

Cymbeline, iii. 3,—

> "———— This gate
> Instructs you how t' adore the heavens; and bows you
> To *a* morning's holy office."

King Henry V. v. 1,—"News have I, that my Doll is dead i' th' spital of *a* malady of France." (By the way, just below, *qu.*,—

> "———— and from my weary limbs
> Honour is cudgelled. Well, bawd, I'll (*Ile*, fol.) turn," &c.)

2 K. Henry IV. ii. 1,—"How comes this, Sir John? Fy, what *a* man of good temper would endure this tempest of exclamations?"[32] Troilus and Cressida, iv. 5,—

> "There's *a* language in her eye, her cheek, her cheek, her lip."

K. Henry V. iv. 3,—"I fear thou wilt once more come again for *a* ransom." Comedy of Errors, i. 2,—

> "So I, to find a mother and a brother,
> In quest of them (unhappy *a*) lose myself."

[32] In this and the next example the quartos omit the *a*. Just above, Mr. Collier reads *cudgelled.—Ed.*

Hamlet, ii. 2,—"What a piece of work is *a* man!"[33] as Julius Cæsar quoted a little above. Timon, iv. 3,—

"—————— Have you forgot me, sir?
Timon. Why dost ask that? I have forgot all men;
Then, if thou grant'st thou 'rt man, I have forgot thee."

I have not the folio at hand; but Knight reads *thou 'rt a man,* whence I conclude that the folio has *a*,[34] as there is no quarto edition of Timon.

In the above instances I have not retained the spelling of the folio, partly through accident. Some of these, it is true, are owing to the near neighbourhood of one or more other *a's*.

On the other hand, there are a few instances in Shakespeare, in which *a* has, as I believe, been erroneously omitted. Taming of the Shrew, v. 2,—

"Is that an answer?
Gre. Ay, and a kind one, too:
Pray God, sir, your wife send you not a worse.
Petr. I hope, better."

"I hope, *a* better." Twelfth Night, iii. 2, near the end: "—— yond gull Malvolio is turned heathen, a very renegade." *Qu.* "is turned a heathen."—4, "He is knight, dubbed with unhacked rapier," &c. "He is *a* knight?" Coriolanus, iv. 5, near the end,—"Peace is a very apo-

[33] The quartos whimsically enough omit the *a* before *piece*, and retain it before *man.*—*Ed.*

[34] The reading, punctuation, and arrangement of the first folio deserve to be recorded:—

"Then, if thou *grunt'st*, th' art a man.
I haue forgot thee." *Ed.*

plexy, lethargy; mulled [*mute*], deaf, sleepy, insensible:" *qu.*, "*a* lethargy." Othello, iv. 3,—

"———— my love doth so approve him,
That even his stubbornness, his checks, his frowns,
(Pr'ythee, unpin me,) have grace and favour in them."

Whence *in them?* it is not in the folio.[35] *Qu.*, "have *a* grace and favour;" as (if an example were wanted), Tempest, iii. 3,—

"Bravely the figure of this harpy hast thou
Perform'd, my Ariel; a grace it had, devouring."

I have met with some instances of the interpolated *a* in other old poets. Ford, &c., Witch of Edmonton, iv. 2, Moxon, p. 202, col. 2,—

"All life is but a wandering to find *a* home;
When we are gone, we 're there."

Dele second *a*. Beaumont and Fletcher, Faithful Friends, ii. 3, Moxon, vol. ii. p. 537, col. 2, ἀμέτρως·

"What cause could you pretend for so foul *a* wrong,
But only we were weak," &c.

Island Princess, iii. 3, p. 247, col. 2,—

"———— Is this violence?
Is it, to fall thus prostrate to your beauty,
A ruffian's boldness? is humility *a* rudeness?
The griefs and sorrows that grow here, an impudence?"

Dele second *a*. Fletcher, &c., Love's Pilgrimage, iv. 2, p. 627, col. 2,—

"What *a* man have they now in the town
Able to maintain a tumult, or uphold
A matter out of square, if need be?

---

[35] The words *in them* appear in the quarto 1622. The folio reading, as emended by Walker, is such as Shakespeare might well have written: on the other hand, the additional words do not look either like a sophistication or a printer's blunder.—*Ed.*

What man. (By the way, the whole, or nearly the whole of this scene is in prose.[36]) Fletcher, Honest Man's Fortune, i. 1, p. 476, col. 2,—

"———————— my first increase of means
Shall offer you *a* fuller payment. Be content
To leave me something."

Dele a, metri gratia; and so ii. 1, p. 479, col. 1,—

"———— we will first set down ourselves
The method of a quarrel, and make choice
Of some frequented tavern, or such *a* place
Of common notice to perform it in."

Middleton, &c., Old Law, v. 1, Moxon's Massinger, p. 439, col. 1,—

"Therefore to be severely punished
For thus attempting *a* second marriage,
His wife yet living."

(Just below, arrange and write,—

"He leads a triumph to the scorn *of't;* which
Unreasonable joy," &c.;

and "*at's* second marriage.") *A* occurs four lines above, and four or five below. Ford and Dekker, Sun's Darling, v. 1, p. 181, col. 2,—"Farewell, frost! I'll go seek *a* fire to thaw me."—The speeches of the Clowns and Folly, in this first part of the scene, are in verse, though erroneously printed as prose,—

"———————————— Farewell, frost!
I'll go seek fire to thaw me."

(In the first speeches, I conjecture,—

"———————————— we are like to have
A fine time of it, neighbours.

---

[36] And so it has been printed by Mr. Dyce, who has also ejected *a* on the authority of the second folio.—*Ed.*

3 *Clown.* Our wives and daughters are, for they are sure
To get by the bargain;
*Al*though our barns be emptied, they'll be sure
To be with bairn for 't. (pron. *barne.*)
. . . .
——— ——— rather than live like beasts.
3 *Clown.* Ay, *and* like horn-beasts, neighbour.
. . . .
It is not a fart matter.")

See for another instance the quotation from Marlowe, S.V., p. 180.

XI.

Certain words used with reference to the agent.

King Henry VIII. i. 1,—

"——— ——— ——— I wonder,
That such a keech can, with his very bulk,
Take up the rays o' th' beneficial sun,
And keep it from the earth."

Beneficial, i.e., beneficent. It is to be observed that the words *benefit* and *beneficial,* in our old writers, almost uniformly involve the idea of a *benefactor,* which has since been dropped, except in cases where the context implies that idea, *e.g., conferring* or *receiving a benefit.* (Compare the similar change in the meaning of *injury ; e.g.,* "the corn has received great injury from the bad weather;" "late hours are very injurious to health," &c.) So understand Comedy of Errors, i. 1,—

"Therefore, merchant, I limit thee this day
To seek thy [help] by beneficial help:
Try all the friends thou hast in Ephesus," &c.

T. N. Kinsman, iii. 6 (Fletcher's part), near the beginning,—

"Would you were so in all, sir! I could wish you
As kind a kinsman, as you force me find [you]
A beneficial foe; that my embraces
Might thank you, not my blows."

Hamlet, i. 3, *init.*,—

"———— as the winds give benefit,
And convoy is assistant, do not sleep,
But let me hear from you."

(As Cymbeline, iv. 2,—

"———— When expect you them?
Captain. With the next benefit o' th' wind.")

King Lear, i. 4,—

"Turn all her mother's pains and benefits
To laughter and contempt."

Hamlet of 1603,—

"And shall I kill him now,
When he is purging of his soule?
Making his way for heauen, this is a benefit,
And not reuenge."

Webster, Dutchess of Malfy, iii. 5, Dyce, vol. i. p. 253,—

"———— The birds that live i' th' field
On the wild benefit of nature, live
Happier than we;"

as we now say, "on the *bounty* of nature;" and see Middleton, quoted in Dyce's note. Massinger, Emperor of the East, iv. 1, Moxon, p. 254, col. 2,—

"———————— In this
The sweetness of your temper does abuse you;
And you call that a benefit to yourself,
Which she, for her own ends, conferr'd upon you."

Perhaps, however, the modern use had already begun to creep in. 2 King Henry VI. i. 3,—

> "As for the duke of York, this late complaint
> Will make but little for his benefit."

So also *artificial* is used with a reference to the agent. Midsummer Night's Dream, iii. 2,—

> "We, Hermia, like two artificial gods,
> Have with our neelds created both one flower," &c.;

deabus artificibus similes. Pericles, v. 1,—

> "If that thy prosperous-artificial feat
> Can draw him but to answer thee in aught,
> Thy sacred physic shall receive such pay," &c.;

the successful exertion of thy art.[37] (By the way, *artful* in our old writers is sometimes used as we now use *artificial.* Beaumont and Fletcher, Queen of Corinth, iii. 1, Moxon, vol. ii. p. 34. col. 1, alluding, of course, to the story of Icarus,—

> "This giant will I fell beneath the earth;
> I will shine out, and melt his artful wings."

In like manner, *effect,* in the old writers, always involves the idea of an *effector. Effectus* and *-um,* hoc est, *quod ab aliquo efficitur.* Sidney, Defence of Poesy, p. 506, l. 15, —"since his [*the poet's*] effects be so good as to teach goodness, and delight the learners of it." Arcadia, B. ii. p. 133, l. 38,—"[*Pyrocles and Musidorus would*] go privately to seek exercises of their virtue, thinking it not so worthy to be brought to heroical effects by fortune, or necessity (like Ulysses or Æneas), as by one's own choice and working." *Ib.* l. 44, "—— they [*P. and M.*] met

---

[37] Walker here adopts, and confirms by his explanation, Steevens's elegant correction. Others read "prosperous *and* artificial."—*Ed.*

an adventure, which, though not so notable for any great effect they performed, yet worthy to be remembered," &c. B. iii. p. 306, l. 25,—"to confirm some of her threatened effects;" see context. Chapman, Il. iv. Taylor, vol. i. p. 116, l. 10, the verb,—

> "———— then the Greeks gave worthy clamours vent,
> Effecting then their first dumb [*i.e., first-dumb*] powers;"

putting into practice their powers of vociferation, which had previously been dumb. See also vi. p, 153. l. 5, *sqq.*,—

> "———— he shunn'd his death direct,
> Holding a way so near not safe, and plotted the effect
> By sending him with letters seal'd," &c.

(In like manner—though the case is not exactly the same—it may be observed that *affair* still retained somewhat of its old etymological connection with *faire*, and was occasionally used in the sense of *doing*, *effort*.
Chapman, Il. xv. vol. ii. p. 58, l. 11,—

> "The Trojans took Jove's sign for them, and pour'd out their affairs
> In much more violence on the Greeks, and thought on nought but fight."

Efforts. xx. p. 202, l. 26,—

> "And this bred fresh desire of moan, and in that sad affair
> The sun had set amongst them all, had Thetis' son not spoke," &c.

l. 153,—

> ——— τοῖσι δὲ πᾶσιν ὑφ' ἵμερον ὦρσε γόοιο.
> καί νύ κ' ὀδυρομένοισιν ἔδυ φάος ἠελίοιο,
> εἰ μὴ 'Αχιλλεὺς, &c.

And so in Chapman, *passim*. This use of *affair*, however,

appears to have been rare; at least there seem to be few passages in the Elizabethan writers, so far as I am acquainted with them, in which it may not be taken in its present sense.)

So *serviceable* is *willing to serve; obedient.* Massinger, Virgin Martyr, ii. 1, towards the end,—

"Therefore, my most lov'd mistress, do not bid
Your boy, so serviceable, to get hence;
For then you break his heart."

Arcadia, B. iii. p. 241, l. 41, "—— for to it was the concourse, one thrusting upon another, who might show himself most diligent and serviceable towards me." P. 252, l. 13, "awfully serviceable," *i.e.*, *reverentially obedient*, or *willing to serve.* Page 296, l. 5: "—— and she, who would never like him for serviceableness, ever after loved him for violence." Here it is *submissiveness;* see context. Continuation of the same work, page 361, l. 17,—"so were these now thrown into so serviceable an affection, that the turning of Zelmane's eye was a strong stern enough to all their motions, wending no way, but as the enchanting force of it guided them." P. 372, l. 19,—"So that she, but then the physician, was now become the patient; and he, to whom her weakness had been serviceable, was now enforced to do service to her weakness." (*But then, i.e., just before;* as we still say *but now.*) Defence of Poesy, p. 491, l. 29,—"the only serviceable courtier without flattery." (As Chaucer; Prologue to the Canterbury Tales, Character of the Squier, *ad fin.* v. 99,—

"Curteis he was, lowly, and servisable.")

Thus, also, *comfortable*—and in like manner *uncomfort-*

able and *discomfortable*—are uniformly applied to a person, or to a thing personified, the idea of will and purpose being always implied in them. Timon, iv. 3 (so I would arrange the lines),—

> "Had I a steward so true, so just, and now
> So comfortable?"

Romeo and Juliet, v. 3,—

> "O comfortable friar! where is my lord?"

All's Well, &c.,—"Be comfortable to my mother, your mistress, and make much of her." King Lear, i. 4,—

> "———— yet have I left a daughter,
> Who, I am sure, is kind and comfortable."

(In As You Like It, ii. 6,—"For my sake be comfortable," the word seems to be used in a passive sense, nearly as Knight explains it, *susceptible of comfort*. See above, "comfort a little.") King Richard II. iii. 2,—

> "Discomfortable cousin!"

See context.

Ford, Lover's Melancholy, v. 1; see context,—

> "———— for, had not Rhetias
> Been always comfortable to me, certainly
> Things had gone worse."

Middleton, &c., Old Law, ii. 2, Moxon's Massinger, p. 423, col. 2,—

> "In troth, Eugenia, I have cause to weep too;
> But, when I visit, I come comfortably,
> And look to be so quited."

Ford, Lady's Trial, iii. 3, near the beginning,—

> "How surely dost thou malice these extremes,
> Uncomfortable man!"

And so, *perhaps*, in Milton, P. L. 1077,—

"And sends a comfortable heat from far,
Which might supply the sun."

And Bunyan, P. P. Part ii.,—"So I saw in my dream that they went on their way, and the weather was comfortable unto them."

XII.

Ingenious, engin, gin, &c.

Cymbeline, iv. 2,—

"———— his body's hostage
For his return.
Bel. My ingenious instrument!
Hark, Polydore, it sounds!"

(Fol. *ingenuous.*) Dyce's note on Webster's Dutchess of Malfi, iii. 2, Dyce's Webster, vol. i. p. 238,—

"———— our weak safety
Rests upon enginous wheels: short syllables
Must stand for periods."

"The quarto of 1640 substitutes 'ingenious.' So Dekker,—

"'For that one Acte gives like an enginous wheele
Action to all.'
The Whore of Babylon, Sig. C 2."

Add Middleton, Triumphs of Integrity, description of one of the pageants, Dyce, vol. v. p. 316,—"those beams, by enginous art, made often to mount and spread like a golden and glorious canopy over the deified persons that are placed under it." Marlowe and Chapman, Hero and Leander, iii. Dyce, vol. iii. p. 51, ed. 1850,—

"All tools that enginous despair could frame."

Chapman, Odyss. i. fol. p. 11,—

"———— consider how thou mayst deprive
Of worthless life these wooers in thy house
By open force or projects enginous.

In these two last examples it means *ingenious;* in Shakespeare, as in the examples quoted from Webster, Dekker, and Middleton, the meaning is, *ingenio factum, artificial, constructed by art;* write therefore—*postulante etiam metro* (for the elision of *y* in *my* is not in Shakespeare's way)—*enginous* or *inginous.* Moreover I would write *ingen'ous* in another passage of the Dutchess of Malfi, i. 1, Dyce, p. 193,—

"———— thy protestation
So ingenious and hearty; I believe it;"

for, although the meaning here is *ingenuous* ("*ingenious* and *ingenuous* were often used for each other;" Whalley ap. Gifford's Jonson, vol. ii. p. 126), yet the pronunciation is evidently the same. On the other hand, in the prologue to Fletcher's Chances, we have *ingenuous* for *ingenious,*—

"My promise will find credit with the most,
When they know ingenuous Fletcher made it, he
Being in himself a perfect comedy."

Pronounce *inginous;* and so in Lord Brooke, Treatie of Humane Learning, St. xliii. (in the same sense Inquisition upon Fame, &c. St. vi.),—

"Yea, Rome itself, while there in her remain'd
That ancient, ingenious austerity,
The Greeks' professors from her walls restrain'd."

So pronounce also, Jonson, Fox, v. 1, near the beginning,—

"Any device, now, of rare ingenious knavery,
That would possess me with a violent laughter," &c.

Or rather write *rare-inginous.*

Ingine or *engine*, as is well known to those conversant in our old writers, was used by them to designate a *contrivance*, whether in the form of an artifice or stratagem, or of a weapon, instrument, or piece of machinery. From the former sense we have the name *Malengin* in Spenser, F. Q. B. v. C. ix. St. v. *ubi vide;* and so understand Bacon, Essay of Superstition, "—the schoolmen were like astronomers, which did feign eccentrics and epicycles, and such engines of orbs, to save the phænomena, though they knew there were no such things;"—*devices.* I find it used in the latter sense as late as the Pilgrim's Progress; P. i. Christian's visit to the House Beautifull,—"They also showed him some of the engines with which some of his (their Lord's) servants had done wonderful things. They showed him Moses's rod; the hammer and nail with which Jael slew Sisera; the pitchers, trumpets, and lamps, too, with which Gideon put to flight the armies of Midian." And he goes on to specify Shamgar's ox-goad, Samson's jaw-bone, David's sling and stone, &c. For *engine*, as is well known, they sometimes used *gin; e.g.*, Beaumont and Fletcher, Queen of Corinth, iii. 1,—

"—————— I should curse my fortune,
Even at the highest, to be made a gin
T' unscrew a mother's love unto her son."

Maid in the Mill, i. 1,—

"Prithee forbear: the gentlewomen——
Mart. That 's it, man,
That moves me like a gin."

So read in Rowley, Noble Soldier, i. 1. 1634, 2nd page,—

> "I would not, for what lyes beneath the Moone,
> Be made a wicked Engine to break in pieces
> That holy Contract."

And, I think, in Webster, Vittoria Corombona, Retrosp. vol. vii. p. 95 (Dyce, vol. i. p. 64),—

> "And by a vaulting engine.
> *Mon.* An active plot;
> He jumpt into his grave."

(*Gin* occurs in this sense in Surrey; Version of Æn. ii. ed. 1631, p. 125,—

> "This fatal gin thus overclamb our walls,
> Stuft with arm'd men."

> "Scandit fatalis machina muros, Fœta armis."

Engine is also used in the strict sense of *ingenium*. Jonson, on Sir John Beaumont's Poems, Gifford, vol. viii. p. 335,—

> "And doth deserve all muniments of praise
> That art, or ingine, on the strength can raise."

Masque of the Fortunate Isles, p. 73-4,—

> "——————— at such a time
> As Christmas, when disguising is afoot,
> To ask of the inventions, and the men,
> The wits, and the ingines that move those orbs!"

Where is an instance of *ingínes* to be found? I imagine that Jonson wrote

> "The wits and th' ingíners that," &c.;

wits (*ingenia*) being associated with *inginers*, as *inventions* with *men*.

XIII.

Writing of the letter O.

Twelfth Night, ii. 3,—

> "O, the twelfth day of December."

Fol. "O the," &c. Read "*O' th'* twelfth," &c. It is the first line of a narrative ballad. (By the way, B. and F., Monsieur Thomas, iii. 3, Moxon, vol. i. p. 481, col. 1, in the enumeration of ballads, for "The Devil and *ye* dainty Dames," read "The Devil and *y^e^* Dainty Dames," which I suppose to be the title of a ballad.[38] In the Two Gentlemen of Verona, the folio has,—

> "Best sing it to the tune of *Light O, Love;*"

meaning, *ut vulg., Light o' Love.*

Beaumont and Fletcher, Women Pleased, ii. 3, fol. 1647 [and f. 1679],—

> "Death, O my soule!" for "Death, o' my soule!"

This last, however, may be a mere erratum, arising from the printer's misunderstanding the author's meaning. *O'* in the forms *o' my truth, o' my life*, &c., is frequently expressed by ô. B. and F., Captain, iii. 3, fol. 1647,—

> "——————— Yes, it shewes very sweetly.
> *Frank.* Nay do not blush Sir, ô my troth it does;"

and just below, "ô my conscience;" a little above, "ô my faith."

---

[38] See Mr. Dyce's note to the passage in his edition, vol. vii. p. 365, where he explains the matter differently. He readily disposes of the "dainty dames," but the "Devil" is more troublesome. He is probably right, though nothing can be more ingenious than Walker's explanation.—*Ed.*

False One, ii. 3,—

"A tempting Devill, ô my life: go off Cæsar."

(In one of Jeremy Taylor's funeral sermons occurs the name *Phelim ó Neale.*) As is also the interjection *O.* Twelfth Night, ii. 4, fol. p. 262, col. 2,—

"——————— lay me ô where
Sad true louer neuer find my graue to weepe there."

M. N. D. v. 1, p. 160, col. 2,—

"O grim look't night, ô night with hue so blacke,
O night, ô night, alacke, alacke, alacke."

As You Like It, iv. 1, p. 201, col. 2,—"ô that woman that cannot make her fault her husbands occasion, let her never nurse her childe herself, &c. And so folio *passim.* Beaumont and Fletcher, Fair Maid of the Inn, ii. 4, fol. 1647, p. 36, col. 2,—

"Pray Sir resolve me, ô for pitty doe."

iii. 2, p. 37, col. 2,—

"——————— ô thou scorne
Of learning, shame of duty."

Demetrius and Enanthe, ii. 1, Dyce, p. 25,—

"But she (forsooth) when I put theis things to her,
(theis thinges of honest Thrift), groanes, ô my conscience,
the load vpon my conscience!"

and so, p. 31, "ô most extremely,"—"ô I have her;"— and elsewhere in the same play.

Daniel, Civil Wars, 1623, *passim; e.g.,* B. i. St. lxxxix. xc. B. v. St. lxviii. Sidney, Arcadia, *passim; e.g.,* B. i. p. 76, ll. 14, 24,—

"This Maide, thus made for ioyes, ô Pan, bemone her;
. . . .
Farre other case, ô Muse, my sorrow tries."

XIV.

Peculiar Mode of Rhyming.

Sonnet cxxxv.,—

"Wilt thou, whose will is large and *spacious*,
Not once vouchsafe to hide my will in thine?
Shall will in others seem right *gracious*,
And in my will no fair acceptance shine?"

This species of rhyme is frequent in Shakespeare and his contemporaries.

Sonnet lxvii.,—

"Ah! wherefore with infection should he live,
And with his presence grace impiety,
That sin by him advantage should achieve,
And lace itself with his society?"

x.,—

"For shame! deny that thou bear'st love to any,
Who for thyself art so unprovident:
Grant, if thou wilt, thou art belov'd of many,
But that thou none lov'st, is most evident."

lxii., *antiquity—iniquity*. Taming of the Shrew, ii. 1,—

"Skipper, stand back: 'tis age that nourisheth.
Tra. But youth in ladies' eyes that flourisheth."

Merry Wives of Windsor, v. 3, about the end,—

"Against such lewdsters, and their lechery,
Those that betray them do no treachery."

Venus and Adonis, St. cliv., somewhat differently, as *spectacles—chronicles*, below,—

"O hard-believing love, how strange it seems
Not to believe, and yet too credulous!
Thy weal and woe are both of them extremes,
Despair and hope make thee ridiculous."

Other poets. Spenser, F. Q., B. ii. C. vii. St. lxii.,—

"I Pilate am, the falsest judge, alas!
And most uniust; that, by unrighteous
And wicked doome, to Jewes despiteous
Deliverd up the Lord of Life to dye."

The following three are curious. Beaumont, Translation of Ovid's Remedy of Love, Moxon, vol. ii. p. 703, col. 1,—

"If she should send her friends to talk with thee,
Suffer them not too long to walk with thee."

Tragicall Historye of Romeus and Juliet, 1562, Var. Shak. vol. vi. p. 297,—

"The nurce that knew no cause why she absented her,
Did doute lest that some sodain greefe too much tormented her."

Jonson, Forest, xi. (10 and 6-syllable lines),—

"——— this bears no brands, nor darts,
To murder different hearts;
But in a calm and godlike unity
Preserves community."

Ford, Fame's Memorial, St. xxx. Gifford, vol. ii. p. 574, *vanity, humanity, urbanity;* xlii. p. 577, *maturity, obscurity, security;* lx. p. 582, *severity, temerity;* lxxxii. p. 587, *servility, nobility;* lxxxviii. p. 589, *prodigality, liberality;* also in many instances, where the lines are of unequal lengths.

Middleton, Wisdom of Solomon Paraphrased, Dyce, vol. v. p. 364,—

"Some blinded be in face, and some in soul;
The face's eyes are not incurable;
The other wanteth healing to be whole,
Or seems to some to be endurable."

383,—

"Thyself art dross to her comparison;
Thy valour weak unto her garrison."

413,—

> "Thus marching one by one, and side by side,
> By the profane, ill-limn'd, pale spectacles,
> Making both fire and fear to be their guide,
> Pull'd down their vain-adoring chronicles."

Fletcher, Faithful Shepherdess, iv. 3, Moxon, vol. i. p. 278, l. ult.,—

> "——————— what men call
> Wonder, or, more than wonder, miracle!
> For sure, so strange as this, the oracle
> Never gave answer of."

Jonson, Cynthia's Revels, Prologue, *init.* Gifford, vol. ii. p. 229,—

> "If gracious silence, sweet attention,
> Quick sight, and quicker apprehension," &c.

Epigram xi.,—

> "At court I met it, in clothes brave enough
> To be a courtier, and looks grave enough
> To seem a statesman."

Daniel, Queen's Arcadia, ii. 4, 1623, p. 355,—

> "And note but how these cankers always seaze
> The choysest fruits with their infections,
> How they are still ordained to disease
> The natures of the best complections."

(Daniel, by the way, deals very little in the *-ïon.*)

W. Browne, Britannia's Pastorals, B. i. Song ii. Clarke, vol. i. p. 70,—

> "The alder, whose fat shadow nourisheth,
> Each plant set near to him long flourisheth."

Beaumont and Fletcher, Wit at Several Weapons, iii. 1,—

"—————— yes, when I complain, sir,
Then do your worst: there I'll deceive you, sir.
Old Knight. You are a dolt, and so I leave you, sir."

Note in Daniel, Civil Wars, B. vii. St. xxxviii.,—

"Sad want, and poverty, makes men industrious,
But law must make them good, and fear obsequious."

Dubartas, i. v. p. 41, col. 1,—

"———————— joining land to land,
House unto house, sea to sea, strand to strand,
Mountain to mountain, and (most-most insatiable)
World unto world, if they could work it possible."

iv. p. 37, col. 2,—

"In brief, mine eye, confounded with such spectacles,
In that one wonder sees a sea of miracles."

(This seems a sort of cross between such rhymes as *credulous—ridiculous*, &c., and the species noted below, art. xvi. *e.g.*,—

"Is there not something more than to be Cæsar?
Must we rest there? it irks t' have come so far.")

Perhaps our old poets were led to this by observing the comparative weakness and inefficiency of a rhyme falling on unaccented syllables; *e.g.*, *vanity—economy;* whence they instinctively called in the aid of the two syllables preceding to render it more sensible.[39]

---

[39] Similar rhymes occur in old German poetry. See Lachmann's Remarks on the Nibelungen, St. 1916 of his edition, p. 239.—*Ed.*

XV.

Another peculiar Mode of Rhyming.

Tarquin and Lucrece, St. li.,—

> "Then Love and Fortune be my gods, my guide!
> My will is back'd with resolution:
> Thoughts are but dreams till their effects be tried;
> The blackest sin is clear'd with absolution:
> Against love's fire fear's frost hath dissolution."

It is *possible* indeed that something may be lost in line 2; but the peculiarity in the metre and rhyme, as the passage at present stands, is one which occurs frequently in the poets of that age. Harrington, Preface to Ariosto, last page:—"Now for them that find fault with polysyllable meeter, we thinke they are like those that blame men for putting suger in their wine, and chide to bad about it, and say they marre all, but yet end with Gods blessing on their hearts. For indeed if I had knowne their diets, I could haue saued some of my cost, at least some of my paine; for when a verse ended with *ciuillitie,* I could easier after the auncient maner of rime, haue made *see* or *flee* or *decree* to aunswer it, leauing the accent vpon the last syllable, then hunt after three syllabled wordes to answere it with *facillitee, gentillitee, tranquillitie, hostillitie, scurrilitie, debillitie, agillitie, fragillitie, nobillitie, mobillitie,* which who mislike, may tast lamp oyle with their eares." King Richard II. ii. 1 (for rhyme seems to be intended; see context),—

> "Whose manners still our tardy apish (*tardy-apish*) nation
> Limps after in base imitation."

Venus and Adonis, St. cxxvii.,—

> "What is thy body but a swallowing grave,
> Seeming to bury that posterity

Which by the rights of time thou needs must have,
If thou destroy them not in dark obscurity?"

These are the only instances I have noticed in Shakespeare.

Dubartas, ii. i. ii. p. 94, col. 2,—

"Man's seed then justly, by succession
Bears the hard penance of his high transgression;"

the only instance, thus far, in the poem.

Ford, Fame's Memorial, 1606, St. iv. Gifford, vol. ii. p. 568 (a juvenile work),—

"Base Fear, the only monument of slaves,
Progenitor to shame, scorn to gentility,
Herald to usher peasants to their graves,
Becomes abjected thoughts of faint servility;
While haughty Fame adorns nobility."

St. ciii. p. 592,—

"He whom we treat of was a president (read *precedent*)
Both for the valiant and judicious;
Both Mercury and Mars were resident
In him at once; sweet words delicious
And horrid battle were to him auspicious," &c.

and so cv. p. 593, cvii. p. 593, cxviii. p. 596, cxxxviii. p. 606, cxlvi. p. 608, cxlvii. p. 608. Jonson, Underwoods, Eupheme, ix. Gifford, vol. ix. p. 74,—

"———— whither they must come
To hear their judge, and his eternal doom;
To have that final retribution,
Expected with the flesh's restitution."

Spenser, Hymne in Honour of Love, xxviii.,—

"Such is the powre of that sweet passion,
That it all sordid basenesse doth expell,
And the refyned mynd doth newly fashion
Unto a fayrer forme, which now doth dwell," &c.

Middleton, Wisdom of Solomon Paraphrased, Dyce, vol. v. p. 350,—a youthful work, I suspect,—

"He that could give such admonition,
Such vaunting words, such words confirming vaunts,
As if his tongue had mounted to ambition,
Or climb'd the turrets which vain-glory haunts."

Chapman and Shirley, Chabot i. 1, near the end, Gifford and Dyce's Shirley, vol. vi. p. 97,—

"————— I must on, [:] I see,
That, 'gainst the politic and privileg'd fashion,
All justice tastes but affectation."

Spenser, Colin Clout, l. 612,—

"There she beholds, with high aspiring (*high-aspiring*] thought,
The cradle of her own creation,
Emongst the seats of angels heavenly wrought,
Most like an angel in all form and fashion."

867,—

"But man, that had the spark of reason's might
More than the rest, to rule his passion,
Chose for his love the fayrest in his sight,
Like as himselfe was fayrest by creation."

Faerie Queene, B. v. C. ii. St. xxviii.,—

"And lastly all that castle quite be raced,
Even from the sole of his foundation,
And all the hewen stones thereof defaced,
That there mote be no hope of reparation
Nor memory thereof to any nation.
All which when Talus throughly had perfourmed,
Sir Artegall undid the evil fashion," &c.

B. iv. c. xii. St. xxxiv. *perfection—inspection*, &c.

Note B. v. C. v. St. xxvi.,—

"Thus there long while continu'd Artegall,
Serving proud Radigund with true subjection ;

However it his noble heart did gall
T' obay a woman's tyrannous direction,
That might have had of life or death election:
But, having chosen, now he might not chaunge.
During which time the warlike Amazon,
Whose wandring fancie," &c.

XVI.

A third peculiar Mode of Rhyming.

The following are instances (the only ones that I have yet discovered in Shakespeare) of a singular mode of rhyming —rhyming to the eye, as at first sight it appears to be— which occurs every now and then in the poets of the Elizabethan (or rather, to use the term which Coleridge coined for the nonce, the Elizabetho-Jacobæan) age. Its origin and explanation are probably to be sought for in our earlier poetry.

Love's Labour 's Lost, v. 2,—

"—————Here was a consent—
Knowing aforehand of our merriment—
To dash it like a Christmas comedy:
Some carry-tale, some please-man, some slight zany,
Some mumble-news," &c.

(On *zany* note, by the way, Donne, Poems, ed. 1633, p. 94,—

"Then write, then I may follow, and so bee
Thy debter, thy 'eccho, thy foyle, thy *zanee*.)

Two Gentlemen of Verona, ii. 1,—

"O jest unseen, inscrutable, invisible,
As a nose on a man's face, or a weathercock on a steeple!"

Pericles of Tyre, i. 2,—

> "Whereas reproof, obedient, and in order,
> Fits kings as they are men, for they may err."

I think the occasion (the winding-up of a *γνώμη*) requires rhyme; see context. But is the passage Shakespeare's? Midsummer Night's Dream, v. i.,—

> "Through which the lovers, Pyramus and Thisby,
> Did whisper often, very secretly."

This is of a piece with the purposely *incondite* composition of this *dramiticle*. So a little above,—

> "This beauteous lady Thisby is *certain*."

We might indeed scan: "Pyram | us and | Thisbý;" but this is not likely. In Sonnet xlv. we have,—

> "For when these quicker elements are gone
> In tender embassy of love to thee,
> My life, being made of four, with two alone
> Sinks down to death, opprest with melancholy."

But Shakespeare was incapable of anything so discordant as this. The other instances, occurring in the places they do, are less offensive; besides that they are from his earlier works. Let any one with a tolerable ear read the Sonnets continuously, and judge. Ought *melancholy* to be pronounced *mélanch'ly?* Instances from other writers. Play of How a Man may Choose a Good Wife from a Bad, 1604, iv. *ad fin.* Old English Drama, vol. i. p. 79,—

> "Then thus resolv'd, I straight will drink to thee
> A health thus deep, to drown thy melancholy."

This, standing as it does at the end of a scene, must be a rhyme of the common sort; the other would be intolerable. And so, *I think*, Jonson, Prologue to the Sad Shepherd,—

> "You shall have love, and hate, and jealousy,
> As well as mirth, and rage, and melancholy."

Dedication to Chapman's Play of All Fools, as printed in Dodsley's Plays, 1825, vol. iv. p. 107; I know not whether *melanch'ly* is from Chapman, or a correction of Dodsley's or Collier's,—

"And drown'd in dark death-ushering melanch'ly,"

rhyming to *vanity*. Play of Hieronimo, Part ii. 1, Dodsley, ed. 2, vol. iii. p. 130 (ed. 1825, p. 109),—

"Aye, aye, this earth, image of melancholy,
Seeks him whom fates adjudge to misery."

I think rhyme is intended. For *seekes* read *suites*.
(By the way, the pronunciation *meláncholy* was also in use; Spenser, F. Q. B. i. C. v. St. iii.—C. xii. St. xxxviii.,—

"To drive away the dull melancholy."

Donne, Poems, ed. 1633, p. 28, Holy Sonnets, i.,—

"Weav'd in my low devout melancholy."

P. 100,—

"Bred in thee by a wise melancholy."

Dubartas, ii. ii. iii. p. 131, col. 2,—

"If this among the Africans we see,
Whom cor'sive humour of melancholy
Doth always tickle with a wanton lust," &c.

Comedy of Errors, iv. 2, l. 4,—

"Ah, Luciana, did he tempt thee so?
Mightst thou perceive austerely in his eye
That he did plead in earnest, yea or no?
Look'd he or red, or pale; or sad, or merrily?"

The twelve-syllable line, if I mistake not, nowhere occurs in Shakespeare, except under certain circumstances, which do not exist here. Perhaps he wrote *merry*. 2 King Henry VI. iii. 2 (not Shakespeare's part, surely),—

"This get I by his death: Ay me unhappy,
To be a queen, and crown'd with infamy."

Rhyme perhaps, from its situation. Taming of the Shrew, i. *ad fin.*,—

"The motion 's good indeed, and be it so:—
Petruchio, I shall be your *ben venuto;*"

at least, if the Italian was rightly pronounced. Can the following be an instance? Romeo and Juliet, v. 3,—

"—————— O, true apothecary!
Thy drugs are quick.—Thus with a kiss I die."

Instances from other writers. In the Prologue and Epilogue to K. H. VIII., consisting together of only 46 lines, it occurs twice, once in each; a sufficient argument, were there no other, to prove that these compositions were not written by Shakespeare. In the Prologue,—

"—————— think, ye see
The very persons of our noble story,
As they were living."

In the Epilogue,—

"All the expected good we are like to hear
In this play at this time, is only in
The merciful construction of good women."

Jonson, Epigram cxiv. Gifford, vol. viii. p. 226,—

"For Cupid . . . .
Hath chang'd his soul, and made his object you,
Where finding so much beauty met with virtue," &c.

For *soule, qu. scope,* *τὸν τοῦ τόξου σκοπόν*?

Sejanus, i. 2, Gifford, vol. iii. p. 36,—

"—————— only a long,
A lasting, high, and happy memory
They should, without being satisfied, pursue;
Contempt of fame begets contempt of virtue."

I think these lines rhyme, from their position; one who is

familiar with the play, or even with this speech, will probably agree with me.

ii. 3, p. 91,—

> "—————— work all my kin
> To swift perdition; leave no untrain'd engin
> For friendship or for innocence."

Here indeed, but that Jonson corrected the folio edition of his works himself, so that such erratum is perhaps unlikely, we might imagine that he had written *gin*, see art. xii. above. v. 1, near the beginning,—

> "Is there not something more than to be Cæsar?
> Must we rest there? it irks t' have come so far,
> To be so near a stay."

Catiline, iii. 1, Gifford, vol. iv. p. 250,—

> "—————— He enjoys rest,
> And ease the while: let the other's spirit toil,
> And wake it out, that was inspired for turmoil."

Peele, Arraignment of Paris, i. 4, Dyce, vol. i. p. 15,—

> "Accounts more honour done to her this day,
> Than ever whilom in these woods of Ida."

And so *ib. ad fin.* p. 16—ii. 1, *init.*, *so—Echo.* The following, ii. 2, Dyce, vol. i. p. 27, is curious,—

> "And for thy meed, sith I am queen of riches,
> Shepherd, I will reward thee with great monarchies."

ii. 1, p. 24,—

> "That Venus is the fairest, this doth prove,
> That Venus is the lovely queen of love.
> The name of Venus is indeed but beauty,
> And men me fairest call per excellency:
> If then the prize be but bequeath'd to beauty,
> The only she that wins the prize am I."

(*Excellency* here is perhaps used as a trisyllable, which, as

I think, is not uncommon: so *excellent* as a dissyllable *passim.* Massinger, Guardian, ii. 4, Moxon, page 348, col. 2,—

> "——— ——— and from their wants
> Her excellences take lustre.")

Peele, *ut supra, ad fin., he—controversy.* And so elsewhere in the same play, *passim.* In King Edward I. it occurs less frequently; in the War of Troy, often. ii. 181,—

> "So Peleus' noble son, the great Achilles,
> That lothly with the Grecians went to seas,
> Clad by his dame in habit of a woman,
> Unworthy cowardice of a valiant man," &c.

Marlowe and Chapman, Hero and Leander, Sestiad, iii. Dyce's Marlowe, vol. iii. p. 47,—

> "Till our Leander, that made Mars his Cupid,
> For soft love-suits, with iron thunders chid."

Sest. v. p. 86,—

> "——— ——— it erected
> To chaste Agneia, which is Shamefac'dness,
> A sacred temple, holding her a goddess."

Sest. iv. p. 58,—

> "And stood not resolute to wed Leander;
> This serv'd her white neck for a purple sphere."

Sest. vi. p. 95,—

> "Men kiss but fire that only shows pursue,
> Her torch and Hero, figure show and virtue."

And so *passim*, throughout the three latter Sestiads; in the two first, which are confessedly Marlowe's, no instance occurs; in the latter part of the third there are, I think, some instances.[40] Webster's Memorials of Honour, Dyce, Appendix, p. 10,—

> "Five cities, Antwerp, and the spacious Paris,
> Rome, Venice, and the Turk's metropolis."

Ford, Fame's Memorial, Gifford, vol. ii. p. 604,—

> "The nine poor figures of a following substance
> Did but present an after-age's mirror,
> Who should more fame than they deserv'd advance,
> And manifest the truth of that time's error."

(This too, as in the case of Shakespeare, was an early work.) Coleridge, Literary Remains, vol. ii. p. 294 [Lectures on Shakespeare, &c. vol. i. p. 295], remarks on B. and F.'s Maid's Tragedy,—"Act i. The Masque:—Cinthia's speech,—

> 'But I will give a greater state and glory,
> And raise to time a noble memory
> Of what these lovers are.'

I suspect that *nobler*, pronounced as *nobiler*, - ᴗ -, was the poet's word, and that the accent is to be placed on the penultimate of *memory*." *Memóry* would be inadmissible. But it is evidently an instance of the anomalous rhyme in question. I am not certain whether the following is intended for rhyme. Double Marriage, v. 2, near the end, Moxon, vol. ii. p. 123, col. 1; see context,—

> "Then build a chapel to your memories,
> Where all my wealth shall fashion out your stories."

---

[40] There are no less than six (besides the one quoted above) in the third Sestiad. I have given the references to passages from Marlowe according to Mr. Dyce's edition of 1850. Walker used the edition wrongly attributed to Mr. Dyce, and disavowed by him.—*Ed.*

Middleton, Witch, i. 2, Dyce, vol. iii. p. 260,—

> "——— ——— o'er steeple-tops,
> Mountains, and pine-trees, that like pricks, or stops,
> Seem to our height; high towers, and roofs of princes,
> Like wrinkles in the earth; whole provinces
> Appear to our sight then" &c.

Spenser, Sonnet li.,—

> "Doe I not see the fayrest ymages
> Of hardest marble are of purpose made,
> For that they should endure for many ages,
> Ne let theyr famous monuments to fade?"

Mother Hubberd's Tale, l. 213,—

> "And his hose broken high above the heeling,
> And his shooes beaten out with traveling."

These two last instances resemble those quoted from the Maid's Tragedy and the Witch just above; compare also those cited below from Barnes, Chapman, Fairfax, Browne, and Cleveland; and the rhyme, thus modified, may be compared to that of which examples have been given in art. xiv. *e.g.*, Tarquin and Lucrece, St. li. The same may perhaps be said of Mother Hubberd's Tale, l. 1240,—

> "——— ——— that never after anie
> Should of his race be void of infamie;"

supposing this to be analogous to that modification of the ordinary rhyme, in which *n* rhymes with *m*.

Lord Brooke (who deals very little in this sort of rhyme), Of Humane Learning, St. cv.,—

> "Hence strive the Schools, by first and second kinds
> Of substances, by essence and existence,
> That Trine, and yet Unitedness divine
> To comprehend, and image to the sense."

Barnes, ap. Dyce's Specimens of English Sonnets, p. 38,—

"But thou gives kingdoms, and makes crowns unstable :
By these I know thy name ineffable."

Beaumont and Fletcher, Mad Lover, iv. 1,—

"—————— that hung himself for love :
This ape, with daily hugging of a glove,
Forgot to eat, and died : This goodly tree,
An usher that first grew before his lady,
Wither'd at root : This, for he could not woo,
A grumbling lawyer : This pied bird a page,
That melted out because he wanted age."

Coleridge, Literary Remains, ii. 303 (Lectures on S. 1849, vol. i. p. 304,—"Here must have been omitted a line rhyming to *tree ;* and the words of the next line have been transposed,—

'—————— This goodly tree,
Which leafless, and obscur'd with moss you see,
An usher this, that 'fore his lady grew,
Wither'd at root : this, for he could not woo,' " &c.

The lost line occurred rather, I think, after *lady* (rejecting Coleridge's emendation), or after *woo*.

Donne, Sat. i. l. 7,—

"And wily statesmen, which teach how to tie
The sinews of a city's mystic body ;"

(ed. 1633, "*jolly* statesmen"!) Fletcher, to Sir Robert Townsend, prefixed to the Faithful Shepherdess,—

"Yet, according to my talent,
As sour fortune loves to use me,
A poor shepherd I have sent,
In homespun gray for to excuse me."

Epilogue to Fletcher's Valentinian (uncertain by whom; see postscript to folio 1647),—

"Then, noble friends, as you would choose a mistress,
(*mistris*, as usual, 1647,)
Only to please the eye awhile, and kiss,
Till a good wife be got; so," &c.

Weber, I think, has *miss*. Can *mistris* have been an erratum for *misse?* (Compare the following passage from Evelyn's Diary, Jan. 9, 1662,—"I saw acted 'the third part of the Siege of Rhodes.' In this acted the faire and famous comedian call'd Roxalana from the part she perform'd; and I think it was the last, she being taken to be the Earle of Oxford's *Misse* (*sic*) as at this time they began to call lewd women.") The word is again noticed, Oct. 9-10, 1671.) If an erratum, compare Fair Maid of the Inn, iii. 2,—

"Or like an angry Chyrurgion, we will use
The roughnesse of our justice;"

of course, *surgeon.*[41]

Beaumont and Fletcher, Knight of the Burning Pestle, ii. 1, near the end, rhyme to all appearance,—

"Till both of us arrive at her request,
Some ten miles off, in the Wild Waltham Forest."

Jonson, Forest, xii.,—

"When gold was made no weapon to cut throats,
Or put to flight Astræa, when her ingots
Were yet unfound."

---

[41] No doubt, and so Seward: both *surgeon* and *chirurgeon* were in use in the Elizabethan age. The case of *mistress* and *miss* seems different. *Miss* was a neologism fifteen years after the first folio was published, and in the passage in question is probably a sophistication by the editor of the folio 1679.—*Ed.*

Spenser, F. Q. B. i. C. vii. St. xliii., we have *mockeries—destinies—felicities—territories;* but here we must scan: *through all | the terri | tories.* In B. iii. C. iv. St. ix.,—

"On the rough rocks, or on the sandy shallowes,"

rhyming to *blowes*, &c., *dele* the second *on*.

Chapman, All Fools, iii. *ad fin.;* Dodsley, vol. iv. p. 155,—

"O, I will gull him rarely with my wench,
Low kneeling at my heels before his fury,
And injury shall be salv'd with injury."

Fairfax's Tasso, C. i. St. lxvi.—

"Prepare ye then, for travail strong and light,
Fierce to the combat, glad to victory:
And with that word and warning soon was dight
Each soldier, longing for near-coming glory:
Impatient be they of the morning bright,
Of honour so them prick'd the memory."

So C. viii. St. xv. *victory—glory—memory.*

But this is rare in Fairfax. Browne, Britannia's Pastorals, Book i. Song v. Clarke, p. 145,—

"As pears, plums, apples, the sweet raspberry,
The quince, the apricot, the blushing cherry."

Chapman, Il. xxiii. ed. Taylor, vol. ii. p. 201, l. 15,—

"——————— I see we have a soul
In th' under-dwellings, and a kind of man-resembling idol."

ii. vol. i. p. 69, l. 29,—

"——————— Iphitis' son, the son of Philacus;
Most rich in sheep, and brother to short-liv'd Protesilaus."

xi. vol. i. p. 242, l. 32,—

"——————— victorious Telamon
Still plied the foe, and put to sword a young Priamides,
Doriclus, Priam's bastard son: then did his lance impress
Pandocus, and strong Pyrasus, Lysander, and Palertes."

P. 246, l. 33,—

"Ulysses, Diomed, our king, Eurypilus, Machaon,
All hurt, and all our worthiest friends, yet no compassion
Can supple thy friend's friendless breast."

xix. vol. ii. p. 149, l. 4 from the bottom,—

"———— and so far were they from hind'ring it,
That to it they were nimble wings, and made so light his spirit,
That from the earth the princely captain they took up to air."

And so xxi. vol. ii. p. 171, l. 3, *sits—spirits;* p. 181, four lines from the bottom, *spirit—it* (unless *spirit* is in these places a monosyllable; for Chapman, who is more licentious in his rhymes than almost any of his contemporaries that I am acquainted with, might *perhaps* have tolerated the conjunction of *it* and *sprite*.) This species of rhyme is rare in Chapman's Iliad. The following is noteworthy:

Il. xxii. vol. ii. p. 191, l. 11,—

"———— in so far opposite state
(Impossible for love t' atone) stand we, till our souls satiate
The god of soldiers."

Is this a variety of the rhyme before us, or merely a piece of carelessness on the part of Chapman? *Satiate* is undoubtedly a trisyllable here. It is just possible, however, that it may be a slip of the pen, or an error of the press for *sate*. (By the way, l. 29,—

"———— cunning words well serve thee," &c.

————————

"But my back never turns with breath; it was not born to bear
Burthens of wounds;"

read (*re ipsa clamante*) *words*.)

Address to the Reader, prefixed to the Iliad,—

"I ———————————— as much abhor
More licence from the words, than may express
Their full compression, and make clear the author."

Sylvester, lines prefixed to his Job Triumphant, p. 449,—

"Sir, you have seen in my Panaretus
A sweet idea of our hopes in you;
A real act of that ideal virtue,
In my St. Lewis royal-virtuous."

Cleveland, Smectymnus, or the Club Divines,—

"I could by letters now untwist the rabble,
Whip *Smec* from constable to constable."

Butler, on Philip Nye's Thanksgiving Beard, 19 (if all be right—I quote from Cooke's edition),—

"From whom he held the most pluralities
Of contributions, donatives, and sal'ries."

Hudibras, P. ii. C. ii. l. 669; I quote from the same edition,—

"And he who made it had read Goodwin,
Or Ross, or Cœlius Rhodogine," &c.

C. iii. 809,—

"Those wholesale critics, who in coffee-
Houses cry down philosophy," &c.

I suspect, however, that in the former couplet we should read *made 't*, and that in the latter there is some corruption he could hardly have meant that we should pronounce—

"Hoúses cry' down phílosóphy,"[42]

inasmuch as I do not recollect another instance of a *trochaic* line in the poem.

---

[42] In this last passage the edition that forms part of "English Poets," 1796, reads, "Houses cry down *all* philosophy."—*Ed.*

Keats must have had some vague recollection of such passages as are quoted in this article, when he wrote in the Epistle to his Brother George, Poems, Smith's edition, p. 71, col. 2,—

"And what we, ignorantly, sheet lightning call,
Is but the opening of their wide portal,
When the bright warder blows his trumpet clear," &c.

Endymion, B. i. p. 4, col. 2,—

"Guarding his forehead with her round elbow,
From low-grown branches, and his footsteps slow
From stumbling over stumps and hillocks small."

Unless indeed he had Chaucer—*delicias suas*—in his mind. In one place, however, he has it exactly; Fragment of Calidore, p. 56, col. 2,—

"And now the sharp keel of his little boat
Comes up with ripple, and with easy float,
And glides into a bed of water-lilies:
Broad-leav'd are they, and their white canopies
Are upward turn'd to catch the heaven's dew."

Note also the following species of rhyme, which is very rare:—

Taming of the Shrew, ii. *ad fin.*,—

"——————————— fathers, commonly,
Do get their children; but, in this case of wooing,
A child shall get a sire, if I fail not of my cunning."

This passage, however, is not Shakespeare's.

Marston's Satires, Prefatory Address; I quote at second-hand,—

"Thou sole [read *soule*] of pleasure, honour's only substance,
Great arbitrator, umpire of the earth,

Whom fleshy [*fleshly?*] epicures call virtue's essence,
Thou moving orator, whose powerful breath
Sways all men's judgments," &c.[43]

Spenser, Visions of Bellay, vii. Todd, vol. vii. p. 512,—

"I saw a river swift, whose fomy billowes
Did wash the grondwork of an old great wall:
I saw it cover'd all with griessy [surely *griesly*] shadowes,
That with black horror did the ayre appall."

Harrington's Ariosto, B. i. St. lvi.,—

"It might be true, but sure it was incredible,
To tell to one that were discreet and wise,
But unto Sacrapant it seemed possible,
Because that love had dazzled so his eyes:
Love causeth that we see to seem invisible,
And makes of things not seen a shape to rise."

St. lxv., *astonished—punished—diminished.* B. iii. St. liii., *unaccessible—impossible—possible.*

XVII.

As, in the sense of *to wit.*

King Henry VIII. iv. 1, point,—

"Where by the Archbishop of Canterbury
She had all the royal makings of a queen—
As, holy oil, Edward Confessor's crown,
The rod, and bird of peace, and all such emblems—
Laid nobly on her."

---

43 See Mr. Halliwell's edition of Marston, printed from the old copies, vol. iii. p. 200, which confirms Walker's two conjectures. His conjecture *griesly* in the next quotation is confirmed by the first folio of Spenser.—*Ed.*

As is here used not in the sense of *for instance,* but in that of *namely, to wit;* it expresses an enumeration of particulars, not a selection from them by way of example. This is a frequent—perhaps, indeed, the one exclusive—signification of *as*, when employed in this construction; *e.g.*, 3 King Henry VI., near the end (a striking instance),—

"What valiant foemen, like to autumn's corn,
Have we mow'd down, in tops of all their pride!
Three dukes of Somerset, &c.
Two Cliffords, as the father and the son;
And two Northumberlands," &c.

This is the true construction of *as* in a number of passages, where it has been, or is likely to be, mistaken for the modern usage.

Hamlet, i. 4, I think,—

"So, oft it chances in particular men,
That for some vicious mole of nature in them,
As, in their birth, &c. ——————————
——————————————
By the[44] o'ergrowth of some complexion, &c.
——————————————
Or by some habit," &c.

2 King Richard II. ii. 1,—

"No, it [*his ear*] is stopt with other flattering sounds,
As, praises of his state; then there are found[45]

---

[44] Walker silently adopts Pope's correction, *the* for *their.* The latter is the reading of the old quartos. It is not English, and is no doubt derived from the last line but one above. The folios are defective here.—*Ed.*

[45] The earliest quartos (those of 1597 and 1598) according to Mr. Collier, read, "As praises of *whose taste the wise* are found." Mr. Collier conjectures *fond* for *found*, but should we not also read *th' unwise* for *the wise?* The reading of the later copies

Lascivious metres, &c. ——————

——————————————

Reports of fashions in proud Italy," &c.

Hence in As You Like It, ii. 7,—

"And one man in his time plays many parts,
His acts being seven ages. *At* first, the infant," &c.

I have no doubt that Shakespeare wrote, "*As*, first," &c. (So in Browne, Britannia's Pastorals, Book ii. Song v. Clarke, p. 295, line 7,—

"—————— 't is sentenc'd so by those,
That here on earth *at* destinies dispose
The lives and deaths of men," &c.;

read *as*.)

It occurs also where only one particular is in question. As You Like It, v. 4, "—but when one of the parties were met themselves, one of them thought but of an *If*, as, 'If you said so, then I said so;' and they shook hands," &c.

XVIII.

Inversion of the Indefinite Article.

Tempest, iv. 1,—

"So rare a wonder'd father, and a wife,
Makes this place Paradise;"

i.e., "so *rare-wonder'd a* father." So King John, iv. 2,—

"Makes sound opinion sick, and truth suspected,
For putting on so new a fashion'd robe."

---

looks to me like a sophistication for the sake of the sense. The variation, however, does not interfere with Walker's interpretation of the word *as*.—*Ed.*

Comedy of Errors, iii. 2, near the end,—

"———— there's no man is so vain
That would refuse so fair an offer'd chain;"

i.e., "so fair- [*fairly-*] offer'd a chain." (Compare Milton's Masque, l. 322, "thy *honest-offer'd* courtesy.") Love's Labour's Lost, i. 1,—

"Or, having sworn too hard-a-keeping oath,
Study to break it," &c.

Beaumont and Fletcher, Island Princess, iv. 3,—

"So brave a mingled temper saw I never;"

i.e., "a temper so well mixed, so happily balanced."

Sir F. Kinaston on Chaucer's Troilus and Cresside, printed 1796, p. 8,—"It cannot be imagined that Chaucer, who was so great a learned scholler, should be ignorant of the story,"—"a scholar so great-learned;" (compare Sidney, Defence of Poesy, p. 493, l. 39,—"I shall not do it without the testimonie of great learned [*great-learned*] men, both ancient and moderne;" p. 517, line 15, "diverse small-lerned courtiers;" Chapman, Lines to the Reader, prefixed to his Iliad, 4th page, old folio, "those great learn'd men ———— that were his [Homer's] commentars;" and Selden as quoted in Gifford's Jonson, vol. i. p. civ., "a common-learned reader.") Chaucer, Frankeleines Tale, l. 11825,—

"Considering the best on every side,
That fro his lust yet were him lever abide,
Than do so high a churlish wretchednesse
Ageins fraunchise, and alle gentillesse."

Chapman, Odyss. xii. note,—"But thus they botch, &c.—imagining so huge a great body must needs have a voice as huge."

XIX.

Certain Preterites used as Participles.

Antony and Cleopatra, ii. 2,—

"———— that the present need
Speaks to atone you.
Lep. Worthily spoken, Mecænas."

Spoke; and so it is printed in Johnson and Steevens's edition, 1793. *Ib.*,—

"———— Will Cæsar speak?
Cæs. Not till he hears how Antony is touch'd
With what is spoke already."

Venus and Adonis, St. clviii.,—

"Hadst thou but bid beware, then he had spoke."

And so I think we should read, Winter's Tale, v. 1,—

"You might have spoke a thousand things that would
Have done the time more benefit."

And so write, Fletcher, Valentinian, i. 3, Moxon, vol. i. p. 442, col. 1,—

"I have spoken too much, sir.
Val. I'll have all.
Aecius. It fits not
Your ears should hear their vanities."

The parliamentary *spoke* is perhaps a relic of antiquity. So *chose*, *took*, &c., in the Elizabethan poets, and indeed much later. *Gave* seems to be used thus, Sonnet clii.,—

"For I have sworn deep oaths of thy deep kindness,
Oaths of thy love, thy truth, thy constancy;
And to enlighten thee, gave eyes to blindness,
To make them swear against the thing they see;
For I have sworn thee fair," &c.

In Chapman, Il. iii. Taylor, vol. i. p. 92, l. 8,—

> "And now my lance hath miss'd his end; my sword in shivers flew;
> And he scapes all;"

flew seems to be the participle.

XX.

Occasional licenses of rhyme in Shakespeare and his contemporaries, more especially as regards the interchange of *m* and *n*. Venus and Adonis, St. xcv.,—

> "What wax so frozen but dissolves with temp'ring,
> And yields at last to ev'ry light impression?
> Things out of hope are compass'd oft with vent'ring,
> Chiefly in love, whose leave exceeds commission."

Sonnet cxx.,—

> "O that our night of woe might have remember'd
> My deepest sense, how hard true sorrow hits;
> And soon to you, as you to me then, tender'd
> The humble salve which wounded bosoms fits!"

Tarquin and Lucrece, St. cxciv.,—

> "The more she saw the blood his cheeks replenish,
> The more she thought he spied in her some blemish."

Venus and Adonis, St. viii., *broken—open;* lxxvi., *open'd—betoken'd;* Sonnet lxi., *open—broken.* Timon of Athens, iv. 3,—

> "———————— I'd exchange
> For this one wish, That you had power and wealth
> To requite me, by making rich yourself."

(As Sir Henry Moody on Fletcher, Moxon's B. and F. vol. i. p. lvii.,—

"Though thou diedst not possess'd of that same pelf,
That nobler souls call dirt, the city, wealth," &c.)

Troilus and Cressida, iii. 3,—

"Great Hector's sister did Achilles win;
But our great Ajax bravely beat down him."

Cymbeline, v. 4,—

"Like hardiment Posthumus hath
To Cymbeline perform'd:
Then, Jupiter, thou king of gods,
Why hast thou thus adjourn'd
The graces for his merits due,
Being all to dolours turn'd."

Other writers. Surrey, ed. 1831, p. 10, *demean—stream*, *some—undone;* p. 27, *mine—time*, *soon—doom;* pp. 28-9, *come—son;* p. 41, *myself—stealth;* p. 48, *rewarded—deserved* (pron. *desarved*); p. 59, *bemoan—swoln;* p. 66, *time—define*.

Spenser, F. Q., B. v. C. v. St. xix., *thondred—sondred—encombred—numbred;* ii. ix. i., alternate rhymes, *adorne—forme*. Hymne in Honour of Beautie, St. xxvi. vv. 6, 7, *reflexion—impression*. Spenser, however, is, I think, very sparing in licenses of this particular kind. Beaumont and Fletcher, Wit at Several Weapons, iv. 1, *ad fin.*, rhyme, I think,—

"These should be sure signs of her affection's truth;
Yet I'll go forward with my surer proof."

Ford, Fame's Memorial, Gifford, vol. ii. p. 588,—

"Sincerest justice is not to discern,
But to defend, aid, further, and confirm."

Lines by J. M., prefixed to the first folio Shakespeare, *init.*,—

"We wonder'd, Shakespeare, that thou went'st so soon
From the world's stage to the grave's tiring-room."

Jonson, Catiline, iii. 2, Gifford, vol, iv. p. 258,—

"His former drifts partake of former times,
But this last plot is only Catiline's."

Play of Hieronimo,[46] Dodsley's Old Plays, vol. iii. p. 60,—

"—————— from farmers that crack barns
With stuffing corn, yet starve the needy swarms."

Middleton, More Dissemblers besides Women, i. 4, *ad fin.*,—

"—————— my master storming
Sent me last night, but I 'll be gone this morning."

Lord Brooke, Of Humane Learning, St. cxvi.,—

"Which being only number, measure, time,
All following Nature, help her to refine."

Lord Brooke's evidence, indeed, is less producible, inasmuch as he is careless—or shall I say obtuse—*in re metrica.* Poem of Massinger to his Son, J. S. upon his Minerva, *ad fin.*, Gifford, vol. iv. p. 595,—

"——————. doth not by chance,
But merit, crown thee with the laurel branch."

Daniel, Complaint of Rosamond, St. cxix. page 144, ed. 1623,—

"Pitiful mouth, quoth he, that living gavest
The sweetest comfort that my soul could wish,
O be it lawful now, that dead thou havest
This sorrowing farewell of a dying kiss."

---

[46] Or rather "The First Part of Jeronimo."—*Ed.*

Donne, Satire vii. l. 9,—

"And wouldst persuade her to a worse offence,
Than that whereof thou didst accuse her wench."

Version of Psalm cxxxvii. St. xi.,—

"Happy, who, thy tender barnes
From the arms
Of their wailing mothers tearing," &c.

Fletcher, Faithful Shepherdess, ii. 3, Moxon, vol. i. p. 271, col. 1,—

"A pair of painted buskins, and a lamb,
Soft as his own locks, or the down of swan."

Cooke, Greene's Tu Quoque, Lamb, ed. 1835, vol. i. p. 60,—

"Thrice happy days they were, and too soon gone,
When as the heart was coupled with the tongue;"

rhyme apparently; see context.

Beaumont, Translation of Ovid's Remedy of Love, Moxon, vol. ii. p. 702, col. 1,—

"Thus must thou school thyself, and I could wish
Thee to thyself most eloquent in this."

On the Marriage of a Beauteous Young Gentlewoman, &c., p. 706, col. 1,—

"Ag'd and deformed Tithon! must thy twine
Circle and blast at once what care and time
Had made for wonder?"

Pericles, ii. Gower's introductory lines,—

"——————————— the ship
Should house him safe, is wreck'd and split."

John Onley, to W. Browne, Clarke's Browne, p. 16,—

"Puff'd with the hope of honour's goal to win,
Runs out of breath, yet furthest off from him."

Ib., p. 17, *come—done.* W. Ferrar's lines, *ib.* 22, *adorn —form.* T. Wenman's, 23, *rhymes—lines.* Britannia's Pastorals, B. i. Song ii. p. 75, penult., *twin—him.* Song i. p. 52, *ad fin.*,—

"When much thou lov'st [*lovest*], most disdain comes on thee,
And when thou think'st to hold her, she flies from thee."

Song ii. p. 74,—

"Sweetly she came, and with a modest blush
Gave him the day, and then accosted thus."

P. 82, penult.,—

"This was the cause them by tradition taught,
Why one flood ran so fast, th' other so soft."

Song iv. p. 118,—

"And to the waking swain it be unknown,
Whether his sheep be dead, or stray'd, or stol'n."

(So Surrey above.)

B. ii. Song i. p. 175,—

"—————— her hands would pass
To serve that purpose, though you daily wash."

Song iii. p. 253, *oft—wrought.* Song iv. p. 271, *oft—bought.* P. 281, *aloft—brought.* B. i. Song iv. p. 110,—

"And as that beast hath legs (which shepherds fear,
Yclept a badger, which our lambs doth tear,)
One long, the other short, that when he runs
Upon the plains, he halts; but when he *runs*
On craggy rocks, or steepy hills, we see
None runs more swift nor easier than he."

Read *comes.* Song v. p. 151,—

"—————— cursed Judas' sin
Was not so much in yielding up the king
Of life to death, as when," &c.

B. i. Song ii. p. 61,—

"And last the little minnow-fish,
Whose chief delight in gravel is."

Spenser, F. Q. ii. x. ix., *time—crime—slime—line;* iv. xi. xxix., *Breane—cleane—stream;* vi. iv. xxiv., *againe—entertaine—faine—ayme;* vi. iii. xxxvi., *offended—contemned—condemned.* The *m-n* rhyme is, I think, very uncommon in Spenser.

Donne, Poems, 1633, Elegy [on a Lady], p. 297,—

"The ravenous earth that now wooes her to be
Earth too, will be a *Lemnia;* and the tree,
That wraps that crystal in a wooden tomb,
Shall be took up *spruce*, fill'd with *diamond.*"

Diamond must be a corruption. *Qu.*,—

"Shall be took up *spice*, fill'd with *amomum*,"

(*i.e.*, cinnamon.) Ámomum, as Sandys's Ovid, xv. ed. 1626. p. 314,—"the gum Of frankincense, and juicy amomum." But perhaps the later edition would set all right. *Lemnia* is an erratum for *limbeck.* It may be merely one of the mistakes of the edition 1633.[47] Play of Ram Alley, iv. Dodsley, vol. v. p. 440, rhyme apparently,—

"We wear small hair, yet have we tongue and wit;
Lawyers close-breech'd have bodies politic."

Play of the Merry Devil of Edmonton, Dodsley, vol. v. p. 242,—

"Then since the first spring was so sweet and warm,
Let it die gently; ne'er kill it [*kill't*] with a scorn."

Rhyme, I imagine; see context. 2 King Henry VI. i. 1; the place seems to require rhyme,—

"Lordings, farewell; and say, when I am gone,
I prophesied,—France will be lost ere long."

---

[47] These blunders are carefully preserved in the ed. 1669.—*Ed.*

H. Killigrew, Play of the Conspiracy, Lamb. ed. 1835, vol. ii. p. 213, the first and third lines rhyming,—

"This is a motion still and soft,
So free from noise and cry,
That Jove himself, who hears a thought,
Knows not when we pass by."

Chapman, Il. xvii. 2nd Argument, vol. ii. p. 96, Taylor, *maintain—same*. Marmyon, Antiquary, iii. 1 (2), Dodsley, x. 49, Madrigal, *become—one—expression*, rhymes apparently. Haughton, Englishmen for My Money, iv. 2, in a rhyming passage,—

"As every plant takes virtue of the sun,
So from her eyes this life and being sprung.
. . . .
Each word thou spak'st (oh speak not so again)
Bore Death's true image on the word engraven."

Chapman, Odyss. xii. p. 185,—

"———— I ————
Chopt it in fragments with my sword, and wrought,
With strong hand, every piece, till all were soft."

Heywood, Four Prentices of London, Dodsley, vol. vi. p. 430, the concluding lines of a scene,—

"This lady as our life we will esteem,
And place her in the honour of a queen."

Harrington, Orlando Furioso, C. iii. St. x.,—

"Long have I looked here for this thy coming,
Being foretold thereof by Merlin's cunning." [48]

v. viii.,—

"Nor thinking this might breed my mistress danger,
I usd this practise in Geneura's chamber."

---

[48] *Coming* and *cunning* rhyme also together C. xliii. St. cxii.—*Ed.*

vi. x., *aloft—sought—brought;* xxxiii. lxxi., *nimble—kindle.* Dubartas, i. iv. p. 35, col. 2,—

"To pour some water of his grace, to quench
Our boiling flesh's fell concupiscence."

vi. p. 57, col. 1, *linage—image.*
Shirley, Narcissus, Gifford and Dyce, vol. vi. page 475, St. 3,—

"But Echo miss'd her aim, for he went back,
And with his hand check'd her unruly one,
As such addresses did good manners lack;
She else perhaps might an embrace have stol'n."

As Surrey and Browne above. Paranymphi, p. 501,—

"—————— These are the myrrh
With which his fanes perfumed are."

This is curious. How did Shirley or his contemporaries pronounce *myrrh?* [49] Fanshawe, Pastor Fido, iii. 2, p. 78; as Cooke above, and Crashawe a little below,—

"———————— make a ring
About me round, and let the sport begin."

ii. 1, p. 47,—

"Blest man, to be transform'd at such a time,
As if this accident thou could'st divine!"

v. 2, p. 160, *time—thine.* 5, p. 179,—

"Or if I have transgress'd so much, wherein
Sinn'd my son so, you will not pardon him?"

The *m-n* rhyme is frequent in this poem.
Crashawe, Music's Duel, l. ii.,—

"There stood she list'ning, and did entertain
The music's soft report, and mould the same
To her own murmurs."

---

[49] Possibly they pronounced *are* as *err;* so even now some persons, Londoners I fancy, say *hev* for *have.—Ed.*

L. 19,—

> "——————— ere the war begin,
> He lightly skirmishes on ev'ry string."

Bishop Corbet, on the Lady Arabella, Poems, 1647, p. 80,—

> "And now my pardon is my epitaph,
> And a small coffin my poor carcase hath."

Id., Journey into France, *ib.* p. 82,—

> "But to believe it you must think
> The Jews did put a candle in 't."

Dryden, Tyrannic Love, iii. 1, Scott's edition, vol. iii. p. 387, *wish—this.* This I believe is exceedingly rare in Dryden's age. Lord Rochester, Satire against Man,—

> "Were I, who to my cost already am
> One of those strange prodigious creatures, man,
> A spirit free to choose."

Oldham, Letter to a Friend, written 1673, Works, ed. 1710, p. 181,—

> "Here rougher strokes, touch'd with a careless dash,
> Resemble the first setting off a face."

All the above rhymes are rather rare in the Elizabethan poets: I speak as far as my knowledge extends. Some of them are particularly uncommon, as *s—sh.*

Instances of such rhymes as *downs—hounds; combines—minds*, &c.; also *wile—child;* both rare, but the latter exceedingly so. Venus and Adonis, St. cxiii.,—

> "Pursue these fearful creatures o'er the downs,
> And on thy well-breath'd horse keep with thy hounds."

This rhyming marriage of *n* with *nd* occurs sometimes, though rarely, in the Elizabethan poets. (I use this epithet here, as elsewhere, in a somewhat wide sense.) It is probably owing to the interchangeableness, in many words of the two terminations, whereof the writers of the age furnish proofs. Compare *drownd*, *gownd*, and other vulgar forms still prevalent. Vulgarisms are seldom corruptions; they are generally relics of antiquity. *Woodbind* occurs in that age; so *cowbind* even now;—on the other hand, *woodbine*, *cowbine*, *bellbine*, are now in use. Cymbeline, iv. 2, fol. p. 389, col. 1,—

> "———————— bring thee all this,
> Yea, and furr'd Mosse besides. When Flowres are none
> To *winter-ground* thy Coarse;"

for *winter-gowne*. (Or indeed *gowne* may have been written in the MS. *gownd*, as the final *e* is often printed *d* in the folio; see art. lxii. on that point.) Instances of this mode of rhyming. Jonson, Forest, xi.,—

> "That falls like sleep on lovers, and combines
> The soft, and sweetest minds
> In equal knots."

Quarles, Argalus and Parthenia, Book i. ed. 1647, p. 13,—

> "So shalt thou wreak thy vengeance by a wile,
> And make the mother bawd to her own child."

Dubartas, i. i. ed. 1641, p. 4, col. 2,—

> "———————— the lowly fields,
> Puft up, shall swell to huge and mighty hills."

And so i. ii. p. 22, col. 1, *hills—fields*.

i. ii. p. 17, col. 2,—

> "But the Heaven's course, not wandring up nor down,
> Continually turns only roundly round."

Drayton (in whom it is, perhaps, particularly rare), Epistle of William de la Poole to Queen Margaret,—

> "The sad investing of so many towns,
> Scor'd on my breast in honourable wounds."

Polybion, Song xi. Delamere,—

"——————————— sees from her shady bowers
The wanton wood-nymphs mixt with her light-footed Fauns,
To lead the rural routs about the goodly lawnds."

Heywood, Four Prentices of London, i. 1, Dodsley, vol. vi. p. 465, rhyme, I imagine,—

"But ere I leave these fair Judæan bounds,
Unto this lion I 'll add all your crowns."

P. 466, the concluding lines of a dialogue,—

"*Soldan.* As loud and proud defiance our drum sounds.
Godfrey. For Christ, my father, conquest and two crowns."

Dubartas again, i. ii. p. 13, col. 1,—

"But if they once perceive or understand
The moony squadrons of proud Ottoman
To be approaching," &c.

Ib. iii. p. 23, col. 1,—

"In Thetis' large cells leaveth nought behind,
Save liquid salt, and a thick bitter brine."

Spenser, Sonnet xix.,—

"The merry Cuckow, messenger of Spring,
His trumpet shrill hath thrise already sounded,
That warnes al Lovers wayte upon their king,
Who now is coming forth with girland crouned."

Fanshawe, Translation of Horace's 16th Epode, p. 308, l. 1,—

"——————— like to the Phocians,
Who left their execrated lands."

Butler has—Butlericè—Epistle of Hudibras to Sidrophel, l. 47, ed. 1716, *crystallines—rinds.* (Or did the form *rines* still linger, and is this a corrupt reading?) I have only met, as far as my observation extends, with two instances in the eighteenth century. Lines in the Gent. Mag. 1735, p. 728, col. 2,—

"And a pack of little hounds
To drive Reynard o'er the downs."

Young, Last Day, B. i, l. 75,—

"While other Bourbons rule in other lands,
And (if man's sin forbids not) other Annes."

Rhymes such as *scorn—thorns*, *arts—impart*, *pursues—due*, occur frequently in Lord Brooke, and in the early part and towards the end of Hall's Satires; and sometimes, though exceedingly seldom, in some of the other poets of this age. The following are the only instances I have noticed in Shakespeare:—

Two Gentlemen of Verona, iii. 1, a mitigated instance,—

"But she did scorn a present that I sent her.
Val. A woman sometimes scorns what best contents her."

King Lear, iii. 6, near the end,—

"When false opinion, whose wrong thoughts defile thee,
In thy just proof repeals, and reconciles thee."

So the quartos, *teste* ed. 1770; which Theobald erroneously altered to "whose wrong *thought defiles* thee." Much Ado, &c., v. 3, *ad fin.* Shakespeare may possibly have written,—

"Come, let us hence, and put on other weeds;
And then to Leonato's we will go.
Claud. And, Hymen, now with luckier issue *speed*,
Than this, for whom we render'd up this woe!"

I have noticed an instance in the Faerie Queene, Book vi. C. vi. St. iii.,—

"——— through the long experience of his dayes
Which had in many fortunes tossed beene,
And past through many perilous assayes,

He knew the diverse went of mortall wayes,
And in the minds of men had great insight;
Which with sage counsell, when they went astray,
He could enforme," &c.

I think Spenser, who is so strict in his rhymes, must have written, by one of his usual licenses, *astrayes*, according to a supposed analogy with certain adverbs, which are written indiscriminately with or without the final *s*. Shepheards Calender, Ægl. x. St. vii.,—

"Abandon then the base and viler clowne;
Lift up thyself out of the lowly dust,
And sing of bloody Mars, of wars, of giusts;
Turne thee to those that weld the awefull crowne,
To doubted knights, whose woundlesse armour rusts,
And helmes unbruzed wexen daylie browne."

Ægl. iv. l. 5,—

"Or bene thine eyes attempred to the yeare,
Quenching the gasping furrowes thirst with rayne?
Like Aprill showre so stream the trickling teares
Adowne thy cheeke, to quench thy thirstie paine."

I have since noticed another instance, F. Q. ii. v. xxxii.,—

"——— a flock of damzelles fresh and gay,
That round about him dissolute did play
Their wanton follies, and light merriment;"

—rhyming to *habiliments* and *ornaments*.

Surely we should read *merriments*.

In Fairfax's Tasso, B. xii. St. lxiii. Knight (Knight has injured Fairfax in several places by injudicious corrections), the alternate rhymes are *blast—cast—lasts*. Read with Singer, *blasts—casts—lasts*. In B. vii. St. lxxxii., *stand—land—bands*, I doubt not we should read *stands* and *lands*, though on this passage I have not consulted Singer. In these places, the alteration, to whomsoever it is owing, no doubt originated in a zeal for grammar. B. xii. St. iv., *feed—deed—weeds;* read *feeds—deeds.* B. viii. St. xxvii., *ran—began—son,* read *run* and *begun,* old forms, the latter of which has only of late become obsolete.

Chapman, Il. xxi. Taylor, vol. ii. p. 175,—

"Pelides, do not stir a foot; nor those waves, proudly curl'd
Against thy bold breast, fear a jot; thou hast us two thy *friends*
(Neptune and Pallas) Jove himself approving th' aid we *lend.*"

Friend, I conjecture, *paullo audacius.* iv. vol. i. p. 114, *foe—goes;* read *foes;* see context. xxiii. vol. ii. p. 214, *ad fin.*, *fist—lists;* read *fists.* I have noticed an instance in Butler; it would not be worth quoting, on account of Butler's habitual license in rhyming, but that it may be considered as one of those archaisms in his writings which I have noticed elsewhere; Miscellaneous Thoughts, line 43, the rabble

"Discharge all damages and costs
Of knights and squires of the post."

Knee—eye, lie—be, geer—fire, seek—like, these—immortalize, and the like, are frequent in Hall's Satires, but—so far at least as I have observed—occur very rarely in the other writers of those times. *Seek—like,* and others with *k,* are found, I think, more frequently than the rest.

Note also *man—on,* and the like, which occur now and then.

Oy—ay are met with sometimes, but very seldom, in the poets of Elizabeth and James's time; perhaps only in the more slovenly writers. I except Daniel, in whom they are frequent. (Here, as elsewhere, I speak only of the poets

I have myself read, which, however, are the majority. Daniel's xxivth Sonnet, alternate rhymes, *annoy—pay*. Poems, ed. 1623, p. 19, Funeral Poem on the Death of the Earl of Devonshire, alternate rhymes, *joy'd—paid*. Complaint of Rosamond, St. cxi. p. 142, alternate rhymes, *stay—way—joy*. Cleopatra, i. p. 465, *destroyer—betray her*. Daniel is, I think, a loose rhymer as regards some particular endings; or is it with him a matter of system? Note the strange rhyme in The Faithful Friends, *ad fin.*,—

"For, whilst I reign, on virtue will I smile,
And honour only with me still prevail."

I suspect that, in the Elizabethan and earlier ages, *ai* was sometimes pronounced as we now pronounce the Greek *αι*. Butler's Miscellaneous Thoughts, l. 449,—

"They that do write in authors' praises,
And freely give their friends their voices."

Id., Satire on the Ridiculous Imitation of the French, l. 109, rhymes, *noise—says*. *Id.*, Ode on Modern Critics, St. v., *oy—ey*,—

"The feeblest vermin can destroy
As soon as stoutest beast of prey."

In the Fragments of a Second Part of the Satire on Human Learning, *Stoics* rhymes to *Cyrenaics*. (By the way, four lines below this latter couplet, for *academics* read *academies*.) I know not whether rhyme was intended in the common proverb,—

"All work, and no play,
Makes Jack a dull boy."

Such rhymes as *discover—mother*, sometimes occur. Flecknoe, Retrospective Review, vol. v. p. 272,—

"———— till you discover
All the beauties of your mother."

I find this even in an early poem of Pope's, the Essay on Criticism, l. 30, at least in ed. 6, Linton, 1719,—

> "These hate as rivals all who write, and others
> But envy wits as eunuchs envy lovers."[50]

Sense—elements, and the like. This, as far as I have observed, is very rare, except in Sylvester.

The following, Browne, Britannia's Pastorals, B. i. Song iii. l. 11, Clarke, p. 89,—

> "————————— in came the watery nymph,
> To raise from sound [*i.e.*, *swoon*] poor Doridon (the imp,
> Whom Nature seem'd," &c.,

may be compared with *wish—this*, &c.

I have noticed, but very rarely, such rhymes as *back—cataract*.[51] Dubartas, i. iv. p. 37, col. 2, *cataract—make*.

Sustain'd—wind, &c. I know not that I have noticed this, except in Chapman's Homer, and that very rarely; *e.g.*, Odyss. i. ed. 1, p. 5. Chapman resorts sometimes to licenses of rhyme scarcely (if at all) authorized by the custom of his age, owing to the unusual demand for rhymes which his translation of Homer involved. Hence, too, Spenser's bold alterations of the forms of words for rhyme's sake. Sylvester too employs some occasionally which are perhaps peculiar to him: i. iv. p. 33, col. 1, *sand—adamant;* ii. iv. iii. p. 225, col. 1, l. 3, *mount—profound;* i. iv. p. 35, col. 2, *months—fronts;* and so vi. p. 54, col. 1, *in't—labyrinth;* and ii. p. 14, col. 1, *out—south*.

---

[50] This couplet now stands thus,—

> "Each burns alike, who can, or cannot write,
> Or with a rival's or an eunuch's spite.—*Ed.*

[51] In O'Connor's Child, Campbell rhymes *backs-cataracts*.—*Ed.*

In Chapman's Iliad, xi. Taylor, vol. i. p. 243, we have,—

"————————— convey'd
The son of Æsculapius, the great physician:
To fleet they flew. Cebriones perceiv'd the slaughter done
By Ajax," &c.

But Chapman wrote *phisition*, according to the common old spelling. [So Butter's folio, p. 152.—*Ed.*] xiv. vol. ii. p. 39,—

"She swore, as he enjoin'd, in all, and strengthen'd all his joys,
By naming all th' infernal gods, surnam'd the Titanoes."

Write (*meo periculo*) *Titanois*. And so I find it to be in the old edition.

Note in Butler, Satire on Human Learning, P. ii. l. 223,—

"Words are but pictures, true or false design'd,
To draw the lines and features of the mind;
The characters and artificial draughts,
T' express the inward images of thoughts."

(Point,—

"——— pictures, true or false, design'd
To draw," &c.;

at least if I understand the construction aright.) So in his Miscellaneous Thoughts, l. 95,—

"The copy of a copy, and lame draught,
Unnaturally taken from a thought;"

I suppose *draught* must be pronounced as *caught*, *taught*.

XXI.

Wistly—wistfully.

K. Richard II. v. 4,—

"*Have I no friend?* quoth he: he spake it twice,
And urg'd it twice together; did he not?

Serv. He did.
Exton. And, speaking it, he wistfully look'd on me;" &c.

Surely, with the folio, *wistly;* and so Knight. The word is frequent in our old poets; *e.g.*, Tarquin and Lucrece, St. cxciv.,—

"She thought he blush'd, as knowing Tarquin's lust,
And, blushing with him, wistly on him gaz'd."

Venus and Adonis, St. lviii.,—

"O what a sight it was, wistly to view
How she came stealing to the wayward boy!"

Passionate Pilgrim, Poem iv. (not Shakespeare's),—

"The sun look'd on the world with glorious eye,
But not so wistly as this queen on him."

Drayton, Muses' Elysium, vii. p. 63,—

"And in my boat I turn'd about,
And wistly view'd the lad,
And clearly saw his eyes were out,
Though bow and shafts he had.
As wistly she did me behold," &c.

In Chapman *wishly*, Il. xi. Taylor, vol. i. p. 245, l. 16,—

"———————— Œacides, that wishly did intend
———————— how deep the skirmish drew
Amongst the Greeks;" &c.

Harrington, Ariosto, xxxvi. xxviii.,—

"Then lookt she wishlie all about the place,
To finde out him that caused all her care."

In the passage from K. R. II. we might possibly read,—

"And, speaking it, look'd wistfully on me;"

but this is very unlikely.[52]

---

[52] "*Wistfully*," says Mr. Knight in his note in the Pictorial Shakespeare, "has crept into the modern editions without authority." This no doubt is true of the Var. 1821, and of such

XXII.

Deserver—undeserver.

Troilus and Cressida, iii. 2,—

"——— give me swift transportance to those fields,
Where I may wallow in the lily beds
Propos'd for the deserver!"

Note the ancient use of *deserver*, absolutely, for "one who deserves *well*." So also *undeserver* is employed. Antony and Cleopatra, i. 2,—

"——————— our slippery people
(Whose love is never link'd to the deserver,
Till his deserts are past) begin," &c.

Ford, Broken Heart, ii. 3, Moxon, p. 58, col. 2,—

"—————— sickness or pain
Is the deserver's exercise."

(As Milton, Samson, 1287,—

"But patience is more oft the exercise
Of saints, the trial of their fortitude.")

Massinger, Emperor of the East, v. 2, Moxon, p. 261, col. 2,—

"We may give poor men riches, confer honours
On undeservers," &c.

---

editions as adopt the vulgate text, called that of Steevens and Malone, but the following modern editions read *wistly:* Rowe's, 1709; Pope's, 1725; Theobald's, 1752; Hanmer's, 1743; Warburton's, 1747; Johnson's, 1765; and Capell's, 1768. I conclude, therefore, that *wistfully* is a comparatively recent sophistication. *Wistly* is the reading, I believe, of all the old copies, except the first and second quartos. These read *wishtly*. *Wistly*, *wishtly*, and *wishly*, seem only various forms of the same word.—*Ed.*

Middleton, Sun in Aries, Dyce, vol. v., p. 303,—

> "What makes less noise than merit? or less show
> Than virtue? 't is the undeservers owe
> All to vain-glory and to rumour still."

By the way, Measure for Measure, v., towards the end of the play, fol. p. 83, col. 2,—

> "Wherein haue I so deseru'd of you
> That you extoll [*spoken ironically*] me thus?"

Vulg., or at least in some editions,—

> "Wherein have I *deserved*[53] *so* of you?" &c.

Possibly, *so undeserv'd.* Milton (I have the quotation from Knight's Quarterly Magazine, vol. ii. p. 378), "the famous (Parliament) I call it, though not the harmless, since none well-affected but will confess, they have deserved much more of these nations than they have undeserved."
Otherwise Spenser, Hymne in Honour of Love, St. xxiii.,—

> "How falls it then, that with thy furious fervour
> Thou dost afflict as well the not-deserver,
> As him that doeth thy lovely heasts despize?"

i.e., "him that does not deserve to be afflicted." Middleton and Rowley, Fair Quarrel, iii. 1, antepenult.,

> "————————————— Noble deserver!
> Farewell, most valiant and most wrong'd of men!"

quasi scribas, Noble-deserver, as *not-deserver* above, *well-deserver*. Bacon, Essay of Suitors,—" If affection lead a man to favour the less worthy in desert, let him do it without depraving or disabling the better deserver."

---

[53] The sophistication *deserved so* was introduced by Pope.—*Ed*.

√

XXIII.

Ovid's influence on Shakespeare.

Allusions to the story of Tereus. (I omit Titus Andronicus, iv. 1,—"Forc'd in the ruthless, vast, and gloomy woods," &c., Metam. vi. 520, *sqq.*, because I believe we are pretty safe in rejecting the whole play as spurious. For the same reason I do not notice ii. 1, near the end,—

"The emperor's court is like the house of fame,
The palace full of tongues, of eyes, of ears;"——

4. "So pale did shine the moon on Pyramus.")

Cymbeline, ii. 2, near the end.

To the discourse of Pythagoras, Metam. xv.; As You Like It, iii. 2; Twelfth Night, iv. 2; 2 K. Henry IV. iii. 1,—

"O Heaven! that one might read the book of fate," &c.

Metam. xv. 262; the same passage is also alluded to in Sonnet lxiv. 3-8. Note especially in K. H. IV.,—

"And see the revolution of the times
Make mountains level, and the continent,
Weary of solid firmness, melt itself
Into the sea!"

"Quodque fuit campus, vallem decursus aquarum
Fecit, et eluvie mons est deductus in æquor.

The simile of the waves in the same passage ("—ut unda impellitur unda") seems to be alluded in Sonnet lx.; compare indeed the whole of this sonnet with the context of Ovid; perhaps also T. and L. cxxxvi., cxxxvii. Possibly, to the story of Bacchus and the Tuscan mariners, Metam. iii. 664, in Ariel's pranks, Tempest, i. 2,—"I boarded the king's ship," &c. (I use the word *allusion*, throughout this article, incorrectly, wherever it seems to imply imitation of, or *conscious* allusion to, particular passages, which is alien from Shakespeare. I only remember three unequivocal instances of it: the first, Two Noble Kinsmen, i. 2, near the beginning,—

> " ——— ——— ——— Who then shall offer
> To Mars's so-scorn'd altar?"

for this scene is certainly Shakespeare's, from Æn. i. 48,— ×

> " Et quisquam numen Junonis adoret
> Præterea, aut supplex aris imponat honorem?"

The second is the concluding line, as I hold it to be, of Troilus and Cressida,—

> "Hope of revenge shall hide our inward woe;"

from Æn. i. 208,—

> "Spem vultu simulat, premit altum corde dolorem;"

and Antony and Cleopatra, ii. 1,—

> " ——— ——— ——— We, ignorant of ourselves,
> Beg often our own harms, which the wise powers
> Deny us for our good; so find we profit
> By losing of our prayers;"

see the well-known passages at the beginning and end of Juvenal's tenth Satire. I have, however noticed two that have the look of imitations. Cymbeline, iv. 2,—

> "Cowards father cowards, and base things sire base;"

(pronounce *sire* as a dissyllable;) compare Horace, Lib. iv. Od. iv. 29,—

> "Fortes creantur fortibus. Et bonis
> Est in juvencis, est in equis patrum
> Virtus;" &c.

(so I would point.) Timon, iv. 2,—

> "Who then dares to be half so kind again?"

this sounds like an echo of ancient poetry. It seems just possible indeed that Shakespeare was thinking not of any Latin poet, but of Chapman's translation of Odyss. ii. 231,

> μή τις ἔτι πρόφρων ἀγανὸς καὶ ἤπιος ἔστω
> σκηπτοῦχος βασιλεὺς, μηδὲ φρεσὶν αἴσιμα εἰδὼς.

But the word *allusion*, in its *correct* use, rather expresses the *unconscious* reproduction, in the poet's mind, of that which had impressed him in reading.)

To the battle of the Lapithæ and the Centaurs, Metam. xii., and the death of Orpheus, Metam. xi. M. N. D. v. 1,—

> "The battle with the Centaurs ————————
> ——————————————————
> ————————— that have I told my love,
> In glory of my kinsman Hercules.
> *Lys.* The riot of the tipsy Bacchanals,
> Tearing the Thracian singer in their rage."

To the story of Arachne and Minerva (with a variety), *ib.* iii. 2,—

> "We, Hermia, like two artificial gods," &c.

To that of Thisbe, and of Medea and Æson, Merchant of Venice, v. 1. (In M. N. D. v. 1,—

> "Whereat with blade, with bloody blameful blade,
> He bravely broach'd his boiling bloody breast;"

he may have been thinking of Ovid, Met. iv. 119, *de eadem re*,—

> "Quoque erat accinctus, demittit in ilia ferrum.
> Nec mora, *ferventi* moriens e vulnere traxit.")

To the cave of Envy, Metam. ii. 761, 2 K. H. VI. iii. 2,—

> " ——— lean-fac'd Envy in her loathsome cave."

To Midas, Merchant of Venice, iii. 2,—

> " ————————— Therefore, thou gaudy gold,
> Hard food for Midas," &c.

To the description of the Sun's chariot in the story of Phaeton, Metam. ii. 107. Cymbeline, v. 5,—

> "———— ———— (he) stakes this ring;
> And would so, had it heen a carbuncle
> Of Phœbus' wheel; and might so safely, had it
> Been all the worth of 's car."

Antony and Cleopatra, iv. 8,—

> "———— ———— ———— I 'll give thee, friend,
> An armour all of gold; it was a king's.
> *Ant.* He has deserv'd it, were it carbuncled
> Like holy Phœbus car."

To the latter part of the story of Phaeton, Two Noble Kinsmen, i. 2, first speech of Valerius. T. G. of Verona, iii. 1,—

> "Why, Phaeton, (for thou art Merops' son,)
> Wilt thou aspire to guide the heavenly car,
> And with thy daring folly burn the world?"

King Richard II. iii. 3,—

> "Down, down, I come; like glist'ring Phaeton,
> Wanting the manage of unruly jades."

(Note by the way, in the play of the Battle of Alcazar, ii. Dyce's Peele, ed. 2, vol. ii. p. 102,—

> "Bassa, wear thou the gold of Barbary,
> And glister like the palace of the Sun,
> In honour of the deed that thou hast done."

Ib. i. *ad fin.*, p. 98, there is an allusion to Envy's cave.) Simile of the river, Metam. iii. 568,—"Sic ego torrentem, qua nil obstabat eunti," &c. Is it fanciful to suppose that this simile caught Shakespeare's fancy, and recurred to him on many occasions? T. G. of Verona, ii. 7; K. John, ii. 2; M. for M. iii. 1, towards the end of the Duke's dialogue with Isabella; Venus and Adonis, lvi., and Tarquin and

Lucrece, xciii. clx. I wish, however, to distinguish between this, which is perhaps only a chance coincidence, such as often misleads commentators by a delusive show of imitation, and the unequivocal allusions which are cited previously and subsequently in this article. K. John, v. 7,—

"To set a form upon that indigest,
Which he hath left so shapeless and so rude."

An allusion to Ovid's "rudis indigestaque moles," Metam. i. 7. So too, I think, 2 K. H. VI. v. 1, where old Clifford says to Richard,—

"Hence, heap of wrath, foul undigested lump!"

Foul, i.e., ugly, ut passim; not *filthy*. And so King Henry calls him, 3 K. H. VI., v. 6, "an indigest deformed lump." The name of Shakespeare's Fairy Queen is borrowed from Ovid, Metam. iii. 173,—

"Dumque ibi perluitur solita Titania lympha."

XXIV.

Meaning of *clamour* in Shakespeare.

King Lear, i. 1,—

"—————— Revoke thy gift;
Or whilst I can vent clamour from my throat,
I'll tell thee, thou dost evil."

In many places it evidently signifies *wailing*. K. L. iv. 3,[54]—

---

[54] This beautiful scene is wanting in the folios and Rowe's edition; the quartos give it very corruptly. The speech before us was outrageously sophisticated by Pope; and his successors, though they properly removed his handiwork, still left the text

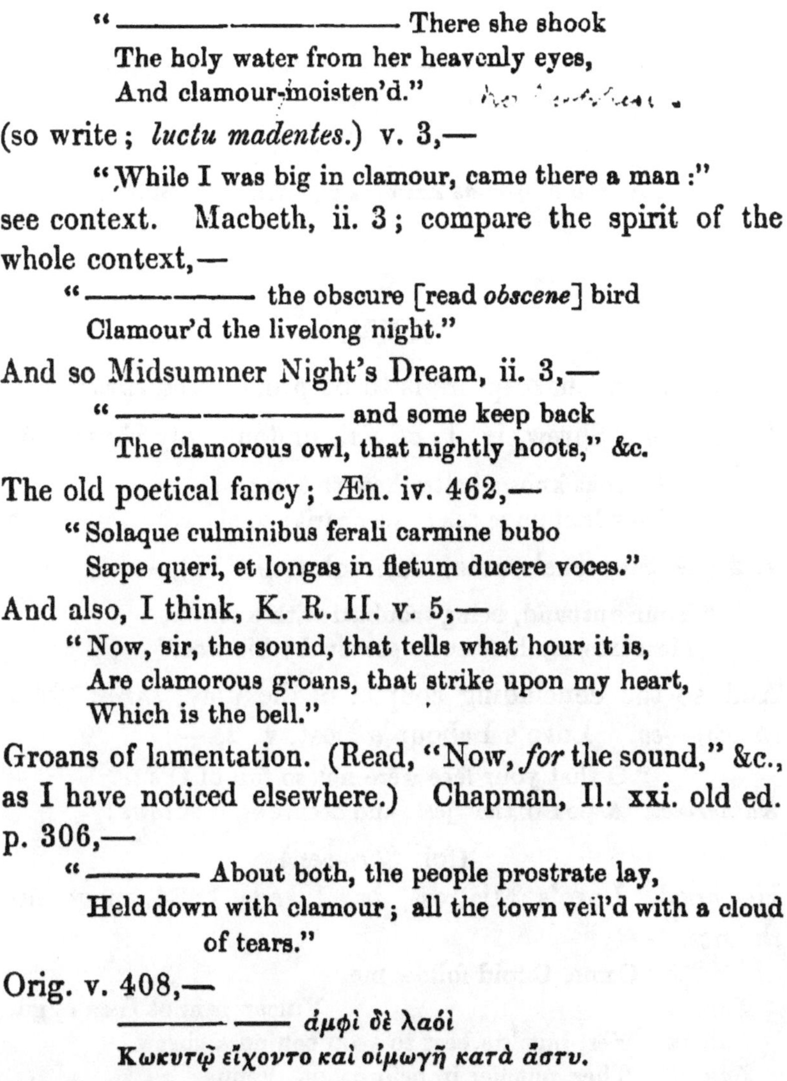

"———— There she shook
The holy water from her heavenly eyes,
And clamour-moisten'd."

(so write; *luctu madentes.*) v. 3,—

"While I was big in clamour, came there a man:"

see context. Macbeth, ii. 3; compare the spirit of the whole context,—

"———— the obscure [read *obscene*] bird
Clamour'd the livelong night."

And so Midsummer Night's Dream, ii. 3,—

"———— and some keep back
The clamorous owl, that nightly hoots," &c.

The old poetical fancy; Æn. iv. 462,—

"Solaque culminibus ferali carmine bubo
Sæpe queri, et longas in fletum ducere voces."

And also, I think, K. R. II. v. 5,—

"Now, sir, the sound, that tells what hour it is,
Are clamorous groans, that strike upon my heart,
Which is the bell."

Groans of lamentation. (Read, "Now, *for* the sound," &c., as I have noticed elsewhere.) Chapman, Il. xxi. old ed. p. 306,—

"———— About both, the people prostrate lay,
Held down with clamour; all the town veil'd with a cloud
of tears."

Orig. v. 408,—

———— ἀμφὶ δὲ λαοὶ
Κωκυτῷ εἴχοντο καὶ οἰμωγῇ κατὰ ἄστυ.

---

in a most unsatisfactory state. I must confess, I do not understand Walker's note; probably there is some mistake of the pen in it, which I cannot correct. The old copies read "moistened *her*;" the critics explain "clamour moisten'd" by "moisten'd clamour." I cannot agree with either.—*Ed.*

P. 307,—

"————— ——————— But now the clamour flew
Up to her turret."

Orig. v. 447,—

κωκυτοῦ δ' ἤκουσε καὶ οἰμωγῆς ἀπο πύργου.

XXV.

Shrew in Shakespeare is to be pronounced *shrow.*

Taming of a Shrew, iv. 1, *ad fin.*, undoubtedly rhyme,—

"He that knows better how to tame a shrew,
Now let him speak; 'tis charity to shew."

v. 2 (see Steevens's note, Var. vol. v. p. 511),—

"Your husband, being troubled with a shrew,
Measures my husband's sorrow by his woe."

And so the concluding couplet of the play, *shrew* (folio, *shrow*)—*so*. Love's Labour 's Lost, v. 2,—

"O that your face were not so full of O's!
Katherine. A pox o' that jest, and beshrew all shrews!"

(fol. *Shrowes.*)

Heywood, Love's Mistress, iv. 1, ed. 1824, page 60, rhymes,—

"Come, Cupid follow me.
Pan. Vulcan cannot [*can't*] go.
Vulcan. Yes, but 'tis best to keep behind a shrew.
Pan. Then put her in before: on, Venus; go."

Greene, K. James IV. iv. Dyce, vol. ii. p. 130; the passage is in rhyme,—

"How look I, Nano? like a man, or no?
Nano. If not a man, yet like a manly shrow."

(Male Dycius, "so written for the sake of the rhyme.") *Shrewd*, which in those times was akin to *shrew* in meaning, was also similarly pronounced; indeed it is often written *shrowd*, and sometimes *shrode*. So *beshrew;* M. of V. iii. 2, folio, page 173, col. 2,—"Beshrow your eyes." *Shrewsbury* is still pronounced by some *Shrowsbury*.

XXVI.

Sneap, &c.

Love's Labour 's Lost, i. 1,—

> "Biron is like an envious sneaping [*envious-sneaping*] frost,
> That bites the first-born infants of the spring."

Compare Milton, Samson Agonistes, 1575,—

> " ——————— which now proves
> Abortive as the first-born bloom of spring,
> Nipt with the lagging rear of winter's frost."

Sneap. Tarquin and Lucrece. St. xlviii.,—

> "So, so, quoth he, these lets attend the time,
> Like little frosts, that sometimes threat the spring,
> To add a more rejoicing to the prime,
> And give the sneaped birds more cause to sing."

Second Maiden's Tragedy, iii. 1, ed. 1824, p. 46,—

> "I think thou'st never done, thou lov'st to talk on 't,
> 'Tis fine discourse, pr'ythee find other business.
> *Servant*. Nay, I am gone, I 'm a man quickly sneap'd."
> [*Exit.*

Snubb'd in fact. It appears as *snubbed* in Bunyan, Holy War, account of Mr. Lustings's trial,—"My Lord, I am a man of high birth, and have been used to pleasures and pastimes and greatness: I have not been wont to be snubbed for my doings, but have been left to follow my will as if it were law." Also spelt *snib* and *sneb*. *Snip*, *nip*, *snap*, *snuff*, *sniff*, all belong to the same family. Marston, Malcontent, iii. 1, Dyce's Webster, vol. iv. p. 81,—"But how stands Mendoza? how is 't with him? *Mal.* Faith like a pair of snuffers, snibs filth in other men, and retains it in himself." Sidney, Arcadia, B. ii. p. 228, l. 14,—

"Thou heardst even now a young man sneb me sore,
Because I red [*counselled*] him, as I would my son."

W. B. Commendatory verses to Massinger, *init.*,—

"I am snapt already, and may go my way;
The poet-critic 's come; I hear him say,
This youth 's mistook, the author's work 's a play."

XXVII.

Peculiar Construction with the Adjective.

Othello iii. 3,—

"This fellow 's of exceeding honesty,
And knows all qualities, with a learned spirit,
Of human dealings."

Quære whether the comma ought not to be expunged after *spirit?* "And knows all qualities with a spirit learned of (*i.e.*, *in*) human dealings." The folio has,—

"And knowes all Quantities with a learn'd Spirit
Of humane dealings."

(I believe I am wrong as to this passage.)[55] This Latinized

---

[55] Steevens's reprint of the quarto 1622 has also a stop after *spirit*, but has a comma after *qualities*. *Quantities* is the absurd reading of all the folios and Rowe. All other editors, I believe,

construction is frequent in Shakespeare. King Lear, iii. 2,—

> "Thou perjur'd, and thou simular man of virtue,
> That art incestuous."

Such I think is the construction of the line.

3 King Henry VI. ii. 6,—

> "Bring forth that fatal screech-owl to our house,
> That nothing sung but death to us and ours."

So construe; and in like manner King Richard II. iii. 2,

> "——— a long-parted mother with her child," &c.

Macbeth iii. 6,—

> "——————— that a swift blessing
> May soon return to this our suffering country
> Under a hand accurst."

Winter's Tale, iv. 3,—

> "———————— 'Pray you, bid
> These unknown friends, to us, welcome."

King Henry VIII. iii. 1,—

> "Bring me a constant woman to her husband."

All 's Well that Ends Well, iii. 4,—

> "——————— Write, write, Rinaldo,
> To this unworthy husband of his wife."

Timon of Athens, iv, 2,—

> "A dedicated beggar to the air."

---

and Mr. Collier's old Corrector agree with the quarto. Notwithstanding Walker's hesitation, I prefer the construction which he has suggested. *Quality* here, as frequently elsewhere, seems to mean *natural disposition*. In this passage the poet has unconsciously described himself. In the next example, the folio, which in general, though less full, is far more correct than the quartos, omits *man*, and prints *simular* with a capital S.—*Ed.*

Sonnet xcviii.,—

> "Yet nor the lays of birds, nor the sweet smell
> Of different flowers in odour and in hue,
> Could make me any summer's story tell,
> Or from their proud lap pluck them where they grew."

(*a summer's story* is *a story suitable to summer;* as *a winter's tale.*)

cxi.,—

> "O, for my sake do you with Fortune chide,
> The guilty goddess of my harmful deeds."

Romeo and Juliet, iii. 1,—

> "Tybalt, the reason that I have to love thee
> Doth much excuse the appertaining rage
> To such a greeting."

1 King Henry IV. v. 4, seemingly,—

> "If it were so, I might have let alone
> Th' insulting hand of Douglas over you."

Cymbeline, v. 5,—

> "—————————— This Posthumus
> (Most like a noble lord in love, and one
> That had a royal lover) took this hint."

Vulg., "a noble lord, in love, and one," &c.[56]

So also, I think, in the Lover's Complaint, St. v.,—

> "Her hair, nor loose, nor tied in formal plat,
> Proclaim'd in her a careless hand of pride."

For *pride* [in the usual sense] has, I think, no place here; and the construction, *a hand of pride*, seems to be modern, and not Elizabethan. I suspect, by the way, that *pride* here means *outward ornament*.

---

[56] This faulty punctuation is that of the folios and Rowe, not of the Vulgate. It was corrected by Pope.—*Ed.*

Sonnet xliv.,—

> "No matter then, although my foot did stand
> Upon the farthest earth remov'd from thee," &c.

i.e., upon the earth farthest removed from thee.

Sonnet lxxxv., I suspect,—

> "My tongue-tied Muse in manners holds her still."

(*Holds her still, i.e., keeps herself silent.*)

Tarquin and Lucrece, St. cxii. (Moxon's ed.),—

> "And let thy misty[57] vapours march so thick,
> That in their smoky ranks his smother'd light,
> May set at noon, and make perpetual night."

i.e., that his light smother'd in their, &c., *may set at noon;* not, *may set in their*, &c. Perhaps the editor of Moxon's ed. meant to indicate this by the comma after *light*.

Taming of the Shrew, Introduction, i.,—

> "—— with declining head into his bosom."

So I think All 's Well, &c. ii. 5,—

> "The ministration and required office
> On my particular."

And perhaps K. Richard II. v. 3,—

> "Mine honour lives, when his dishonour dies,
> And my sham'd life in his dishonour lies."

Antony and Cleopatra, i. 2, —

> "—————— the letters too
> Of many our contriving friends in Rome
> Petition us at home."

(Pronounce *Rome*, as usual, *Room;* this removes the jingle between *Rome* and *home.*) *Contriving* here is not *managing* or *plotting*, but *sojourning; conterentes tempus.* See the

---

[57] Mr. Collier reads *musty*, with the first edition.—*Ed.*

Variorum notes on Taming of the Shrew, i. 2, near the end (where, however, the true reading is *convive*). Φίλων ἐν Ῥώμῃ διαγόντων. Tarquin and Lucrece, St. cx., Address to Night,—

"Grim cave of death, whispering conspirator,
With close-tongued treason, and the ravisher!"

Dele comma after *conspirator*. The construction is, I think, *whispering with*, &c. Hamlet, iii. 1,—

"This something-settled matter in his heart."

Antony and Cleopatra, iv. 8,—

"Bear our hack'd targets like the men that owe them."

So Warburton, rightly I think, construes this passage. 2 King Henry IV. i. 3,—

"With an incensed fire of injuries."

i.e., "a fire *incensed of* (*kindled by*) injuries."

Two Noble Kinsmen, i. 1, perhaps an instance,—

"——————— whilst we dispatch
This grand act of our life, this daring deed
Of fate in wedlock."

This deed which dares fate. Tempest, v. 1,—

"——————— Whe'r thou be'st he or no,
Or some enchanted trifle to abuse me,"

is, I suspect, a case of the same kind; *some trifle produced by enchantment to abuse me;* for *some trifle to abuse me,* seems unlike the Elizabethan English.[58] 1 K. H. IV. v. 1, near the beginning,—

"A prodigy of fear, and a portent
Of broached mischief to the unborn times."

---

[58] Compare, however, Bonduca, v. 2,—

"In love too with *a trifle to abuse me.*"

This example may also serve to cast out from the Tempest that

A portent of mischief broached to, &c., for he could not be a portent to *future* times. Othello, ii. 3,—

"There comes a fellow, crying out for help;
And Cassio following him with determin'd sword
To execute upon him."

(Ought *him* in the second line to be expunged?) *Dele* comma after *sword;* and perhaps after *course*. ii. 3,—

"————— How am I then a villain,
To counsel Cassio to this parallel course,
Directly to his good?"

Sonnet xxviii. comes under this head,—

"And each, though enemies to either's reign,
Do in consent shake hands to torture me."

Macbeth, i. 7, near the end of the act,—

"————— When in swinish sleep
Their drenched natures lie, as in a death."

So in other old writers preceding and contemporary. Chaucer, House of Fame, B. ii. ed. 1602, fol. 266, col. 2,—

"Till he saw the Scorpioun,
Which that in Heven a signe is yet,
And he for fere lost his wit
Of that, and let the reynes gone
Of his horse." (*i.e.*, *horses.*)

---

enchanted devil, which Mr. Collier's Old Corrector raised to *abuse* his disinterrer. Was the Old Corrector acquainted with the Parliament of Love, iv. 2, or is this a mere chance coincidence?—

"Make use of reason, as an exorcist
To cast this devil out, that does abuse you."

For *trifle* add from Ford, Fancies, &c. iv. 1,—"Why you know I am an ignorant, unable *trifle* in such business." Sun's Darling, i. 1,—

"————— scourge hence this *trifle*."

ii. 1,—

"This lady, call'd the Spring, is an odd *trifle*."—*Ed.*

Persones Tale, ed. 1798, vol. ii. p. 337,—"A man, which is in a dropping hous in many places, though he eschew the dropping in o place, it droppeth on him in another place."—Man of Lawes Prologue, v. 4489,—

"The dreint Leandre for his faire Hero."

Lord Surrey's Poems, ed. 1831, p. 5,—

"To blind their eyes (*eyen?*) which else should see
My speckled cheeks with Cupid's hue."

P. 14, "the wedded birds so late." P. 18,—

"With dazed eyes we oft by gleams of love
Have miss'd the ball."

P. 89, Eccles. chap. iii., "the grafted plants with pain." P. 93, "their gotten good with strife." P. 107, Version of Psalm lxxiii., so construe,—

"So shall their glory fade; thy sword of vengeance shall
Unto their drunken eyes in blood disclose their errors all."

P. 156, Version of Æneid iv., "the stricken hind with shaft."

Play of Edward III., Lamb's Specimens, ed. 1835, vol. ii. p. 269,—

"—————— your progenitor,
Sole reigning Adam on the universe,
By God was honour'd," &c.

Sackville, Gorboduc, v. 2, p. 82, ed. 1820,—

"A ruthful case! that they, whom duty's bond,
Whom grafted law, by nature, truth, and faith,
Bound to defend their country and their king,
Even they should give consent," &c.

Dele comma after *law*. iv. 2, p. 72,—

"When greedy lust in royal seat to reign
Hath reft all care of Gods, and eke of men," &c.;

So construc. Spenser, Sonnet lxxxi.,—

"Fayre, when her breast, like a rich-laden barke,
With precious merchandise, she forth doth lay."

Expunge the comma after *barke*. Faerie Queene, B. iii. C. ii. St. xxi. (of Merlin's mirror),—

"It was a famous present for a prince,
And worthie worke of infinite reward."

Second Maiden's Tragedy, iv. 1,—

"Well, sir, since you've begun to make my lord
A doubtful man of me, keep on that course."

v. 2,—

"———————— this the disquieted body
Of my too resolute child in honour's war."

Kyd, Cornelia, iv., chorus (I quote from Collier's Annals of the Stage, vol. iii. p. 212),—

"Meddling with nothing but his own,
While gazing eyes at crowns grow dim."

Peele, War of Troy, Dyce, 2nd ed., vol. ii. p. 181 (of Achilles),—

"Clad by his dame in habit of a woman,
Unworthy cowardice of a valiant man."

So construe. Friar Bacon, &c., Dyce's Greene, vol. i. p. 207,—

"———————— this base attire
Better befits an humble mind to God
Than all the show of rich habiliments."

Fanshawe's Querer por Solo Querer, Lamb, ed. 1835, vol. ii. p. 244,—

"This should be that so famous Queen
For unquell'd valour and disdain."

P. 249,—

"Zelidaura, star divine,
That do'st in highest orb of beauty shine;
Pardon'd Murd'ress, by that heart
Itself, which thou dost kill," &c.

Richard Brome on Fletcher, B. and F., ed. 1647, 35th Poem, Seward, vol. i. p. 56, title,—"To the Memory of the Deceased but Ever-living Author, in these his Poems, Mr. John Fletcher." The erroneous comma after *Author* does not appear in the 1647 edition. Beaumont and Fletcher, Valentine, iii. 1, Moxon, vol. i. p. 448, vol. i.,—

"————————— such a one
That had an itching husband to be honourable,
And groan'd to get it."

Captain, iv. 5, Moxon, vol. i. p. 368, col. 2,—

"For safety of your soul, and of the soul
Of that too wicked woman yet to die."

King and No King, iv. 3, Moxon, vol. i. p. 70, col. 1,—

"For that brave sufferance you speak of, brother,
Consists not in a beating and away;
But in a cudgell'd body from eighteen
To eight-and-thirty, in a head rebuk'd
With pots of all size,[59] daggers, stools, and bedstaves."

(Vulg., comma after *body*.) Loyal Subject, ii. 6, vol. i. p. 326, col. 1,—

"Nor had you known this now, but for this pickthank,
That lost man in his faith! he has reveal'd it."

iv. 5, vol. 1, p. 337, col. 1,—

"Believe me, fellow, here will (*here 'll*) be lusty drinking,
Many a wash'd pate in wine, I warrant thee."

---

[59] Write *size'*; at any rate the word is plural. See S. V., art. li. In the original manuscript, by a slip of the pen, Walker had written *sorts*.—*Ed.*

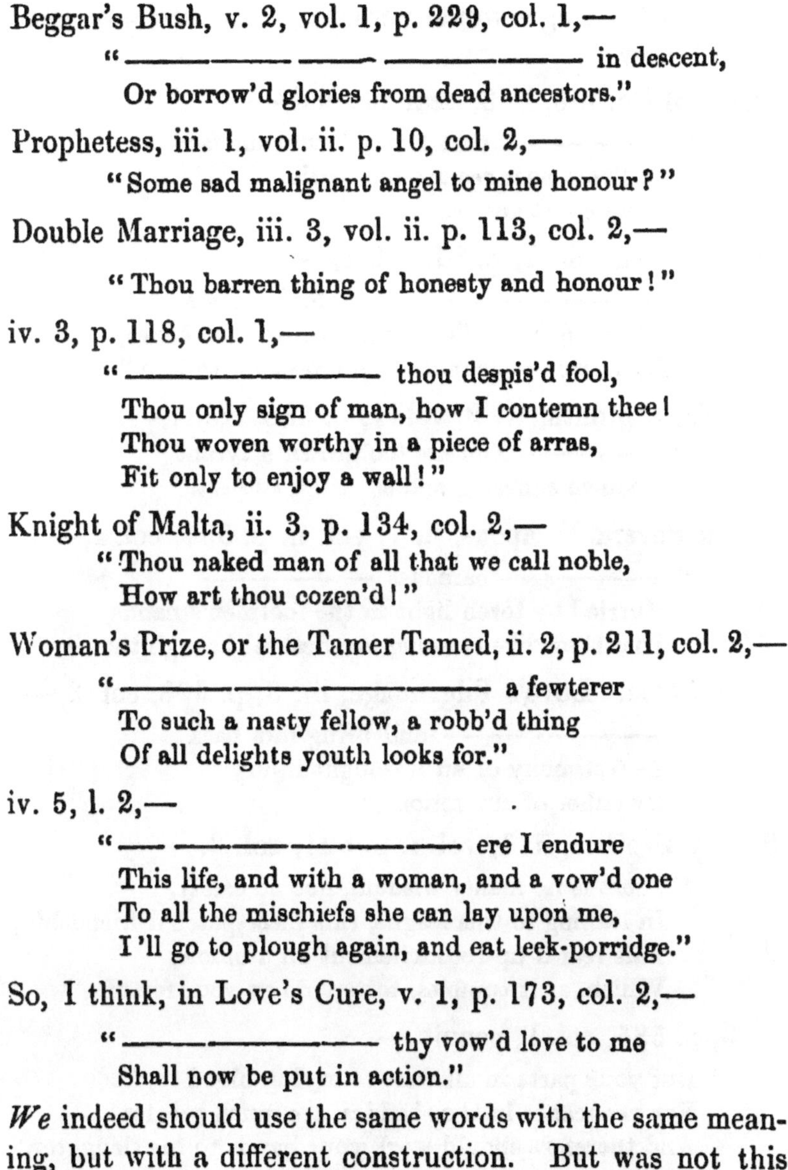

Beggar's Bush, v. 2, vol. 1, p. 229, col. 1,—

"———————— ——— ———————— in descent,
Or borrow'd glories from dead ancestors."

Prophetess, iii. 1, vol. ii. p. 10, col. 2,—

"Some sad malignant angel to mine honour?"

Double Marriage, iii. 3, vol. ii. p. 113, col. 2,—

"Thou barren thing of honesty and honour!"

iv. 3, p. 118, col. 1,—

"—————————— thou despis'd fool,
Thou only sign of man, how I contemn thee!
Thou woven worthy in a piece of arras,
Fit only to enjoy a wall!"

Knight of Malta, ii. 3, p. 134, col. 2,—

"Thou naked man of all that we call noble,
How art thou cozen'd!"

Woman's Prize, or the Tamer Tamed, ii. 2, p. 211, col. 2,—

"———————————————— a fewterer
To such a nasty fellow, a robb'd thing
Of all delights youth looks for."

iv. 5, l. 2,—

"——— ———————————— ere I endure
This life, and with a woman, and a vow'd one
To all the mischiefs she can lay upon me,
I'll go to plough again, and eat leek-porridge."

So, I think, in Love's Cure, v. 1, p. 173, col. 2,—

"—————————— thy vow'd love to me
Shall now be put in action."

We indeed should use the same words with the same meaning, but with a different construction. But was not this very syntax, in its first origin, a corruption of the old Latinized one? And in like manner, many other of the

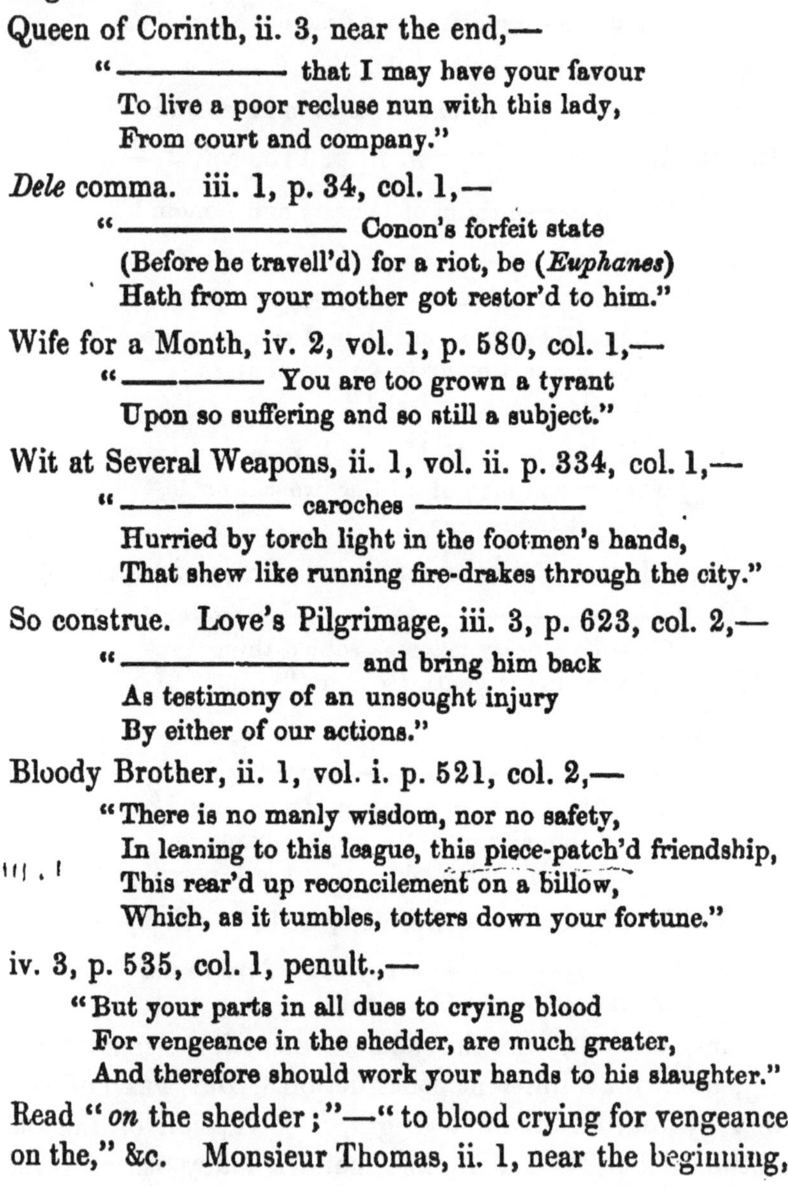

above-cited passages would perhaps, *quoad verba*, be good English now.

Queen of Corinth, ii. 3, near the end,—

"———— that I may have your favour
To live a poor recluse nun with this lady,
From court and company."

Dele comma. iii. 1, p. 34, col. 1,—

"———— Conon's forfeit state
(Before he travell'd) for a riot, be (*Euphanes*)
Hath from your mother got restor'd to him."

Wife for a Month, iv. 2, vol. 1, p. 580, col. 1,—

"———— You are too grown a tyrant
Upon so suffering and so still a subject."

Wit at Several Weapons, ii. 1, vol. ii. p. 334, col. 1,—

"———— caroches ————
Hurried by torch light in the footmen's hands,
That shew like running fire-drakes through the city."

So construe. Love's Pilgrimage, iii. 3, p. 623, col. 2,—

"———— and bring him back
As testimony of an unsought injury
By either of our actions."

Bloody Brother, ii. 1, vol. i. p. 521, col. 2,—

"There is no manly wisdom, nor no safety,
In leaning to this league, this piece-patch'd friendship,
This rear'd up reconcilement on a billow,
Which, as it tumbles, totters down your fortune."

iv. 3, p. 535, col. 1, penult.,—

"But your parts in all dues to crying blood
For vengeance in the shedder, are much greater,
And therefore should work your hands to his slaughter."

Read "*on* the shedder;"—"to blood crying for vengeance on the," &c. Monsieur Thomas, ii. 1, near the beginning,

"The sharp and nipping air of our cold climate,
I hope, is all, which will as well restore
To health again th' afflicted body by it," &c.

Middleton, Witch, ii. 1, Dyce, vol. iii. p. 284,—

"Thou that retain'st an envious soul to goodness!"

Id., Triumphs of Truth, Dyce, vol. v. p. 230,—

"That crown of stars shews her descent from heaven;
That robe of white, fill'd all with eagles' eyes,
Her piercing sight through hidden mysteries."

Id., Wisdom of Solomon, &c., p. 427,—

"O tossed fantasies in folly's ship!"

Rowley, Noble Spanish Soldier, iv. 1, 3rd page of the act,—

"Go fetch the mark'd out lamb for slaughter hither;"

And the following, iii. 2, 8th page of the act, seems to me somewhat similar in construction,

"———————— is there not here
A promising face of manly princely virtues?"

A face of virtues, for old English, looks to me suspicious.

Shirley, Arcadia, iv. 2, Gifford and Dyce, vol. vi. p. 223,—

"———————— do not give
Your strength and trust to th' mercy of those slaves,
Inhuman villains to us."

Id., Narcissus, p. 487, St. 4,—

"Out of the ground a lovely flower betrays
His whiter leaves, and visibly did rear
His tufted head, with saffron-colour'd rays:

so we should undoubtedly construe it.

Passionate Pilgrim, xv.,—

"How sighs resound
Through heartless (?) ground,
Like a thousand vanquish'd men in bloody fight!"

Sidney, Arcadia, B. ii. p. 133, l. 40,—" And so they went away from very unwilling people to leave them," &c.

Jonson, Poetaster, iv. 7, Gifford, vol. ii. p. 496,—

"Thy life may chance be shorten'd by the length
Of my unwilling speeches to depart."

i.e., the speeches of me unwilling, &c., a double Latinism.

Epistle to a Friend, vol. viii. p. 368,—

"It is a call to keep the spirits alive
That gasp for action, and would yet revive
Man's buried honour, in his sleepy life,
Quick'ng dead Nature to her noblest strife."

Masque of Neptune's Triumph, p. 31,—

"But where's your antimasque now, all this while?
I hearken after them.
Poet. Faith, we have none.
Cook. None.
Poet. None, I assure you, neither do I think them
A worthy part of presentation," &c.

Sad Shepherd, i. 2, vol. vi. p. 262,—

"(He) Is so distracted, as no sought relief
By all our studies can procure his peace."

ii. 1, p. 281,—

"——————— where'er you spy
This browder'd belt with characters, 'tis I."

Silent Woman, iii. 2, vol. iii. p. 415,—"you have done both him and me grace to visit so unprepared a pair to entertain you."

Play of Solomon and Perseda, D 3; so construe,—

"But is there no reward for my false dice?
Erast. Yes sir, a garded suit from top to toe."

Tomkins, Albumazar, v. 11, Dodsley, vol. vii. p. 193,—

"——————— O wonderful!
Admir'd Albumazar in two transmutations!"

" admired on account of two transmutations which he has wrought."

Massinger, Virgin Martyr, iv. 1, Moxon, p. 17, col. 1,—

" Age on my head hath stuck no white hairs yet,
Yet I 'm an old man, a fond doating fool
Upon a woman."

Daniel, Civil Wars, B. i. St. lxxxv.,—

"For now this absent lord, out of his land
Where, &c. ——————————————
Gave time to them at home, that had in hand
Th' ungodly worke."

Dele comma after *lord*. The " lord " is Richard II., absent in Ireland. I have noticed, I think, several instances of this syntax in the Civil Wars.

Quarles, Argalus and Parthenia, B. i. p. 12, ed. 1647,—

" And leave to after times an enter'd name
I' th' calendar of fools."

Chapman, Bussy d'Ambois, v. 1, Old English Plays, vol. iii. p. 338,—

"Forgive it (my hand) for the blood with which 'tis stain'd,
In which I writ the summons of thy death:
The forced summons, by this bleeding wound,
By this, here in my bosom, and by this,
That makes me hold up both my hands embrued
For thy dear pardon."

The summons forced by, is, I imagine, the construction here; not *μα τόδ' ἕλκος*. *Ib.* iv. 2, *init.* p. 310,—

"I am suspicious, most honour'd father,
Of some of Monsieur's cunning passages,
That his still ranging and contentious nose thrills
To scent the haunts of mischief, have so us'd
The vicious virtue of his busy sense," &c.

For *nose thrills*, read *nosethrills*, an old spelling of *nostrils*.

"His nostrills still ranging and contentious (*contendentes*) to scent," &c. *Ib.* i. 1, p. 237,—

"—————— If Epaminondas
(Who liv'd twice twenty years obscur'd in Thebes)
Had liv'd so still, he had been still unnam'd,
And paid his country nor himself their right;
But putting forth his strength, he rescued both
From imminent ruin; and like burnish'd steel,
After long use he shin'd."

Read and point,—

"—————— and like burnish'd steel
After long *rust*, he shin'd."

See Dyce, Remarks, pp. 20, 21, on the "proneness" of our early printers "to blunder in words commencing with the letter *v*." Among the examples he quotes is *rise* for *vse*. Chapman, Byron's Tragedy, Lamb's Specimens, ed. 1835, vol. i. p. 105,—

"——— Or if th' unsettled blood of France,
With ease and wealth, renew her civil furies,
Let all my powers be emptied in my son;
To curb and end them all, as I have done."

Same Play, Retrosp., vol. iv. p. 362,—

"———— if in midst of winter
To make black groves grow green; to still the thunder;
And cast out able flashes from my eyes,
To beat the lightning back into the skies,
Prove power to do it, I can make it good."

Dele comma after *eyes*.

Chapman, Odyss., xi. fol. p. 163,—

"——— Neptune still will his opposure try
With all his laid-up anger, for the eye
His lov'd son lost to thee."

Il. x. Taylor, vol. i. p. 226,—

> "Which to Minerva, Ithacus did zealously advance
> With lifted arm into the air;"

so construe. i. p. 65, the Abantes are called "*swift men on foot;*" so Commentary on xiii. vol. ii. p. 27, *those just men of life.* xviii. vol. ii. p. 122,—

> "——— that the crying blood for vengeance of my friend,
> Mangled by Hector, may be still'd."

Commentary on Il. xiii. p. 30, "— that unknown secret to himself —." (The following transposition of a similar kind, xv. p. 62, is worth noticing here,—

> "————————— his spirit touch'd them deep,
> And turn'd them all before the fleet into a wall of brass;"

i.e., "turned them all into a wall of brass before," &c. v. 566, ἐν θυμῳ δὲ βάλοντο ἔπος· φράξαντο δὲ νῆας ἕρκεϊ χαλκείῳ.) xxi. p. 172, l. 2, "the op'd vein against him." And so I imagine xxiv. p. 231, l. 9,—

> "————————— then like a fair young prince,
> First-down chinn'd, and of such a grace as makes his looks convince [*i.e.*, *subdue, captivate*]
> Contending eyes to view him, forth he went to meet the king."

(*Contending* is not *contesting*, but *striving*, *contendentes*, *ut passim apud* C.—By the way, l. 22, "the prince turn'd deity," strange as the expression is, might seem to be justified by iii. vol. i. p. 93, l. 5, "Helen—knew—the deified disguise;" though I doubt whether the latter is really parallel; but I would read "the *prince-turn'd* deity,"[60] on account of Odyss. i. p. 6, l. 6,—

> "————— In a throne he plac'd
> The man-turn'd goddess.")

---

[60] Walker's conjecture is confirm'd by Nathaniel Butter's folio, which inserts the hyphen.—*Ed.*

Odyss. ix., fol., p. 136, speaking of Polyphemus' club,—

> " —————————— 'T was so vast,
> That we resembled it to some fit mast,
> To serve a ship of burthen," &c.

Dele comma after *mast.* See for another instance, S. V. p. 245.

Spenser, Faery Queene, B. ii. C. vii. St. xvii.; so construe,—

> "Then gan a cursed hand the quiet wombe
> Of his great-grandmother with steele to wound,
> And the hid treasures in her sacred tombe
> With sacriledge to dig."

Perhaps even the following passage comes under this head, iii. iii. xiv.,—

> "Untill the hardy mayd (with Love to frend)
> First entering, the dreadful Mage there fownd," &c.;

"bold through the aid of Love." And the following, ii. v. xxxii.,—

> "There he him found all carelesly displaid,
> In secrete shadow from the sunny ray," &c.;

secrete from, &c.; i. vi. xvii.,—

> "And how he slew with glauncing dart amisse
> A gentle hynd," &c.

St. xlv.,—

> "They gan to fight retourne; increasing more
> Their puissant force, and cruell rage attonce,
> With heaped strokes more hugely than before."

C. xii. St. xxvii.,—

> "Witnesse the burning altars that he swore,
> And guilty heavens of his bold perjury."

B. iii. C. viii. St. xxx. Proteus is described as

> "An aged sire with head all frowy hore,
> And sprinckled frost upon his dewy beard."

St. xxxii.,—

> "And blubberd face with tears of her faire eyes."

And so I think, C. xii. St. xxvi.,—

> "All which disguized marcht in masking-wise
> About the chamber."

Fairfax's Tasso, C. ii. St. v.,—

> "Within the Christians' church, from light of skies,
> An hidden altar stands, far out of sight," &c.

Dele comma after *skies*. C. xiii. St. li. comes nearly under this head,—

> "Now, now the fatal ship of conquest lands."

C. v. St. xxiii.,—

> "With such false words the kindled fire began
> To ev'ry vein its poison'd heat to reach;"

" the fire kindled with such false words." And so viii. xvii.,

> "His visage shone, his noble looks did flame
> With kindled brand of courage bold and stout."

So construe. xi. xxxvii.,—

> "—————— in their trenches deep
> The hidden squadrons kept themselves from scath."

As also vii. l.,—

> "Yet long'd he for th' appointed day to fight."

xii. xlvi.,—

> "A mass of solid fier, burning bright,
> Roll'd up in smould'ring flames there brusteth out;
> And there the blust'ring winds add strength and might,
> And gather close the 'spersed flames about."

Harrington's Ariosto, C. xxvi. St. xi.,—

"Maganza men of one side, merchant-like,
Brought laden moyles, with gold and costly ware."[61]

Play of Tancred and Gismunda, iv. 4, l. 11. Dodsley, vol. ii. p. 210,—

"Upon thy false dissembling heart with us;"

(*false-dissembling;*) *thy heart which dissembles falsely with us.* Edwards, Damon and Pithias, Dodsley, vol. i. p. 237,—

"———————— I know for my parte,
That a heavy pouch with goulde makes a light harte."

Fletcher, Demetrius and Enanthe, v. 3, p. 103,—

"———— your urgd on Anger to the highest."

And so I imagine Ford, Love's Sacrifice, ii. 2, Moxon, p. 81, col. 2; see context. "— a very curious eye might repute it as an imaginary rapture of some transported conceit, to aim at an impossibility;" &c. *Dele* comma after *conceit.* (Just below, "a *substantial* love" is a love such as one bears for a real living person, not for a mere picture.)

Waller, at Penshurst, l. 38, Cook's edition, p. 33,—

"—————————— hie thee to the sea,
That there with wonders thy diverted mind
Some truce, at least, may with this passion find."

On the Prince's Escape, l. 3, p. 13,—

"With British bounty in his ship he feasts
Th' Hesperian princes, his amazed guests,
To find that wat'ry wilderness exceed
The entertainment of their great Madrid."

---

[61] Compare the original,—

"Giungean dall' una parte i Mangazesi,
E conducean con loro i muli carchi
D' oro e di vesti e d' altri ricchi arnesi."—*Ed.*

Herrick, Clarke, vol. i. p. 165, cclxxxiv.,—

"Methought I saw, as I did dream in bed,
A mantling vine, about Anacreon's head;"

Dele comma after *vine*, [and, in the preceding example, after *guests*.] P. 136, ccxxv. The Bubble,—

"To my revenge, and to her desperate fears,
Fly, thou made bubble of my sighs and tears."

Butler, Hudibras, P. iii. C. ii. l. 1103,—

"Denounc'd and pray'd, with fierce devotion,
And bended elbows on the cushion;" &c.

Milton has it; *e.g.*, Paradise Lost, xii. 233,—

"—————— informing them by types
And shadows, of that destin'd seed to bruise
The Serpent."

But in his Latinized diction it is less noticeable.

I observe in Green's Spleen, near the end, speaking of wine,

"————— the dispersive bowl
Of cloudy weather in the soul."

XXVIII.

Perspective, *directive*, &c., are frequently used by Shakespeare and his contemporaries, so to speak, in a passive sense.

Two Gentlemen of Verona, iv. 4,—

"What should it be, that he respects in her,
But I can make respective in myself,
If this fond Love were not a blinded god?"

Troilus and Cressida, ii. 2,—

"We turn not back the silks upon the merchant,
When we have spoil'd them; nor the remainder viands
We do not throw in unrespective sieve,
Because we now are full."

Play of Hieronimo (First Part of Jeronymo), Dodsley, edition 1825, vol. ii. p. 58, Andrew addresses Bellimperia,—

"Respective dear, O my live's [*lives*, life's] happiness," &c.

On the other hand, Romeo and Juliet, iii. 1,—

"Away to heaven, respective lenity,
And fire-eyed fury be my conduct now!"

Glapthorne, Dedication to Albertus Wallenstein, speaks of "my respective service to you (his patron)." By the way in Daniel's Hymen's Triumph, iv. 3, I would write in one word,—

"——————— I am content to speak
With him, he speaks so prettily, so sweet,
And with so good-respective modesty."

Beaumont and Fletcher, Little French Lawyer, ii. 3,—

"——————— What 's thy name?
La-Writ. My name is Cock-a-two: use me respectively,
I will be cock of three else."

Troilus and Cressida, iii. 3,—

"The providence that 's in a watchful state
Knows almost every grain of Plutus' gold;
Finds bottom in th' uncomprehensive deeps;" &c.

i. 3,—

"———— limbs are his (the opinion's) instruments,
In no less working, than are swords and bows
Directive by the limbs."

Othello, i. 3, is somewhat in the same way,—

"Whereof by parcels she had something heard,
But not distinctively;"

at least if ***distinctively*** is the true reading ;[62] see Var. notes. Julius Cæsar, ii. 1,—

> "——————— do not stain
> The even virtue of our enterprise,
> Nor th' insuppressive mettle of our spirits
> To think that," &c.

And so I think All 's Well, &c., i. 2,—

> "——————— his plausive words
> He scatter'd not in ears, but grafted them
> To grow there, and to bear ;"

worthy of applause. iv. 1, Parolles says,—"What shall I say I have done? it must be a very plausive invention that carries it :"—*i.e., plausible.* Heywood, Four Prentices of London, Dodsley, vol. vi. p. 466, Robert of Normandy, congratulating Charles and Godfrey on their escape, says,

> "——————— Let us rejoice,
> And to your plausive fortunes give our voice."

Woman Killed with Kindness, Dodsley, vol. vii. p. 261,—

> "——————— Is this a dream?
> Or do my waking senses apprehend
> The pleasing taste of these applausive news?"

news worthy of acclamation ; compare *plausive* above. As You Like It, iii. 2,—

> "Run, run, Orlando; carve on every tree
> The fair, the chaste and unexpressive she."

---

[62] *Distinctively* seems a mere sophistication by the editor of the second folio for *instinctively*, the nonsensical reading of the first. The quartos have *intentively*, which the critics tell us was used in the sense of *attentively*, But in this particular passage it seems to mean either *all at a stretch*, or, *so as to comprehend the story as a whole.—Ed.*

Where Malone quotes Milton's Hymn on the Nativity, noticed below. Jonson, Alchemist, ii. 1, Gifford, vol. iv. p. 68,—

> "——————— But these two
> Make the rest ductile, malleable, extensive;"

i.e., extensible; see context. Drayton, Barons' Wars, B. ii. St. lviii.,—

> "With such brave raptures, from her words that rise,
> She made a breach in his impressive breast," &c.

Marmyon, Antiquary, Dodsley, vol. x. page 83,—"'Tis so, that all women thirst man's overthrow; that's a principle as demonstrative as truth; 'tis the only end they were made for;" &c. Herrick, Clarke, vol. i. cclxxiv. p. 161,

> "Then this immensive cup
> Of aromatic wine,
> Catullus, I quaff up
> To that terse muse of thine."

And so vol. ii. ccclxxix. p. 165,—

> "Give way, give way; now, now my Charles shines here,
> A public light, in this immensive sphere."

Milton, Lycidas, l. 176,—

> "And hears the unexpressive nuptial song,
> In the blest kingdoms meek of joy and love."

Hymn on the Nativity, l. 115,—

> "Harping in loud and solemn quire
> With unexpressive notes to Heaven's new-born Heir."

Did this usage originate in the unmanageable length of some of the adjectives in *able* and *ible*, as *unsuppressible, uncomprehensible?*

Some of our later poets have occasionally employed this license in imitation of their predecessors.

Akenside, Pleasures of Imagination, B. i. l. 434,—

"———— sound her (Virtue's) brow
To twine the wreath of incorruptive praise."

l. 124,—

"———— Then the inexpressive strain
Diffuses its enchantment."

Mason, in one of the choruses of the Elfrida, after Milton, as Akenside above,—

"Though now you circle yon eternal throne
With harpings high of inexpressive praise."

Cary's Dante, Paradise, C. ix. l. 72,—

"That voice, which joins the inexpressive song,
Pastime of heaven," &c.

Southey, in a poetical letter to Allan Cunningham, describes Bilderdijk the Dutch poet as

"In knowledge and in inexhaustive stores
Of native genius rich."

Id., Inscriptions, xli. Poems, vol. iii. p. 166,—

"———— Contemplate now,
What days and nights of thought, what years of toil,
What inexhaustive springs of public wealth
The vast design requir'd."

Cary, Translation of Pindar, Nemean vi. l. 5, p. 152,—

"For them, an indestructive mansion
Abideth in the skies."

XXIX.

On the other hand, adjectives in *able* and *ible*, both positive and negative ones, are frequently used by old writers in an *active* sense. (Compare the Latin, *e.g.*, Oceano dissociabili, Hor.; and compare also the occasional active use of verbals in τος in the Greek tragedians; *e.g.*, Soph. Trach. 445. εἴ τι τῷ 'μῷ τανδρὶ —μεμπτός εἰμι. Æsch. Eumen. 236, Scholefield, ἔπου δὲ μηνυτῆρος ἀφθέγκτου φραδαῖς.) Proclamation of Protector Somerset, Tytler's Reigns of Edward VI. and Mary, somewhere about page 205 (I quote from the British and Foreign Review), the king's subjects are required to repair to Hampton Court "in most defensible array, with harness and weapons to defend his most royal person," &c. Shakespeare, 2 King Henry IV. ii. 3,—

> "———— ———— to abide a field
> Where nothing but the sound of Hotspur's name
> Did seem defensible."

King Henry V. iii. 3,—

> "Enter our gates, dispose of us and ours,
> For we no longer are defensible."

Hence our present *Fencibles*. As You Like It, ii. 5,— "He is too disputable for my company." Chaucer, Merchantes Tale, Canterbury Tales, l. 9931,—

> "O soden hap, o thou fortune unstable,
> Like to the scorpion so deceivable,
> That flatrest with thy head whan thou wolt sting."

Shakespeare, Twelfth Night, iv. 3; see context,—

> "———————— there's something in't
> That is deceivable."

Bacon, Essay of Deformity,—"therefore, it is good to consider of deformity, not as a sign which is more deceiveable, but as a cause which seldom faileth of the effect." Sidney, Arcadia, B. ii. p. 179, l. 29,—"this colour of mine, which she (in the deceivable style of affection) would entitle beautiful." Bunyan, Holy War, ed. 1791, p. 21,—"Diabolus

—— made this further deceivable speech to them, saying," &c. And p. 40, ult., margin,—" Very deceivable language." Shakespeare, Sonnet xxxvi.,—

> " In our two loves there is but one respect,
> Though in our lives a separable spite,
> Which though it alter not love's sole effect,
> Yet doth it steal sweet hours from love's delight."

i.e., a spiteful fortune that separates us. (Compare *Oceanus dissociabilis.*) Tarquin and Lucrece, *ad fin.*,—

> "The Romans plausibly did give consent
> To Tarquin's everlasting banishment ;"

i.e., by acclamation ; the converse of *plausive* above. (On the other hand, Jonson, Every Man Out of His Humour, iii. 3, Gifford, vol. ii. p. 110, Shift talks of " taking tobacco plausibly in any ordinary, theatre, or the tiltyard," &c.) Note Sidney, Arcadia, v. 449, ult., " —— all the whole people —— confirmed with an united murmur Pyrocles' demand——. Euarchus, though neither regarding a prisoner's passionate prayer, nor bearing overplausible ears to a many-headed motion, yet well enough content to win their liking with things in themselves indifferent," &c.——*not being influenced in his determination by any inordinate love of popular applause.* All 's Well, &c., i. 3,—

> " Yet in this captious and intenible sieve
> I still pour in the waters of my love
> And lack not to lose still."

(*Tenable* or *tenible* in the passive sense, Hamlet, i. 2,—

> " —— ———————— I pray you all,
> If you have hitherto conceal'd this sight,
> Let it be tenable in your silence still."

In the Hamlet (so called) of 1603 it is written *tenible ;*

perhaps this was Shakespeare's spelling, for the folio has *treble*. And so on the other hand, as I have noticed elsewhere, Hamlet, v. 1, p. 278, col. 2, the folio has,—" Oh *terrible* woer [*woes*, I think, not *woe*], Fall ten times trebble," &c.) King Henry V. ii. 4,—

> " He sends you this most memorable line,
> In every branch truly demonstrative," &c.

iv. 7,—

> " I wear it for a memorable honour,
> For I am Welch, you know, good countryman ; "

i.e., *commemorative*. Note too, iii. 4, dialogue between the princess Katharine and Alice,—" ces sont mots de son mauvais, *corruptible*, grosse, et impudique," &c. Cymbeline, iii. 2,—

> " Some griefs are med'cinable ; that is (*that's ?*) one of them,
> For it doth physic love."

Othello, i. 3,—" why, the power and corrigible authority of this lies in our wills." Jonson, Poetaster, ii. 1, Gifford, vol. ii. p. 419,—" Do not I bear a reasonable corrigible hand over him, Crispinus ?" Black Book, Dyce's Middleton, vol. v. p. 528,—" being moved both with his penetrable (*i.e.*, *piercing*, *affecting*) petition, and his insufferable poverty." Beaumont and Fletcher, Coxcomb, v. 2, Moxon, vol. ii. p. 303, col. 2,—

> " I do not mock, nor lives there such a villain
> That can do any thing contemptible
> To you ; but I do kneel, because it is
> An action very fit and reverent
> In presence of so pure a creature."

Play of Soliman and Perseda, 1529, B. 2,—" I have rejected with contemptible frowns the sweet glances of many amorous girls." (Here it is spelt *contemptable*.) Jonson,

Cynthia's Revels, ii. 1, Gifford, vol. ii. p. 259,—"He does naturally admire his wit that wears gold lace or tissue; stabs any man that speaks more contemptibly of the scholar than he." I notice this in Gaudentio di Lucca; ed. 1776, p. 93, note,—"Signor Redi, being an Italian, one cannot wonder that he speaks contemptibly of the northern people; the Italians call them all Barbari." Is this a slip of the author's pen? And so perhaps Twelfth Night, ii. 1,—"A lady, sir, though it was said she much resembled me, was yet of many accounted beautiful; but, though I could not, with such estimable wonder, overfar believe that, yet thus far will I boldly publish her;" &c. W. Browne's Britannia's Pastorals, B. ii. Song ii. Clarke's ed. p. 201; I have corrected the punctuation,—

> "No less did all this quaint assembly long
> Than doth the traveller: this shepherd's song
> Had so ensnar'd each acceptable ear,
> That, but a second, nought could bring them clear
> From an affected [*i.e., beloved* or *desired*] snare."

Spenser, F. Q. B. vi. C. viii. St. iii.,—

> "Who after thraldome of the gentle Squire
> Which she beheld with lamentable eye,
> Was touched with compassion entire,
> And much lamented his calamity," &c.

C. iv. St. xxix.,—

> "Then thus began the lamentable Dane;" &c.

see context.—Sidney, Arcadia, B. ii. page 97, l. 23, "the lamentable party;" see context; and so understand "a lamentable tune," three lines above; and B. iii. p. 255, l. 30, "who in vain had lamentably cried unto him to stay." Holinshed, ap. Taylor's ed. of Chapman's Iliad, vol. i. p. 127, note *c*, says the Irish are "sufferable of infinite pains." (*Pains* is here *labour.*) Chapman, Preface to his Translation of Achilles' Shield; I quote from Dyce's Remarks on Knight and Collier, p. 156, "—— for neyther doe common dispositions keepe fitte or plausible consort with iudiciall and simple honestie, nor are idle capacities comprehensible of an elaborate Poeme." King Richard III. iii. 7,—

"—————————— my desert,
Unmeritable, shuns [*shames*] your high request."

Julius Cæsar, iv. 1, Lepidus is called "a slight unmeritable man." Browne, Religio Medici, B. i. Sect. xlvii., "—— and indeed I found [*i.e.*, *within myself*] upon a natural inclination, an inbred loyalty unto virtue, that I could serve her without a livery, yet not in that resolved and venerable way, but that the frailty of my nature, upon an easy temptation, might be induced to forget her."

(*Comfortable*, Art. xi. above, is perhaps something in point. It may also be noticed that *terrible* is sometimes used for *fearful;* the converse of the present usage. King Lear, i. 2,—"What paper were you reading? *Edmund.* Nothing, sir. *Gloster.* No? what needed then that terrible despatch of it into your pocket?" Jonson, Bartholomew Fair, iv. i, Gifford, vol. iv. p. 471,—"Beshrew him, he startled me: I thought he had known of our plot. Guilt 's a terrible thing.")

So I think Kyd, Cornelia, v. Dodsley, vol. v. p. 298; see context,—

"Incessantly lamenting th' extreme loss,
And suspirable death of so brave soldiers."

Coriolanus, iv. 5, near the end,—"Let me have war, say I; it 's sprightly, waking, audible and full of vent. Peace is a very apoplexy, lethargy; mulled [read *mute*], deaf,

muddied

sleepy, insensible," &c. So *detestable* seems to be used, Sidney's Arcadia, iii. p. 410, l. 13, "—— kill yourself, to make me (whom you say you love) as long as I after live, change my loving admiration of you to a detestable abhorring your name." Measure for Measure, v. 1,—

"He would not, but by gift of my chaste body
To his concupiscible intemperate lust,
Release my brother."

Milton, Paradise Lost, ix. 563,—

"How cam'st thou speakable of mute?"

Cary uses *limitable* after the analogy of these old forms; Translation of Pindar, Nemean, iii. p. 138,—

"And he, unbidden, safe, pursued
Of that wild marish every secret flood,
Until he reach'd the limitable bourne,
That mark'd his late return."

Darley's Sylvia, ii. 2, describing a swan on the water,—

"—————————— Beautiful!
She is the lady of the reed-girt Isles!
See! how she swells her navigable wings,
And coasts her sedgy empire keenly round!"

This, however, I think, is accidental, though Darley knows and loves the old poets.

XXX.

Far and *near* used as *comparatives.*

1 King Henry IV. iii. 1,—

"And giv'st such sarcenet surety for thy oaths,
As if thou never walk'dst further than Finsbury."

I would read,—

"As if thou ne'er walk'dst fur' than Finsbury."

Compare Winter's Tale, iv. 3,—

> " ———————— we'll bar thee from succession;
> Not hold thee of our blood, no, not our kin,
> Far than Deucalion off."

Quasi *farrer, furrer?* In Chaucer we have *ferre*, further; House of Fame, Book ii. l. 92,—

> "But er I bere the much ferre,
> I wol the tel what I am."

(Note, As You Like It, i. 3,—

> "Alas, what danger will it be for us,
> Maids as we are, to travel forth so far!"

Does not Shakespeare's instinctive love of euphony require that we should here pronounce, perhaps write, *fur?* πόῤῥω.) *Near* for *nearer*, a contraction from the old *negher*, for which latter see Chaucer. Macbeth, ii. 3, near the end,—

> "There's daggers in men's smiles; the near in blood,
> The nearer bloody."

Perhaps *near* here is for *nearer*. Death of Robert Earl of Huntingdon, quoted by Steevens, Var. Shakespeare, 1793, vol. xiv. p. 562,—

> "In you, i' faith, the proverb's verified;
> You are early up, and yet are ne'er the near."

Wyatt, Version of Psalm vi. ed. 1831, p. 207,—

> "That dread of death, of death that ever lasts,
> Threateth of right, and draweth near and near."

Songs and Sonnets, p. 42,—

> "Your sighs you fetch from far,
> And all to wry [*conceal*] your woe;
> Yet are ye ne'er the narre:
> Men are not blinded so."

King Richard II. v. 1,—

> "Better far off, than, near, be ne'er the near."

Churchyard, quoted by Malone, *ib.* Greene, Friar Bacon and Friar Bungay, Dyce, vol. i. p. 167,—

"You're early up, pray God it be the near."

Alluding, as Dyce observes, to the proverb, Early up and never the nearer (as in R. Earl of Huntingdon, above). Daniel, Letter of Octavia to Antony, St. xxxv.,—

"Whereof when he had made relation,
I was commanded to approach no near."

Drayton, Eclogue, vii.,—

"Much will be said, and ne'er a whit the near."

And so Uncertain Poets. Chalmers, vol. ii. p. 405, col. 2,

"Shall I thus ever long, and be no whit the near?"

Butler, Hudibras, P. ii. C. ii. l. 381,—

"These reasons may perhaps look oddly
To th' wicked, though they evince [Let. *evincunt*] the godly;
But if they will not serve to clear
My honour, I am ne'er the near."

And so C. iii. l. 579,—

"But if it be, 't is ne'er the near,
You have a wrong sow by the ear."

Ford, 'Tis Pity She 's a Whore, iii. near the end,—

"*Don.* Is this a churchman's voice? dwells justice here?
Flo. Justice is fled to heaven, and comes no nearer."

Neare, I suspect; see context. Fairfax's Tasso, B. viii. St. xxvii.,—

"But still the light approached near and near."
"Più e più ognor s' avvicinava intanto
Quel lume."

Harrington's Ariosto, B. i. St. xix.,—

"Had you me ta'en or slain, your gain were none,
Sith you were ne'er the near your love therefore."

B. xi. St. xiv.,—

> "And still the near and nearer that he goes,
> The plainer sound he heard of sturdy blows."

B. xiv. St. lxxxii.,—

> "Silence is centinel of all this band;
> And unto those he coming doth discern,
> To come no neare, he beckons with his hand."

B. xxxix. St. lxviii.,—

> "So did the damsels chafe, and sigh, and fret,
> That they to Agramant no near could get."

Chaucer also has *ferrest* for *farthest*. I learn this from Tyrwhitt's Glossary, where the word is given in its place. Under the word *nere* for *nearer*, it also gives, as a Chaucerian phrase, *ferre ne nere* for *later nor earlier*. In the Knightes Tale, l. 1449, we have *derre* for *derer* (*dearer*); Arcite

> "—— bare him so in pees and eke in werre,
> Ther n'as no man that Theseus hath derre."

Gammer Gurton's Needle, i. 3, Dodsley, vol. ii. p. 14, l. 13,

> "*Hodge.* And is not then my breches sewid up, to morrow that I shuld were?
> *Tib.* No, in faith, Hodge, thy breches lie, for all this never the nere."

And so in another passage of this play, to which I have lost the reference.[63] Sidney, Arcadia, p. 87, l. 14; I retain the original spelling,—

> "She went, they staid; or rightly for to say,
> She staid in them, they went in thought with hyr:
> Klaius indeede would faine haue puld away

[63] I have observed the following passages:—p. 17, "my neele is never the nere"; p. 78, "cham never the nere my neele"; and p. 58, the full form, "Then we be never the nearer for all that you can tell."—*Ed.*

This mote from out his eye, this inward burre,
And now, proud Rebell gan for to gainsay
The lesson which but late he learn'd too furre:" &c.

P. 91, l. 10 (where *narre* for *nearer* also occurs; perhaps both are *meant* for *rusticisms*),—

"As Venus bird the white, swift, louely Doue,
(O happie Doue that art compar'd to her!)
Doth on her wings her vtmost swiftnesse proue,
Finding the gripe of Falcon fierce not furre:
So did Uran: [,] the narre, the swifter moue
(Yet beautie still as fast as she did sturre,") &c.

Fur for *far* occurs in Astrophel and Stella, Sonnet xcvi. l. 12, p. 564, l. 4,—

"But, but, (alas!) night's side the odds hath *fur*;"

rhyming to *stur* (*i.e.*, *stir*) in l. 10 of the sonnet; both, no doubt, altered for the sake of the rhyme. And so C. ii. ll. 11 and 13, p. 566,—

"But feeling proof makes me (they say) mistake it furre;"

rhyming to *sturre*. *Farer* for farther is frequent in Ramsay's Gentle Shepherd; *e.g.*, i. 1, ed. Edinb. 1820, p. 51,—

"For ilka sheep he hae, I'll number ten,
And should, as ane may think, come farer ben."

2, l. 5, p. 57,—

"Gae farer up the burn to Hobbie's How."

XXXI.

It may safely be laid down as a canon, that the word *spirit* in our old poets, wherever the metre does not compel us to pronounce it dissyllabically, is a monosyllable. And this is almost always the case. The truth of the above rule is evident from several considerations. In the first place, we never meet with other dissyllables —such, I mean, as are incapable of contraction—placed in a similar situation; the apparent exceptions not being really exceptions (see S. V. *passim*). Another argument is founded on the unpleasant ripple which the common pronunciation occasions in the flow of numberless lines, interfering with the general run of the verse; a harshness which, in some passages, must be evident to the dullest ear. Add to this the frequent substitution of *spright* or *sprite* for spirit (in all the different senses of the word, I mean, and not merely in that of *ghost*, in which *sprite* is still used); also *spreet*, though rarely (only in the ante-Elizabethan age, I think, as far as I have observed); and sometimes *sp'rit* and *sprit*. (For the double spelling, *spright* and *sprite*, one may compare *despight* and *despite;* which in like manner subsequently assumed different meanings, *despight* being used for *contempt*, *despectus;* Coriolanus, iii. 1,—

"——— Thou wretch! despight o'erwhelm thee!"

Perhaps, too, it would be better to write *spight* in Milton, L'Allegro, l. 45,—

"Then to come in spite of sorrow,
And at my window bid good morrow;"

in joyous scorn of it.) *Spright* or *sprite*. Sackville, Gorboduc, iv. 2, ed. 1800 (I think;[64] the same edition which is referred to in my other quotations from this play),—

[64] The edition of 1820 reads *spirit;* Dodsley, ed. 1825, which apparently preserves the old spelling, reads *sprite*. In Porrex's speech above,—

"If my owne servant hired to this fact, (*i.e.*, to poison me)
And moved by *trouth with* to work the same," &c.;

"Many can yield right grave and sage advice
Of patient sprite to others wrapt in woe," &c.

Fairfax's Tasso, B. xiv. St. xlv.,—

"So learned, cunning, wise, myself I thought,
That I suppos'd my wit so high might climb
To know all things that God had fram'd or wrought,
Fire, air, sea, earth, man, beast, sprite, place and time."

Heywood, Woman Killed with Kindness, Dodsley, ed. 1825, p. 285,—

"But when my tears have wash'd my black soul white,
Sweet Saviour, to thy hands I yield my sprite."

Tempest, i. 2, fol. p. 4, col. 2,—

"I will be correspondent to command,
And doe my spryting, gently."

Harrington's Ariosto, B. xvi. St. xxxiv.,—

"This speech, by him utter'd with so good spright,
With voice so audible, with comely grace,
Incensed them with such desire to fight," &c.

Sidney, Arcadia, B. ii. p. 113, l. 23,—

"O Chastity, the chief of heavenly lights,
Which makes us most immortal shape to wear,

(*i.e., which most of all mak'st us; quæ potissimum facis, ut nos*, &c.)

Hold thou my heart, establish thou my sprights:
To only thee my constant course I bear."

Astrophel and Stella, Sonnet xlvii.,—

"—————— am I borne [*i.e., born*] a slave,
Whose neck becomes such yoke of tyranny?
Or want I sense to feel my misery?
Or sprite, disdain of such disdain to have?

---

surely we ought to read, not "truth with *hate*," as the ed. 1590 has it, but "moved by *oath withal*."—*Ed.*

Spenser, Hymne in Honour of Love, St. xvi.,—

> "For, having yet in his deducted spright
> Some sparks remaining of that heavenly fire,
> He is enlumind with that goodly light."

(Spenser's evidence is perhaps less adducible on account of his love of antique forms.) *Spright* for *spirit* occurs with a similar rhyme, Hymne in Honour of Beautie, Sts. xvi. xxxiv.; Hymne of Heavenly Love, vi. vii. xvi. xl.; of Heavenly Beautie, i. ii. xxxvii. xliii. Shakespeare, Tarquin and Lucrece, St. xviii.,—

> "For then is Tarquin brought unto his bed,
> Intending weariness with heavy spright;"

rhyming with *night* and *fight*. Venus and Adonis, St. cxlvii.,

> "Even so the timorous yelping of the hounds
> Appals her senses, and her spright confounds."

xxxi.,—

> "And now Adonis, with a lazy sprite," &c.

rhyming to *sight*. Fletcher, Faithful Shepherdess, iv. 2, where Alexis recovers from fainting; Moxon, vol. i. p. 278, col. 1,—

> "See, he gathers up his sprite,
> And begins to hunt for light."

ii. 3, vol. i. p. 271, col. 1,

> "—————————— I'll swear she met
> Me 'mongst the shady sycamores last night,
> And loosely offer'd up her flame and spright
> Into my bosom."

Jonson, Poetaster, iii. 1, near the beginning, Gifford, vol. ii. p. 431,—

> "I drink as I would write,
> In flowing measure fill'd with flame and sprite."

Id., Underwoods, lix. Elegy, Gifford, vol. viii. p. 409,—

"Yet should the lover still be airy 'and light
In all his actions, rarified to sprite."

Epigram xix. p. 162, "On Sir Cod, the Perfumed,"—

"That Cod can get no widow, yet a knight,
I scent the cause: he woos with an ill spite."

Daniel, Cleopatra, iv. 2, p. 472, ed. 1623,—

"Look how a stray'd perplexed traveller
. . . .
Cheers up his tired sprites."

In the First Part of Jeronimo, Dodsley, vol. iii. p. 83,—

"This should not be 'mong men of virtuous sprit:
Pay tribute then, and receive peace and writ:"

read *spright* and *right*.

I have quoted some of the above passages for the sake of the rhyme, which proves that there can be no erratum in the case. *Spright* continued in use some time after the Elizabethan age. Cowley, Davideis, B. i. l. 93, of Satan,

"Once gen'ral of a gilded host of sprights,
Like Hesper leading forth the spangled nights."

Cotton, Voyage to Ireland (performed about 1670), C. i. Chalmers's Poets, vol. vi. p. 273, col. 2,—

"From thence we set forth with more mettle and spright,
Our horses[64*] were empty, our coxcombs were light."

Spreet. Bishop Bale, God's Promises, v. Dodsley, vol. i. p. 31; David is addressing the Almighty,—

"— thy godly sprete, which thu [*i.e., thou*] in me didst plant."

vi. vol. i. p. 35, speaking of Christ,—

"Upon whom alwayes the sprete of the lorde shall be,
The sprete of wysdome, the sprete of heavenly practyse,
And the sprete that wyll all godlynesse devyse."

64* *Qu.*, purses. See context. *Horses* occurs two lines below.-*Ed.*

Gammer Gurton's Needle, printed from the edition of 1575, i. 2, Dodsley, vol. ii. p. 10,—

"By Gog's soule, there they syt as still as stones in the streite,
As though they had ben taken with fairies, or els with some
ill spreet."

ii. 1, p. 28, rhymes, *meete—spreete.*

Poem by Churchyard, 1593, quoted in Var. Shakespeare, vol. vii. p. 187,—

"Her colour changde, her cheerfull lookes
And countenance wanted spreete;
To sallow ashes turnde the hue
Of beauties blossomes sweete."

Historye of Romeus and Juliet, 1562, Var. Shakespeare, vol. vi. p. 318, l. ult.,—

"Beside the great contentednes my sprete abydeth in."

But everywhere else in this poem it is printed *sprite.* I am not sure that I have noticed this spelling in the Elizabethan age; [65] there are several passages, however, in which euphony seems to require that the word should be so pronounced, although *sprite* must have been the ordinary pronunciation. Yet I doubt. *Sprite* and *night* were not *exactly* the same. Merchant of Venice, v. 1,—

"The notions of his *spirit* are dull as *night.*"

Love's Labour 's Lost, iv. 3,—

"Devils soonest tempt resembling *spirits* of *light.*"

Sonnet lxxx.,—

"O, how I faint when I of you do *write,*
Knowing a better *spirit* doth use your name,
And in the praise thereof spends all his *might.*"

---

[65] Perhaps Walker omitted *elsewhere,* as the last two examples belong to the reign of Elizabeth.—*Ed.*

Fairfax, B. xvi. St. xxix.,—

"His noble *spright* awaked at that *sight.*"

Drayton, Idea, Æglogue vi. (I have the quotation from the Variorum Shakespeare, vol. ii. p. 204),—

"Who would not die, when Elphin now is gone,
Living that was the shepherd's [*shepherds'*] true *delight*,
With whose blest *spirit* (attending him alone)
Virtue to heaven directly took her *flight?*"

Spenser, Faery Queen, B. i. C. xii. St. xxxix.,—

"Yet wist no creature whence that hevenly sweet
Proceeded, yet each one felt secretly
Himselfe thereby refte of his sences meet,
And ravished with rare impression in his sprite."[66]

In Spenser it is evidently used as a license, after his manner. In Shakespeare, at least, I know not how to conceive the possibility of such cacophony. The pronunciation must have varied between the two, but *spright* evidently predominated. Perhaps some poets (and even speakers) used them indiscriminately, as convenience dictated.

Sprit. Harrington's Ariosto, B. xiii. St. xlvi.,—

"But all your sprits and forces all assemble."

Sidney, Arcadia, B. ii. p. 222, l. 33,—

"The flying sprits [*i.e., winds*] which trees by rootes vp teare."

Sp'rit. This is not very frequent. Bishop Hall, Easter Anthems, supplemental volume to his works, 1660, and Chalmers, vol. v. p. 348, col. 2,—

"What state? attendance of each glorious sp'rit;"

---

[66] The second folio spells the word *spreete*, but Walker probably follows Todd, who, I fancy, printed from the first quarto.—*Ed.*

rhyming to *light*. Lord Brooke, Alaham, ii. 3, Works, 1633, p. 31,—

"With shaking thoughts no hands can draw aright:
True hearts, to do unnobly, have no sp'rit."

Sonnet ciii. p. 251, *sp'rit* rhymes to *infinite*. lxxxiii. p. 229, *unites—sp'rits*. v. *ad fin.*, p. 163, *delights—sp'rits*. Note by the way Alaham, ii. 4, *init.*, p. 33,—

"Who ever have observ'd the work of *spirits*,"

rhyming to *delights;* and so Sonnet lxv. p. 210, *spirit—light;* so also in the play of Tancred and Gismund, i. 2, near the end, Dodsley, vol. ii. p. 176, *rites—spirits*, alternate rhymes. Dubartas, i. vii. p. 61, col. 2,—

"—————— I hope to cancel quite
This profane thought from your unsettled sp'rit."

Butler, Hudibras, P. iii. C. iii. 153, ed. 1716,—

"Quoth he, I know your constant rate,
And frame of sp'rit, too obstinate."

Note Lord Brooke, Sonnet xcix. p. 246,—

"For on this sp'rituall cross condemned lying."

Butler, Satire on the Age of Charles II., l. 176,—

"In sp'ritual and carnal ignorance."

Hudibras, P. iii. C. ii. 73,—

"But by their sp'ritual attaints
Degraded from the right of saints."

Also Golding's Phillis, Introduction, St. ii., as quoted in the Variorum Shakespeare, vol. ii. p. 253,—

"Oh you high sp'rited paragons of witte."

An additional argument might be drawn, if it were necessary, from the numerous passages in which the dissyllabic pronunciation of *spirit* renders a line positively unmetrical, or inharmonious to a degree beyond what the poet's ear could possibly have tolerated. Examples : Shakespeare, M. for M. i. 1,—

> " ——————— 't were all alike
> As if we had them not. Spirits are not finely touch'd
> But to fine issues."

Antony and Cleopatra, i. 2,—

> "There's a great spirit gone!—thus did I desire it."

Sonnet, lvi.,—

> "To-morrow see again, and do not kill
> The spirit of love with a perpetual dulness."

No one, who is familiar with Shakespeare's Sonnets, and has an ear, can tolerate this.

Daniel, Civil Wars, B. vii. St. xxxiv. ed. 1623, p. 182,—

> "For, other motions, other int'rests heere,
> The acting spirits vp and awake doe keepe."

Hymen's Triumph, iii. 4, p. 300,—

> "Ah worthy Thirsis, entertaine that spirit
> Whatever else thou doe;"

contrary to the "monosyllabo-teleutic" flow of this poem.

Drummond, ap. Dyce's Sonnets, p. 95,—

> "If my spirit with itself holds lasting strife."

Rowley, Noble Spanish Soldier, iii. 1, 1634, 3rd page of the act,—

> " ——————— being only daughter
> To such a brave spirit as the duke of Florence."

Dubartas, ii. iii. i. p. 154, col. 1,—

> "The Spirit, whom all good spirits in spirit adore."

Drayton, Polyolbion, Song xii. ed. 1753, p. 893,—

> "The most redoubted spirits that Denmark here addrest."

xxii. p. 1074,—

> "Who with words full of spirit his fighting soldiers cheer'd."

Ib., p. 1072,—

> "Which in his mighty spirit still rooted did remain."

So, too, Chapman in his Iliad frequently concludes the former division of his long line with this word, *e.g.*, xiii. Taylor, vol. ii. p. 24, l. 25,—

> "——— for she that brought thee forth not utterly left me
> Without some portion of thy spirit, to make me brother thee."

xv. p. 55, l. 14,—

> "Be strong, said he, for such a spirit now sends the god of breath."

Spenser, Faery Queene, B. iv. C. ii. St. xxxiv.,—

> "————— through infusion sweete
> Of thine own spirit which doth in me survive," &c.

No *Spenserian* ear can tolerate this, if *spirit* be taken as a dissyllable. And so C. ii. of Mutabilitie, St. xxii.,—

> "————— with subtill influence
> Of his thin spirit, all creatures to maintaine
> In state of life."

B. ii. C. xii. St. li., last line,—

> "That still it breathed forth fresh spirit and wholesome smell."

B. vi. C. iv. St. xxxv.,—

> "This little Babe, of sweete and lovely face,
> And spotlesse spirit in which he may enchace
> Whatever formes ye list thereto apply," &c.

Ford, Love's Sacrifice, ii. 4, Moxon, p. 85, col. 2,—

> "————— you will say
> I was a good, cold, easy-spirited man,"

read in conjunction with the entire scene. Massinger,

Roman Actor, iv. 2, p. 159, col. l. ult.; here *spi-rit* would be unmetrical, *Massingero judice*,—

"But for Augusta so to lose herself,
That holds command o'er Cæsar and the world,
Were poverty of spirit. Thou must—thou shalt, &c."

Beaumont and Fletcher, Custom of the Country, ii. 1, *ad fin.*,

"Nor will I curb my spirit; I was born free,
And will pursue the course best liketh me."

Herbert, Temple, Church Porch,—

"Sink not in spirit: who aimeth at the sky,
Shoots higher much than he that means a tree."

(Compare for the sentiment, Sidney, Arcadia, B. ii. p. 120, l. 24,—"Who shoots at the midday sun, though he be sure he shall never hit the mark, yet as sure he is, he shall shoot higher, than who aims but at a bush.") Herrick, Clarke, vol. ii. ccccclxviii.,—

"Ravish'd in spirit, I come, nay more, I fly
To thee, blest place of my nativity!"

Spi-rit would raise a ripple on the smooth surface of Herrick's verse. Note by the way the word *to sprighten*, Marston, Malcontent, 1604; I quote here from the Variorum Shakespeare, vol. xiv. p. 67, "—he is the most exquisite in forging of veins [*qu.?*] [67] spright'ning of eyes, dyeing of hair, sleeking of skins, blushing of cheeks," &c. And *sprightful*. King Richard II. i. 3,—

"The Duke of Norfolk, sprightfully and bold,
Stays but the summons of th' appellant's trumpet."

---

[67] Possibly the corruption is not in *veins* but in *forging*, which seems a misprint for *purging*. A little before we have, "it purifieth the blood, smootheth the skinne, inlifeneth the eye, strengthneth the *veines*," &c.—*Ed.*

Glapthorne, Lady's [Ladies'] Privilege, i. 1, Old English Drama, 1825, vol. ii. p. 3 of the play,—

> "That fatal music rapp'd [*i.e., rapt*] his sprightful sense,
> Like jovial hymns at nuptials."

Massinger, Bondman, ii. 1, *init.*,—

> "So, so, 'tis well: how do I look?
> *Marullo.* Most sprightfully."

Chapman, Il. xiii. Taylor, vol. ii. p. 22, l. 25,—

> "The Phthian and Epeian troops did spritefully assail
> The godlike Hector rushing in."

ii. vol. i. p. 62, antepenult., *spiritful*,—

> "———— that with their spiritful cry
> The meadow shrieks again;"

but xii. p. 258, l. 6, as a trisyllable,—

> "———— the man, so late so spiritful,
> Fell now quite spiritless to earth."

Dedicatory Sonnet to Lord Southampton,—

> "———— high and spiritful alarms."

Sylvester, i. iii. p. 23, col. 1, ed. 1641,—

> "Our sprighful pulse the tide doth well resemble,
> Whose outside seems more than the midst to tremble."

I notice also *sprightless*, Shirley, Witty Fair One, iv. 3, l. 3,—"The world and the devil are tame and sprightless temptations, poor traffic, to this staple commodity of whoring." Sylvester, i. vi. p. 55, col. 2,—

> "———— Whoso doth not admire
> His spirit, is sprightless."

l. vii. p. 62, col. 1,—

> "The spirit is spright-less if it want discourse."

Merry Wives of Windsor, i. 4,—"A softly-sprighted man, is he not?" Since the above note was written, I have met with the following passages:—Malone, note on M. N. D.

iii. 2, Var. Shakespeare, vol. v. 272,—" In the old editions of these plays many words of two syllables are printed at length, though intended to be pronounced as one. Thus spirit is almost always so written, though often used as a monosyllable." *Id.*, note on K. John, v. 2, Var. Shakespeare, vol. xv. p. 353,—" Many dissyllables are used by Shakespeare and other writers as monosyllables, as *whether*, *spirit*, &c., though they generally appear at length in the original editions of these plays." Gifford, note on Jonson's Penates, Jonson, vol. vi. p. 491,—" It may not be amiss to notice here, once for all, that our old poets, with few exceptions, pronounced this word (*spirit*) as if it were written *sprite*. It rarely occurs as a dissyllable in the writers of Jonson's age."

Perhaps it would be desirable, wherever the word occurs as a monosyllable, to write it *spright*, in order to ensure the proper pronunciation of the line. I prefer *spright* to *sprite;* inasmuch as the latter invariably carries with it a spectral association; although the old writers, in those passages where they write the word monosyllabically, use sometimes the one form, sometimes the other. Fairfax, Tasso, B. xvi. St. xxix.,—

> "His noble *sprite* awaked at that sight;"

where *spright* would manifestly be inadmissible.

XXXII.

Please as a personal and impersonal verb.

All 's Well that Ends Well, ii. 3,—

> "To each of you one fair and virtuous mistress
> Fall when Love please!"

Is not the construction *when please Love, quando placuerit Cupidini, ἐπὴν δόξῃ τῷ Ἔρωτι?* Both this and the other were indeed in use. Twelfth Night, v. 1,—

"———————— What shall I do?
Olivia. Even what it please my lord, that shall become him."

Much Ado, &c. ii. 3,—"her hair shall be of what colour it please God." Winter's Tale, iv. 3,—

"If you may please to think I love the king,
And, through him, what is nearest [*near'st*] to him," &c.

Here *si tibi placeat* is the more suitable meaning. King Richard III. ii. 2,—

"Where every horse bears his commanding rein,
And may direct his course as please himself."

Taming of the Shrew, iii. 2, the editions[68] have,—

"———— ———— I will not go to-day,
No, nor to-morrow, nor till I please myself.
. . . .
For me, I'll not be gone till I please myself."

And so the folio. Read, however, *metri gratia,* "till please myself." *What you please* would thus be originally ὅ τι ἄν σοι ἀρέσκῃ· and so of *if you please.* As You Like It, Epilogue,—"I charge you, O women, for the love you bear to men, to like as much of this play as please you."

---

[68] This is true only of the folios, Rowe's, and the more recent editions, for, in the last verse of the quotation, Pope coolly altered *be gone* to *go,* and was followed by all the earlier editors but Capel, who, like Walker, omitted *I,* and restored *be gone.* In the verse above, this omission is not absolutely necessary for the metre, but it is not likely that the poet varied the phrase. In the quotation from Fairfax, *O* seems a misprint for *So.—Ed.*

Perhaps there is a double meaning *here; as may be acceptable to you.* Fairfax's Tasso, C. ii. St. lxxv.,—

"Thy ships to bring it [*i.e., your provision*] are, perchance, assign'd:
O! that you live as long as please the wind!"

Drayton, Idea, Sonnet li.,—

"Calling to mind, since first my love begun,
Th' uncertain times oft varying in their course,
How things still unexpectedly have run,
As 't please the fates, by their resistless force;" &c.

Massinger, Bondman, iv. 2, Moxon, p. 89, col. 2,—

"——————————— show a cause
That leads you to this desperate course, which must end
In your destruction.
Grac. That as please the Fates;" &c.

Sidney, Arcadia, B. iii. p. 304, l. 32; see context, "—— and thereof is indeed (when it please you) more counsel to be taken." Dekker, Old Fortunatus, O. E. Drama, 1831, p. 79—

"———— your pains [*i.e., punishments*] shall ring
Through both your ears to terrify your souls,
As please the judgment of this mortal king."

i.e., as he shall determine your sentence.

Instances of the other syntax with *please* in the subjunctive.

1 K. Henry IV. i. 2,—

"Yet herein will I imitate the sun,
Who doth permit the base contagious clouds
To smother up his beauty from the world,
That when he please again to be himself,
Being wanted he may more be wonder'd at."

Hamlet, iii. 2,—

"———————— and blest are those,
Whose blood and judgment are so well commingled,

That they are not a pipe for fortune's finger
To play what stop she please."

King Henry VIII. ii. 2,—

" ———— ———— all men's honours
Lie in one lump before him, to be fashion'd
Into what pitch he please."

1 King Henry VI. iii. 2,—

"Now, quiet soul, depart when Heaven please," &c.

2 King Henry VI. iii. 1,—

"By flattery hath he won the commons' hearts;
And, when he please to make commotion,
'Tis to be fear'd, they all will follow him."

Marlowe, Translation of B. i. of Lucan, Dyce, vol. iii. p. 285,

" ———— Here every band applauded,
And, with their hands held up, all jointly cried
They 'll follow where he please."

Jonson, Entertainment at Althorpe, Gifford, vol. vi. p. 471,

"This is Mab, the mistress fairy,
That doth nightly rob the dairy,
And can hurt or help the churning,
As she please, without discerning."

Silent Woman, ii. 1, Gifford, vol. iii. p. 370,—"Then you must keep what servants she please, what company she will." Beaumont and Fletcher, King and No King, i. 1, Moxon, vol. i. p. 53, col. 1,—

"But let him freely send for whom he please;" &c.

Monsieur Thomas, ii. 5, vol. i. p. 475, col. 1,—

"She is not married?
Val. Not yet.
Cel. Nor near it?
Val. When she please.

Queen of Corinth, iii. 1, vol. ii. p. 36, col. 1,—

"———————— tell him, for his marrying,
He may dispose him how and when he please."

Island Princess, ii. 1, *ad fin.* vol. ii. p. 238, col. 1,—

"———————— That 's the most cruelty,
That we must keep him living.
2 *Moor.* That 's as he please;
For that man that resolves needs no physician."

Massinger, Maid of Honour, v. 1, near the beginning,—

"———————— for my fine favourite,
He may graze where he please."

Tailor, Hog hath Lost his Pearl, v. 1, Dodsley, vol. vi. p. 382,—

"Great Crœsus shadow may dispose of me
To what he *pleaseth.*
Lightfoot. So speaks obediency."

Metri gratia,[69] *please.*

Tomkis, Albumazar, i. 5, Dodsley, vol. vii. p. 123,—

"———— the bunch of planets new found out,
Hanging at th' end of my best perspicil,
Send them to Galileo at Padua:
Let him bestow them where he please."

Marmyon, Antiquary, i. 1 (it should be 2), Dodsley, vol. x. p. 19,—

"———— by that time she 'll get strength
To break this rotten hedge of matrimony [,]
And after have a fair green field to walk in,
And wanton where she please."

Spenser, Faery Queene, B. ii. C. vii. St. xvii.

"Then if thee list my offred grace to use,
Take what thou please of all this surplusage."

---

[69] *Please* here may be better Elizabethan English, but *pleaseth* scarcely violates the metre. See S. V., art. ix.—*Ed.*

Fairfax's Tasso, B. xvii. St. lii.,—

> "Thou worthy art that their disdain and ire
> At thy commands these knights should both appease,
> That 'gainst thy foe their courage hot as fire
> Thou may'st employ both when and where thou please.'

I conjecture, that it was the form with *you, e.g., what you please, how you please*—where the words might bear two different constructions—which gave rise to the error in question.

XXXIII.

INSTANCES of *when*, and similar particles—as also of *who, whose,* &c.—joined with the subjunctive of other verbs besides *please*. I have included under this head some other passages of analogous construction.

Daniel, Sonnet xl.,—

> "Thou canst not die, whilst any zeal abound
> In feeling hearts, that can conceive these lines."

Dekker and Middleton, Honest Whore, part 1, i. 1, near the end; the lines are in rhyme,—

> "If ever, whilst frail blood through my veins run,
> On woman's beams I throw affection,
>
> . . . .
>
> Let me not prosper, Heaven!"

Fletcher, Purple Island, B. i. St. xxii.,—

> "Oft therefore have I chid my tender Muse;
> Oft my chill breast beats off her flutt'ring wing:
> Yet when new spring her gentle rays infuse,
> All storms are laid, again[70] to chirp and sing."

---

[70] The edition of 1633 has *I 'gin,* which seems the genuine reading. *Again,* however, appears in Southey's "British Poets,"

Lord Brooke, Mustapha, i. 2, p. 87,—

"———————— this crafty slave,
Careless in which he make the other's tomb."

Drayton, Polyolbion, Song x.,—

"This scarce the Muse had said, but Cluyd did quickly call
Her great recourse, to come and guard her while she glide
Along the goodly vale," &c.;

as in Daniel and Dekker and Middleton just above; for it can hardly, I think, be *glide* for *glided*, as *rise* for *rose*, *light* for *lighted*. (A false analogy, I suspect.) Can this be the syntax in Tarquin and Lucrece, St. cxcii.?

"For they whose guilt within their bosoms lie,
Imagine every eye beholds their blame."

Dekker, Old Fortunatus, ed. 1831, p. 80,—

"———————— those that (like him) do muffle
Virtue in clouds, and care not how she shine,
I'll make their glory, like to his, decline."

Fletcher, &c., Bloody Brother, iii. 2, Moxon, vol. i. p. 530, col. 1, Song, *init.*,—

"Come, Fortune's a whore, I care not who tell her."

Cary, Inferno, C. v. l. 21, if in point,—

"Look how thou *enter* here; beware in whom
Thou *place* thy trust; let not the entrance broad
Deceive thee to thy harm."

(Under this head may be noticed, though not exactly similar, the following passage from Daniel's Hymen's Triumph, ii. 4, *init.* p. 238, ed. 1623,—

"Here comes my long expected messenger,
God grant the news he bring may make amends
For his long stay.")

---

and therefore is probably not a mere slip of Walker's pen. I must confess, I do not quite understand the passage with either reading.—*Ed.*

Sir John Beaumont, Description of Love, ap. Clarke's Helicon of Love, 1844, p. 71, St. iii.,—

"Love is like youth, he thirsts for age,
He scorns to be his mother's page;
But when proceeding time assuage
The former heat, he will complain,
And wish those pleasant hours again."

Sidney, Arcadia, B. i. p. 82, l. 36, is somewhat in point,—

"Then do I shape to myself that form which reigns so within me,
And think there she do dwell, and hear what plaints I do utter."

Ib., p. 88, l. 33,—

"They false and fearful do their hands undo,
Brother his brother, friend doth friend forsake,
Heeding himself, cares not how fellow do,
But of a stranger mutual help doth take."

P. 94, l. 31,—

"Away, ragg'd rams! care I what murrain kill?"

B. ii. p. 228, l. 26,—

"I con thee thank, to whom thy dogs be dear;
But commonly like curs we them entreat,
Save when great need of them perforce appear."

B. iii. p. 262, l. 35,—

"——— if I prevail, you give your gifts to me;
If you, on you I lay what in my office be."

Defence of Poesy, p. 501, l. 37,—"For suppose it be granted, that which I suppose with great reason may be denied, that the philosopher, in respect of his methodical proceeding, teach more perfectly than the poet, yet do I think," &c.

Astrophel and Stella, Sonnet lxxiii. p. 545,—

"Love still a boy, and oft a wanton is,
School'd only by his mother's tender eye:
What wonder then if he his lesson miss,
When for so soft a rod dear play he try?"

Kyd, Cornelia, i. 1, Dodsley, vol. ii. p. 247,—

> "'Tis not enough (alas) our power t' extend,
> Or overrun the world from east to west,
> Or that our hands the earth can comprehend,
> Or that we proudly do what like us best."

Shelley has, in one or two passages of his poems, adopted the same idiom in the case of *when*, not however through imitation of the old poets, but from a supposed analogy. Revolt of Islam, C. v. Hymn, St. 6,—

> "——————— Almighty Fear,
> The Fiend-God, when our charmed name he hear,
> Shall fade like shadow from his thousand fanes."

C. vii. St. xxii.,—

> "——— like those illusions clear and bright,
> Which dwell in lakes, when the red moon on high
> Pause ere it waken tempest."

Tennyson, vol. ii. p. 193 (φιλολογώτερος),—

> "And wheresoe'er thou move, good luck
> Shall fling her old shoe after."

Vol. 1, p. 224, (an instance?)—

> "Make Knowledge circle with the winds;
> But let her herald, Reverence, fly
> Before her to whatever sky
> Bear seed of men or growth of minds."

XXXIV.

The word *God* omitted or altered.

Measure for Measure, ii. 2, fol. p. 67, col. 1,—

> "Let her haue needtul, but not lauish meanes,
> There shall be order for 't.

Pro. 'Saue your Honour.
Ang. Stay a little while: y' are welcome: what's your will?
Isab. I am a wofull Sutor to your Honor."

And so the Var. 1821 reads and arranges, only altering *for 't* to *for it*. Did the editor mean the words *'Save your honour* to be the complement of the supposed former part of the verse, "*There shall be order for it*"?[71] Read and arrange,—

"*God* save your honour.
Ang. Stay a little while.
Y' are welcome: what's your will?
Isab. I am," &c.;

the name of God having been omitted by the editor of the folio in deference to the well-known act of parliament against profaneness; or having been, perhaps, struck out by the licensers of the press. For the same reason the word *God* has been in various places altered to *Heaven*, *Jove*, or the like. *Ib.*, below, read,—

"—————— At what hour to morrow
Shall I attend your lordship?"
Ang. At any time 'fore noon.
Isab. *God* save your honour!
Ang. From thee; even from thy virtue."

Also ii. 3, near the end,—

"*God's* grace go with you! *Benedicite!*"

And Winter's Tale, i. 2,—

"Your precious self had then not crost the eyes
Of my young playfellow.
Herm. *God's* grace to boot!"

---

[71] Perhaps; but he and other editors followed the lead of Pope in printing *for it* at length. As to *'Save*, all the folios prefix the apostrophe, and so Rowe, Pope, Theobald, Hanmer, Warburton, and Johnson; Capell and most recent editors omit it.—*Ed.*

Tempest, ii. 1, perhaps verse,—

"*God* save his majesty!

Ant. Long live Gonzalo!"

In all these passages the metre requires the supplement. Othello, ii. 2, *ad fin.* fol. p. 319, col. 1, l. 2,—"Blesse the Isle of Cyprus, and our Noble Generall Othello;" and so Knight. Vulg., "*Heaven* bless," &c. Read *God.* And so I imagine in numberless other prose passages, where the word has been expunged; *e.g.*, Two Gentlemen of Verona, ii. 1,—

"O '*give ye* good ev'n! here's a million of manners."

Merry Wives of Windsor, ii. 3,—"'*Bless thee*, bully doctor. *Shallow.* '*Save you*, master doctor Caius. . . . . *Slender.* '*Give you* good morrow, sir." iii. 1,—"'*Save you*, good sir Hugh! *Evans.* '*Pless you* from his mercy sake, all of you." 2 King Henry IV. v. 5,—

"Save thy grace, king Hal! my royal Hal!

. . . .

Save thee, my sweet boy!"

Romeo and Juliet, ii. 2,—

"Lady, by yonder blessed moon, I swear," &c.

The folio (page 60, col. 1) omits *blessed*, and has *vow* for *swear*. Can this also have originated in the Profanation Act?

Instances of substitution.

Love's Labour's Lost, v. 2,—

"This fellow picks up wit as pigeons pease,
And utters it again, when Jove doth please."

King John, v. 7,—

"The Dauphin is preparing hitherward,
Where, heaven he knows, how we shall answer him.'

Read "*God* he knows," as Comedy of Errors, v. 1,—

> "——————— the chain,
> Which, God he knows, I saw not."

(Compare too King Richard III. i. 3,—

> "Small joy have I in being England's queen.
> *Q. Mary.* And lessen'd be that small, God I beseech him.").

Two Gentlemen of Verona, iv. 4,—

> "Yet I will woo for him; but yet so coldly,
> As, heaven it knows, I would not have him speed."

(In King Richard II. ii. 2, iii. 2, and v. 2,[72]—

> "*God* for his mercy! what a tide of woes
> Comes rushing on this woful land at once!"
>
> . . . .
>
> "*God* for his Richard hath in heavenly pay
> A glorious angel;" &c.
>
> . . . .
>
> "*God* for his mercy! what treachery is here!"

(Print ? after *here*, I think;) the folio has *Heaven* for *God;* whence in the second passage the most un-Shakespearian antithesis of *Heaven* and *heavenly*.)

Instances of unnoticed or noteworthy omission and substitution in other Writers.

Omission.—Fletcher, &c., Love's Pilgrimage, iv. 1, Moxon, vol. ii. p. 625, col. 1,—

> "'*Slight, sir!*" yonder is a lady veil'd."

"*God's* light." Even Fletcher—still more Massinger, to whom I imagine this scene belongs—would not have tole-

[72] The quartos have *God* in all the three passages. Mr. Collier's Old Corrector does not seem to have noticed this sophistication. All the old copies, I fancy, place a note of interrogation after *here.*—*Ed.*

rated an *acephalous* line like this. Jonson, Sad Shepherd, ii. 2, Gifford, vol. vi. p. 288,—

"'*Slid*, I thought the swineherd would have beat me,
He look'd so big."

Massinger, Fatal Dowry, ii. 1, Moxon, p. 271, col. 1; see context,—

"For me, my portion provide in heaven!"

Read "my portion, *God* provide" (*Ibid.*, iii. 1, Moxon, p. 276, col. 2, insert, I think,—

"————— sure a legion
Of [ ] *devils* has possest this woman.")

Marston, Antonio and Mellida, P. i. i. 1, Old English Plays, 1814, vol. ii. p. 122,—

"'*Precious*, what a slender waist he hath!"

Here perhaps we should write "'*Ods* or '*Uds* precious;" though this, one would think, would hardly have offended against the profaneness act. iii. 2, p. 151,—

"'*Sfoot*, methinks I am as like a man."

v. 2, p. 179,—

"'*Sfoot*, a sits like Lucifer himself."

Beaumont and Fletcher, Love's Cure, ii. 2, Moxon, vol. ii. p. 161, col. 2,—

"And seen poor rogues retire, all gore, and gash'd
Like bleeding shads.
Lucio. *Bless us*, sister Clara,
How desperately you talk!"
"*God* bless us."

May, Old Couple, iii. 2 (not 1, as in Dodsley), vol. x. p. 414,—

"They are [*Th' are*] the last couple in hell.
Dotterel. *Save* you, gallants!"

Read "*God* save you," &c.

Substitutions.—Play of Ram Alley, iii. Dodsley, vol. v. p. 415,—

> "For Jove's love, speak."

Massinger, City Madam, iv. 4, Moxon, p. 334, col. 2,—

> "——— you were tickled when the beggars cried
> *Heaven* save your honour!"

Such omissions, &c., are common in the old plays.

XXXV.

Terminations attached to one Adjective, affecting others.

Measure for Measure, iv. 6,—

> "The generous and gravest citizens
> Have hent the gates."

i.e., "the most generous (*i.e.*, *noble*) and grave." (Compare, for this sense of *generous*, Chapman, Il. xiv. Taylor, vol. ii. p. 40,—

> "————— the parts so generous
> Ixion's wife had;"

i.e., *her noble or princely graces*. Il. xv. vol. ii. p. 56,—

> "————— all the generous
> They call'd t' encounter Hector's charge."

Jonson, Poetaster, v. 1, Gifford, vol. ii. p. 524, "as I am generous," *i.e.*, *as I am a gentleman by birth.*)

This idiom is not unfrequent in the Elizabethan poets. Heywood, Rape of Lucrece, i. 2, *init.*,—

> "This place is not for fools: this parliament
> Assembles not the strains of idiotism,
> Only the grave and wisest of the land."

Jonson, Forest, xi.,—

"It is a golden chain, let down from heaven,
Whose links are bright and even,
That falls like sleep on lovers, and combines
The soft, and sweetest minds
In equal knots."

Fairfax's Tasso, B. xvii. S. lx.,—

"—— keep them well in mind, till in the truth
A wise and holier man instruct thy youth."
("———————— sin che distingua
Meglio a te il ver più saggia e santa lingua.")

B. xix. St. lxxiii.,—

"—— had I liberty to use this blade,
Who slow, who weakest is, soon should be seen."
("———————— chi sia più lento.")

And so I think B. xviii. St. lxxii.,—

"—— where the wall high, strong, and surest was,
That part would he assault, and that way pass."
("La' dove il muro più munito ad alto
In pace stassi, ei vuol portar l'assalto.")

Chapman, Odyss. vi. p. 91,—

"—— one of fresh and firmest spirit would change
T' embrace so bright an object."

Hudibras, P. iii. C. i. 567; see context,—

"Of which the true and faithfull'st lover
Gives best security to suffer."

C. ii. 743, the adverb similarly used,—

"We never fail to carry on
The work still, as we had begun;
But true and faithfully obey'd,
And neither preach'd them hurt, nor pray'd."

So Beaumont and Fletcher, Love's Cure, v. 3, Moxon, vol. ii. p. 174, col. 2, "—it hath therefore pleased his sacred majesty,—as a sweet and heartily-loving father of his people,—to order and ordain, &c.," *i.e.*, "as a sweetly and heartily loving," &c.

Goffe, Courageous Turk, 1632, ii. 3,—

> "The vain and haughtiest minds the sun e'er saw."

Play of Ram Alley, i. Dodsley, vol. v. p. 373,—

> "—————————— let's in,
> And on with all your neat and finest rage."

John Onley, Lines to W. Browne, Clarke's Browne, vol. i. p. 17,—

> "Fair Muse of Browne, whose beauty is as pure
> As women brown, that fair and long'st endure."

Compare Shakespeare, Sonnet lxxx.,—

> "But since your worth (wide, as the ocean is)
> The humble as the proudest sail doth bear."

Beaumont and Fletcher, Pilgrim, ii. 2,—

> "———— Then thou should'st have brav'd me,
> And, arm'd with all thy family's hate, upon me
> Done something worthy feat:[73] Now poor and basely
> Thou sett'st toils to betray me.

Here again, as elsewhere occasionally, we have the adverbial termination. So King Richard III. iii. 4 (the *ly* preceding),

> "His grace looks cheerfully and smooth this morning."

Othello, iii. 4,—

> "Why do you speak so startingly and rash."

Merchant of Venice, iii. 2,—

> "The dearest friend to me, the kindest man,
> The *best condition'd* and *unwearied* spirit
> In doing courtesies," &c.

---

[73] Read *fame* for *feat*, I think. For other emendations see Mr. Dyce's Beaumont and Fletcher, vol. viii. p. 30, note *o*.—*Ed.*

This usage, whereby the *latter* of two superlatives copulated with *and* is changed into a positive, is frequent in Shakespeare and his contemporaries.[74] Jonson, Induction to Cynthia's Revels, Gifford, vol. ii. p. 228,—"the only best and judiciously penn'd play of Europe."

Daniel, Hymen's Triumph, iii. 4, ed. 1623, p. 301,—

> "——————— creatures built ———
> ——— of the purest and refined clay
> Whereto th' eternal fires their spirits convey."

Middleton, Witch, i. 2, Dyce, vol. iii. p. 269,—

> "Call me the horrid'st and unhallow'd thing
> That life and nature tremble at."

I notice in Ramsay's Gentle Shepherd, Sang x.,—

> "Its mony times sweeter and pleasing to me."

XXXVI.

Sometimes, something, nothing, with a shifting accent.

Julius Cæsar, ii. 1,—

> "——————————— Am I yourself
> But, as it were, in sort or limitation,
> To keep with you at meals, comfort your bed,
> And talk to you sometimes? Dwell I but in the suburbs
> Of your good pleasure?"

Write,—

> "And talk *t' you* sometimes? Dwell I but *i' th'* suburbs," &c.

---

[74] This usage seems to have grown obsolete in the time of Mr. Collier's Old Corrector, who has altered *unwearied* to *unwearied'st*.—*Ed.*

(This last allusion, by the bye, is connected with what follows,—

"———— ———— if it be no more,
Portia is Brutus' harlot, not his wife."

So by the way, Lover's Complaint, St. xxxiii.,—

"Take all these similes to your own command;"

read *t' your.*) *Sómetimes* and *sometímes*, or rather *sometímes* and *sómetimes*, were both current in Shakespeare's time; *e.g.* (if instances be worth quoting), Hamlet, ii. 2,—

"You know, sometimes he walks for hours together," &c.

and v. 2,—

"Our indiscretion sometimes serves us well,
When our deep plots do fail."

(Compare *wherefóre* and *whérefore;* S. V. art. xi.)

In like manner *sómething* and *nóthing* were not unfrequent in Shakespeare's time. The former, and I suppose also the latter, though I happen only to have noticed the former, are common in the earlier English poetry. Note that Surrey always lays the stronger accent on the final syllable of such words. Winter's Tale, ii. 2,—

"She is, something before her time, deliver'd."

As if he had said "some *whit* before," &c.,—

"———— ———— I cannot speak
So well, nothing so well; no, nor mean better."

King Richard II. ii. 2,—

"———— ———— my inward soul
At nothing trembles; at something it grieves [75]
More than with parting from my lord the king."

[75] Perhaps another instance occurs at the close of the Queen's next speech,—

(Var. *some thing.*) See context. King Richard III. i. 2,—

"———— But, gentle lady Anne,
To leave this keen encounter of our wits,
And fall something into a slower method," &c.

Romeo and Juliet, v. 3,—

"———— whistle then to me,
As signal that thou hear'st something approach."

To one that reads the play continuously it is evident that the ear demands *something*. Fol. (which, by the way, has *hearest*), *some thing;* whereas just below it reads,—

"The boy gives warning, *something* doth approach."

Taming of the Shrew, v. 2,—

"Padua affords this kindness, son Petruchio.
Petr. Padua affords nothing but what is kind."

The double accent restores harmony to the line. Troilus and Cressida, iii. 1, Pandarus's song,—

"Love, love, nothing but love, still more!"

In fact, just before the folio has, 14th page of the play, col. 1,—"*Par.* I, good now loue, loue, *no thing* but loue. *Pan.* In good troth it begins so." Othello, iv. 1,—

"———— What trumpet is that same?
Iago. I warrant, something from Venice."

Warrant as a monosyllable, S. V. art. iv. p. 65. I hardly know whether the Hamlet of 1603, C 3, is worth quoting,

"It beckons you, as though it had something
To impart to you alone."

"so heavy sad,
As, though in thinking on *no thought* I think,
Makes me with heavy nothing faint and shrink."

Surely common sense requires us to read *no thing* for *no thought*. —*Ed.*

Other Poets.—Chaucer, Frankeleines Tale, Tyrwhitt, v. 11256,—

> "——— in his songes somewhat wold he wray
> His wo, as in a general complaining;
> He said, he loved, and was beloved nothing."

Beaumont and Fletcher, Bonduca, ii. 3, Moxon, vol. ii. p. 55, col. 2,—

> "Speak of us nobly; keep your oaths to-morrow,
> And do something worthy your meat. Go, guide 'em."

In some passages, *e.g.*, Middleton, Roaring Girl, iv. 1, Dyce, vol. ii. p. 506,—

> "——————— I see 't so plain,
> That I could steal 't myself.
> *Sir Alex.* Perhaps thou shalt too,
> That or something as weighty; what she leaves," &c.;

it might be better to write *some thing*. Same play, v. 2, p. 550,—

> "——— his son's revenues, which are less,
> And yet nothing at all till they come from him."

This last, if alone, would weigh nothing, the "accentual trochee" in the second place being frequent in Middleton. When I speak of a trochee in the second place, I mean of course one preceded by an iambus in the first, for a line beginning with two trochees would, in such blank verse as that of our Elizabethan dramatists, sound intolerably harsh; whence in the passage first quoted from Middleton, *something* must necessarily be an iambus. Play of How a Man may Choose a Good Wife, &c., near the end,—

> "————— A good wife will conceal
> Her husband's dangers, and nothing reveal
> That may procure him harm."

Here it would be more convenient perhaps to write *no thing*.

1 K. Henry VI. i. 1, near the end,—

"I am left out: for me nothing remains."

The flow of this play requires *nothing*. Beaumont and Fletcher, Coxcomb, iv. 8, near the end of the act,—

"—————— I cannot tell,
But I fear shrewdly I should do something
That would quite scratch me out o' th' calendar."

Island Princess, iii. 1, Moxon, vol. ii. 244, col. 2,—

"———— what ails the princess?
I know nothing she wants.
Quisar. Who's that with you?"

Love's Cure, ii. 2, vol. ii. p. 162, col. 2,—

"—— if you will bestow something, that I
May wear about me, it shall bind all wrath."

Same Play, i. 3, p. 157, col. 1,—

"————— though thy breeding
I' th' camp, may plead something in the excuse
Of thy rough manners."

Fletcher, Faithful Shepherdess, iv. 5, vol. i. p. 281, col. 1,

"And as a little infant cries and bends
His tender brows, when rolling of his eye
He hath espied something that glitters nigh
Which he would have," &c.

Sómething would be quite irreconcileable with the flow of this play. Drinking-Song in Gammer Gurton's Needle,

"Though I go bare, take ye no care,
I am nothing a-cold."

Daniel, Philotas, iv. 2, ed. 1623, p. 237,—

"I do confess indeed I wrote something
Against this title of the son of Jove."

Cleopatra, v. 2, p. 473,—

"Well did our priests discern something divine
Shadow'd in thee."

Two Noble Kinsmen, v. 1,—

"———————— and i' th 'self-same place
To seat something I would confound: So hoist we
The sails, that must," &c.

In the Dedication to the folio Shakespeare *something* is printed *some-thing;* "But since your L. L. haue beene pleas'd to thinke these trifles some-thing," &c., which looks somewhat like Jonson's scientific mode of spelling, being meant to indicate that the associated words, which were hardly yet recognized as one compound word, were in fact such. Crawshaw, ap. Retrosp. vol. i. p. 237. [Wishes to his (supposed) mistress. Ed. 1670, p. 127],—

"Soft silken hours;
Open sunnes; shady bow'rs;
'Bove all, nothing that low'rs."

The metre of the poem—see context—requires *nothing* With regard to the "trochaic" word in the second place, which is common in the Italian poets, and frequent in Milton, but which rarely occurs in the Elizabethan poets (except, as above noticed, in Middleton, and possibly in one or two others, for I am not acquainted with them all), it may be observed, that it is scarcely ever found in Shakespeare. Comedy of Errors, i. 1,—

"Therefore, merchant, I'll limit thee this day
To seek thy [help] by beneficial help."

(*Beneficial,* by the way, means *beneficent;* see art. xi. above.) So the folio and all subsequent editions; yet I almost suspect some mistake, from the harshness of the verse; which, however, is somewhat softened, if we lay the stronger accent (*more veterum*) on the latter syllable of *therefore*. See S. V. art. xi. Measure for Measure, near the end,—

> "Th' offence pardons itself. Dear Isabel,
> I have a motion much imports your good."

In Troilus and Cressida, iii. 3,—

> "—————— O, let not virtue seek
> Remuneration for the thing it was:
> For beauty, wit,
> High birth, vigour of bone, desert in service,
> Love, friendship, charity, are subjects all," &c.

we should arrange,—

> "For beauty, wit, high birth, vigour of bone,
> Desert in service,
> Love, friendship," &c.;

by which the passage will be otherwise improved in more ways than one. (It is possible, by the way, that some words may be lost after *service*.) Tarquin and Lucrece, St. ccxi.,—

> "Thy eye kindled the fire that burneth here."

This is unlike the ordinary rhythm of the Tarquin and Lucrece, yet not, I think, so unlike as to render it suspicious; and there is no other ground of misgiving. Two Noble Kinsmen, i. 3, not far from the beginning; the whole act bears indisputable marks of Shakespeare's hand,

> "——————— which shall be then
> Without further requiring.
> *Emilia.* How his longing
> Follows his friend!"

v. i., for surely this scene is Shakespeare's also,—

> "—————— To Phœbus thou
> Add'st flames hotter than his; the heavenly fires
> Did scorch his mortal son," &c.

King Richard III. iii. 1,—

"What think'st thou? is it not an easy matter
To make William lord Hastings of our mind?"

Timon of Athens, i. near the end,—

"I doubt whether their legs be worth the sums
That are given for 'em."

Winter's Tale, iv. 3,—

"—————————— now here,
At upper end o' th' table, now i' th' middle;
On his shoulder, and his: her face o' fire
With labour," &c.

Cymbeline, iv. 2,—

"The smile mocking the sigh, that it would fly
From so divine a temple," &c.

Coriolanus, iii. 2,—

"And thus far having stretch'd it, (here be with them,)
Thy knee bussing the stones, (for in such business
Action is eloquence," &c.)

I suspect something is lost,—

"—————————— thy knee
Bussing the stones, (for in such business
Action is eloqueuce," &c.)

Taming of the Shrew, Induction, near the end,—

"'Tis much. Servants, leave me and her alone."

But how much of this play is Shakespeare's?

[To return to the main subject.] Robin Hood Ballads, ed. Smith, 1844, p. 60, col. 1, l. 121,—

"The beggar then thought all was wrong,
They were set for his wrack,
He saw nothing appearing then,
But ill upon warse back."

("*Warse*' back," I suppose.)

Browne, Britannia's Pastorals, B.i. Song ii. Clarke, p. 84,—

"But stay, methinks I hear something in me,
That bids me keep the bounds of modesty."

Browne's rhythm requires *something*.

Jonson, Every Man in his Humour, iv. 8,—

"Why, woman, grieves it you to ope the door?
Belike, you get something to keep it shut."

Marmion, Antiquary, iv. 2 (not 1), Dodsley, vol. x. p. 64,—

"My suit no sooner ended, but came in
My jealous husband.
Lionel. That was something indeed!"

For the two last hemistichs seem to form one line.

May, Old Couple, iv. 4 (not 1, as in Dodsley), *ib.*, p. 403,—

"—————— he can expound,
But understands nothing. One thing in him
Is excellent," &c.

(I am not quite sure of this passage. See context.)

Donne, Anatomy of the World, First Anniversary, 1633, p. 250,—

"——— 'tis in vain to dew or mollify
It with thy tears, or sweat, or blood: nothing
Is worth our travail, grief, or perishing,
But those rich joys," &c.

Beaumont and Fletcher, King and No King, v, 3, early in the scene,—

"Though I have done nothing but what was good,
I dare not see my father."

Otherwise the flow would be unlike Beaumont and Fletcher.

Rule a Wife, &c., iv. 3, Moxon, vol. i. p. 361, col. 2,—

"—————— as mad as a French tailor,
That has nothing in 's head but ends of fustians."

Shirley, Imposture, v. 3, Gifford and Dyce, vol. v. p. 258,—

"—————————— I could, if you
Durst hear me, say something, perhaps, would take
Your charity."

XXXVII.

Double Forms of some Proper Names.

Midsummer Night's Dream, ii. 3,—

"Transparent *Helena!* Nature here shows art," &c.

Read *Helen*, as in half a dozen other passages in the play. A few lines below, the folio has,—

"Not Hermia but Helena now I love:"

the quarto F. (teste Var.) omits *now*. I do not think, however, that *now* can be dispensed with. The editions follow the quarto in question. Read *Helen;* and so likewise iii. 2,—

"Be not afraid; she shall not harm thee, Helena;"

to avoid the trisyllabic termination; see S. V. art. liii. (All 's Well, &c., i. 1,—"No more of this, *Helena*, go to," &c. Should we not write *Helen*, as everywhere else in the play?) So in Othello the verse requires that we should write Desdemon, iii. 1, fol. p. 322, col. 2,—

"Give me advantage of some breefe Discourse
With Desdemon alone."

So the folio prints the name in several other passages; 3, p. 323, col. 1,—

"Not now (sweet Desdemon) some other time."

iv. 2, p. 331, col. 2,—

"Ah Desdemon, away, away, away."

v. 2, p. 337, col. 2,—

> "Poore Desdemon:
> I am glad thy Father's dead."

Ib., p. 338, col. 1,—

> "Oh, Desdemon! dead Desdemon: dead. Oh, oh."

This spelling ought to be restored in the above passages. Knight has done so in all but the first, where he doubtless supposes it to be an erratum. But he is wrong, I think, in saying that it is "clearly used as an epithet * of familiar tenderness." It seems to be like *Helen* for *Helena*, and similar double forms. Perhaps also we should read *Desdemon* in iii. 3, fol., p. 323, col. 2,—

> "Farewell my Desdemona, Ile (vulg. *I will*) come to thee strait."

But of this last I much doubt. Pericles, v. 1,—

> "Where's the lord *Helicanus?* he can resolve you."

Should we not write *Helicane*, as ii. Gower's second speech, and Sc. 4 of the same act, *passim?* Two Gentlemen of Verona, ii. 4,—

> "Know you Don Antonio, your countryman?"

Qu., *Antonie;* as *Don John*. Two Noble Kinsmen, v. 3,—

> "—————— be plighted with
> A love that grows as you decay!
> *Arcite.* *Emily,*
> To buy you I have lost," &c.

Emilia. Winter's Tale, iv. 3,—

> "We are not furnish'd like Bohemia's son,

---

* *Epithet*, for *title* or *designation*, a solecism, which has been of late creeping into our language.—*W.*

Nor shall appear in *Sicilia* [76]——

Camillo. My lord,

Fear none of this," &c.

Sicilie. Twelfth Night, ii. 3,—" *Marian*, I say;—a stoop of wine!" Marian occurs nowhere else in Twelfth Night. Can it ever have been synonymous with *Maria* and *Mary?*

Isabel, in Measure for Measure, appears to be sometimes pronounced as Isbel. So Marlowe, K. Edward II., Dodsley, vol. ii. p. 376,—

"God save queen Isabel, and her princely son."

Harrington's Ariosto, B. iii. St. liv.,—

"Three worthy children shall of her be seen,

——————————————

Isabell by name, Alfonso, and his brother."

B. xxiii. St. lxxv.,—

"Poor Isabell shedding tears for tender heart."

So B. xxiv. St. lxxv.—B. xxix. St. xxiv.

Other poets. In the play of Lust's Dominion, Dyce's Marlowe,[77] vol. iii., read *Philippo* for *Philip*, *passim:* in that of Soliman and Perseda, *passim*, for *Ferdinando* read *Fernando*

---

[76] *Sicilia* is the reading of the first folio, *Sicily* of the second. For *appear* Mr. Collier's Old Corrector reads *appear't.* This is scarcely English, but it suggested to me what I suspect to be the genuine reading,—

"Nor shall appear *so* in Sicilia."

My lord seems to be *extra metrum.* The *dash* after Sicilia is modern.—*Ed.*

[77] This edition has been disavowed by Mr. Dyce. I have not seen it. In the play, as it is given in "Old English Plays," vol. i., *Philip*, *Philippo*, *Lord Philip*, and *Prince Philip*, all occur in situations where they suit the metre. In several passages, no doubt, *Philip* is wrong.—*Ed.*

(both forms are used in the play); and D 3, p. 3, *Ferdinand*. Fletcher, &c., Love's Pilgrimage, iv. 1, Moxon, vol. ii. p. 627, col. 2,—

"————— ——— Yes, sir, all happiness
To that fair lady, as I hope.
Gent. Marc-Antonio!"

This part is Massinger's (*meo periculo*), and his metre demands *Marc-Antonie*, and so read v. 2, as in the passage from the Two Gentlemen of Verona, quoted above,—

"——————— I have heard so much
Will keep me deaf for ever! No, Marc-Antonio,"[78] &c.

and 5, p. 634, col. 1,—

"——— ——— I'll have pistols ready
Quickly.
Phil. She is not here.—Marc-Antonio,
Saw you not Leocadia?"

On the other hand, v. 4, p. 632, l. 1,—

"And, which is worse, even Marc-Antony
Would be call'd just," &c.;

the dissyllabic *even* looks suspicious; I think, "e'en Marc-Antonio," &c.

XXXVIII.

The final *s* frequently interpolated and frequently omitted in the first folio.

Merchant of Venice, iv. 1,—

"Bring us the letters; call the messenger."

---

[78] So Moxon's edition, to which Walker refers, and the second folio; but the first folio, the best authority (not that authority is worth much in a case of this kind) has *Mark-antonie*.—*Ed.*

The folio has *messengers*. The interpolation of an *s* at the end of a word—generally, but not always, a noun substantive—is remarkably frequent in the folio. Those who are conversant with the MSS. of the Elizabethan age may perhaps be able to explain its origin. Were it not for the different degree of frequency with which it occurs in different parts of the folio,—being comparatively rare in the Comedies (except perhaps in the Winter's Tale), appearing more frequently in the Histories, and becoming quite common in the Tragedies,—I should be inclined to think it originated in some peculiarity of Shakespeare's handwriting. Most of the passages in question have been already corrected; but I believe that there are several which still require to be reformed. As, however, my alterations may in some instances appear rash and licentious, owing to the reader's not being aware of the exceeding frequency of this corruption, and the freedom of emendation which, in consequence, we are justified in using, I shall proceed to give a number of instances in which, even according to the universally received text (Knight's blind adherence to the folio in these passages is hardly to be reckoned an exception), the error in question has taken place; comprising the far greater part of those which I have noticed; and shall then subjoin the other passages, hitherto unquestioned, in which I also conceive it to exist.

Comedies.—Two Gentlemen of Verona, i. 2, p. 22, col. 1,—

"——————— sith so prettily
He couples it, to his complaining *Names*,"[79]

---

[79] In several other of these examples some modern editors as well as Mr. Knight retain the interpolated final *s*, but I have not thought it advisable to multiply footnotes in specifying all.—*Ed.*

is perhaps not in point; for I see some editions retain *names*. 3, near the end, p. 23, col. 1,—

"Sir Protheus, your *Fathers* call's for you."

Comedy of Errors, iii. 2, l. 4, p. 91, col. 1,—

"Shall loue in *buildings* grow so ruinate?"

Midsummer Night's Dream, i. 1, p. 147, col. 1,—

"As you on him, Demetrius *dotes* on you."

iv. 1, p. 158, col. 1,—

"Me-thinks I see these things with parted eye,
Where euery *things* seemes double."

As You Like It, i. 3, p. 189 (misprinted 187), col. 1,—

"Tell me whereon the *likelihoods* depends."

Twelfth Night, iii. 1, near the beginning, p. 264, col. 2,— "So thou maist say the *Kings* lyes by a begger, if a begger dwell near him."—P. 265, col. 1,—

"But *wisemens* folly falne, quite taint their wit."

(For "wise men, folly fall'n, quite," &c.)

Merchant of Venice, iii. 1, near the beginning, p. 172, col. 2,

"— if my *gossips* report be an honest woman of her word."

Histories.—King John, ii. (iii. 1, of modern editions) p. 8, col. 2, penult.,—

"———————— here I and *sorrowes* sit;"

quod male retinet Knightius. iii. 1, p. 9, col. 1,—

"Let not the howres of this vngodly day
Weare out the *daies* in Peace."

iv. 3, p. 17, col. 1,—

"Sir, sir, impatience hath his priuiledge.
Bast. 'Tis true, to hurt his master, no *mans* else."

King Richard II. i. 3, p. 26, col. 1,—

"———————— true to *Kings* Richards Throne."

1 King Henry IV. i. 1, p. 46, col. 2,—

"And he hath brought vs smooth and *welcomes* newes."

v. 2, l. 6, p. 70, col. 1,—

"He will suspect vs still, and finde a time
To punish this offence in *others* [80] faults."

3, p. 71, col. 1,—

"And thou shalt finde a King that will reuenge
Lords Staffords death."

2 King Henry IV. i. 3, p. 78 (the former of the two pages so numbered), col. 1,—

"Thus haue you heard our *causes*, and kno our Means."

iv. 3, near the end, p. 92 (the second of the three pages so numbered) col. 2, "the sherris warmes it, and makes it course inwards, to the parts *extremes*." ii. 2, p. 81, col. 1,

"I will imitate the honourable *Romaines*[81] in breuitie;"

quod male retinet Eques. 4, p. 84, col. 2, near the bottom,—"For one of them, shee is in Hell alreadie, and burnes poore *Soules*." v. 2, p. 97, col. 2,—

"My Father is gone wilde into his Graue,

———————————————

And with his *Spirits*, sadly I suruiue,
To mocke the expectation of the World."

---

[80] This blunder first appeared in the quarto 1613 (see Capell's Various Readings), from which edition, according to Mr. Collier, the 1st folio was copied. It is found also in the 2nd folio, but was corrected in the 3rd. Many of the instances adduced by Walker are peculiar to the 1st folio.—*Ed.*

[81] This palpable blunder runs through all the old copies, and deforms very many modern editions. It seems to have escaped Mr. Collier's Old Corrector.—*Ed.*

King Henry V. i. 2, p. 71, col. 1,—

"O let their bodyes follow my dear Liege
With *Bloods*, and Sword and Fire, to win your Right."

Col. 2,—

"Who busied in his *Maiesties* surueys
The singing Masons," &c.

2 King Henry VI. iv. 10, *init.*, p. 143, col. 1,—

"Fye on Ambitions: fie on myself."

3 King Henry VI. iii. 2, p. 159, col. 1,—

"'Twere pittie they should lose their Fathers *lands*.
Wid. Be pittiful, dread Lord, and graunt it then."

King Richard III. iii. 7, p. 192, col. 2,—if indeed this is a case of error,—

"Call them againe, I am not made of *Stones*;"

So too King Lear, v. 3, p. 38 (misprinted for 308), col. 2,

"———— O your (*you*) are men of *Stones*."

and Pope and others read *stone*, though the Variorum, I think, retains *stones*. A similar phrase occurs, Merchant of Venice, iv. 1, p. 178, col. 1, penult.,—

"And plucke commiseration of his state
From brassie bosomes, and rough hearts of *flints*." [82]

But the fact of the same error being so often repeated leads me to doubt whether it is an error at all. K. Richard III. iv. 1, p. 193, col. 2, *ad fin.*,—

"So foolish *Sorrowes* [83] bids your Stones farewell."

---

[82] Keye's quarto has *flints*; Roberts's and the 2nd folio *flint*. In the passage from K. Lear all the old copies have *stones*.

[83] First corrected properly by Rowe. The 4th folio had previously introduced the sophistication *Sorrows bid*. In the quotation below from Troilus and Cressida, the editions that I have consulted, except Hanmer's only, read *ingratitudes*.—*Ed.*

As King John, ii. above. King Henry VIII. v. 2, p. 230, col. 2,—

"Good Man, those ioyfull tears shew thy true *hearts*."

Troilus and Cressida, iii. 3, 17th page of the play, col. 1,

"A great siz'd monster of *ingratitudes*."

Ib., near the bottom,—

"————— the welcome euer smiles,
And *farewels* goes out sighing."

i. 3, 6th page, col. 2,—

"————— With tearmes vnsquar'd
Which from the tongue of roaring Typhon dropt,
Would *seemes* Hyperboles."

Tragedies.—Coriolanus, v. 5, p. 30, col. 1,—

"That Pages blush'd at him, and men of heart
Look'd wond'ring each at *others*."

Titus Andronicus, ii. 4, p. 39, col. 1, stage direction,—"*Boths* fall in." *Ib.*,—

"I beg this boone,—————
That this fell fault of my accursed Sonnes
Accursed, if the *faults* be prou'd in them.
King. If it be prou'd? you see it is apparant."

iii. 1, p. 42, col. 2,—

"Beg at the gates *likes* Tarquin and his Queene."

2, near the end, p. 43, col. 1,—

"Flattering my *selfes*, as if it were the Moore."

iv. 1, p. 43, col. 2,—

"Or slunke not Saturnine, as Tarquin *ersts*."

P. 44, col. 1,—

"Oh doe ye read my Lord what she hath *writs*?"

The erratum in question is particularly frequent in this play. Romeo and Juliet, i. 1, p. 54, col. 1,—

"Have you importun'd him by any meanes?
Moun. Both by myselfe and many *others* Friends."

iii. 1, p. 65, col. 1,—

"I charge thee in the Princes *names* obey."

Ib.,—

"Could not take truce with the vnruly spleene
Of *Tybalts* deafe to peace,"

which, however, may have originated in what follows, "but that he Tilts," &c.

5, p. 70, col. 1,—

"Vtter your grauitie ore a Gossips *bowles*
For here we neede it not."

Timon, iv. 3, p. 90, col. 2,—

"Raise me this Begger, and deny 't that Lord,
The *Senators* shall beare contempt Hereditary,
The Begger native Honor."

King Lear, iv. 6, p. 304, col. 1, l. 2. "Place (*Plate*) *sinnes* with Gold, and the strong Lance of Justice, hurtlesse breakes: Arme it in ragges," &c.

Othello, i. 3, p. 314, col. 2,—

"——————— I neuer yet did heare:
That the bruized heart was pierc'd through the *eares*."

iii. 3, p. 324, col. 2,—

"Foh, one may smel in such, a will most ranke,
Foule *disproportions*, Thoughts vnnaturall."

iv. 1, p. 329, col. 2,—

"——————— I shifted him away,
And layd good *scuses* vpon your Extasie."

Here, however, it is possible that Shakespeare may have

written "scuses *on*[84] your," &c. Antony and Cleopatra, i. 5, p. 344, col. 2,—

"—————— Bee'st thou sad or merrie,
The violence of either thee becomes,
So do's it no *mans* else."

Cymbeline, ii. 3, p. 377, col. 1,—"I have assayl'd her with *Musickes*,[85] but she vouchsafes no notice."

(The following are heaped together miscellaneously.)

Othello, i. 1, p. 310, col. 1,—

"At Rhodes, at Ciprus, and on *others* grounds
Christen'd, and Heathen."

Col. 2,—

"What a fall [full] Fortune do's the *Thicks*-lips owe."

Macbeth, iii. 1, p. 139, col. 2,—

"To make them Kings, the *Seedes* of Banquo Kings."

(Atque ita Eques !)[86] We have indeed, in Chapman and Shirley's Chabot, ii. 3, Gifford and Dyce's Shirley, vol. vi. p. 108,—

"And I advanc'd you not to heap on you
Honours and fortunes, that, by strong hand now
Held up, and over you, when heaven takes off
That powerful hand, should thunder on your head,
And after you crush your surviving *seeds*."

---

[84] But the quarto 1622 has *scuse, vpon*.—*Ed.*

[85] Not merely the three other folios and Mr. Knight, but Rowe, Pope, and Theobald, retain *musics*. It is therefore not superfluous to show that, in this particular point, the authority of the first folio is next to nothing.—*Ed.*

[86] Not Eques but Collierius. Mr. Collier, however, in his edition of 1853, has received *seed*, following the example of the Old Corrector.—*Ed.*

But this play is grossly corrupt. (The passage is from Juvenal, Sat. x. 104.) King Lear, i. 1, p. 284, col. 2,—

"To come betwixt our *sentences* and our power."

P. 285, col. 1,—

"Since that respect and *Fortunes* are his love."

This, however, may have arisen from *respects of fortune* being in the printer's thoughts. i. 4, p. 287, col. 2,—

"He saies my Lord, your *Daughters* is not well."

v. 1, p. 306, col. 1,—

"Your businesse of the world hath so an end,
And machination ceases. Fortune *loues* you."

3, p. 307, col. 1,—

"————— for your claime faire *Sisters*,
I bare [*barre*] it in the interest of my wife."

Othello, iv. 1, p. 329, col. 2,—

"Poore Cassio's smiles, gestures and light *behauiours*."

Antony and Cleopatra, i. 4, p. 343, col. 2,—

"——— ——— ——— You
Shall finde there a man, who is th' *abstracts* of all faults,
That all men follow."

v. 2, p. 366, col. 2,—

"————— sawcie Lictors
Will catch at vs like Strumpets, and scald Rimers
Ballads vs out a Tune."

iv. 12, p. 362, col. 1,—

"————— shee Eros has
Packt cards with *Cæsars*, and false plaid my Glory
Vnto an Enemies triumph."

v. 2, p. 368, col. 1,—

"She levell'd at our *purposes*, and being Royall
Tooke her owne way;"

and so, indeed, the Variorum reads. Cymbeline, i. 5, p. 372, col. 1,—"The one may be solde or giuen, or if there were wealth enough for the *purchases*, or merite for the guift." Col. 2,—"I will lay ten *thousands* Duckets to your Ring." 7, p. 374, col. 1,—

"——— ——— but most miserable
Is the *desires* that's glorious."

Timon, i. 2, p. 81 (the second page so numbered), col. 2, "Oh *ioyes*, e'ne made away er't can be borne." Julius Cæsar, v. 1, p. 127, col. 2,—

"You shew'd your *teethes* like Apes."

Othello, iv. 1, p. 329, col. 1,—

"Worke on,
My Medicine *workes*."

Timon, i. 1, p. 82 (properly 80), col. 2,—

"*Comes* shall we in,
And taste Lord Timon's bountie."

Hamlet, ii. 2, p. 264, col. 1,—

"And neuer did the Cyclops hammers fall
On Mars his *armours*," &c.

iii. 2, p. 269, col. 1,—

"Sir, I cannot.
Guild. What, my Lord?
Ham. Make you a wholesome answere: my wits diseas'd. But sir, such *answers* as I can make, you shal command."

In the list of actors prefixed to the folio, *Heminge* is called *Hemmings*. This, however, may perhaps be otherwise explained; such names are often sigmatized in common parlance.

Some of the above, perhaps, are not in point, owing to their originating in other causes.

Hence we are warranted in correcting the following passages, in which, through the means of the folio, the established text has been corrupted. Winter's Tale, iii. 2,—

"What wheels? racks? fires? What flaying? boiling,
In *leads*, or *oils*?"

Anglice, "In *lead*, or *oil*." 2 King Henry VI. iii. 1,—

"The duchess, by his subornation,
Upon my life, began her devilish *practises*."

Practise; a triple ending is inadmissible in this play; and in the same way, Titus Andronicus, v. 2,—

"And will o'erreach them in their own *devices*,"

read *device*, to avoid the double ending, the absence of which, by the way, is characteristic (as has been observed by critics) of a certain time and school, to which this play evidently belongs. Timon of Athens, i. 2.—

"———————— the best of happiness,
Honour and *fortunes*, keep with you, Lord Timon!"

Evidently *fortune*. iii. 5, "And for I know," &c. Read, and (I think) arrange,—

"And, for I know
Your reverend ages love security,
I'll pawn my victories, all my honour, to you
Upon his good *return*."

Julius Cæsar, i. 2,—

"Tell me, good Brutus, can you see your face?
Bru. No, Cassius; for the eye sees not itself,
But by reflexion from[87] some other *things*.
Cas. 'Tis just:
And it is very much lamented, Brutus,

[87] Walker tacitly adopts Pope's correction. The folios, and the modern editions from Capell's inclusive, read "reflexion *by* some," &c. The cause of the blunder is obvious.—*Ed.*

> That you have no such *mirrors*, as will turn
> Your hidden worthiness into your eye."

Read *thing*, and probably *mirror*. So with *some* in several other places. *Ib.*,—

> "——————— and Cicero
> Looks with such ferret and such fiery eyes,
> As we have seen him in the Capitol,
> Being crost in conference by *some senators*."

All's Well, &c., i. 2,—

> "I, after him, do after him wish too,
> Since I nor wax nor honey can bring home,
> I quickly were dissolved from my hive,
> To give *some labourers* room."

(*Dissolvèd*, as Browne, Brit. Past. ii. 4, Clarke, p. 274,—

> "——————— frost and snow,
> Seldom dissolved by Hyperion's ray."

For the sense of the word, *i.q.*, *released*, *solutus*, compare Chapman, Il. xv. Taylor, vol. ii. p. 49,—

> "None durst dissolve [*unchain*] thee."

Odyss. viii. fol. p. 119, Neptune

> "——————— propitiate
> Was still for Mars, and pray'd the God of fire
> He would dissolve him."

v. 344,—

> "——————— λίσσετο δ' αἰεὶ
> Ἥφαιστον κλυτοεργὸν, ὅπως λύσειεν Ἄρηα.)

Hamlet, v. 2,—

> "——— but in my terms of honour
> I stand aloof; and will no reconcilement,
> Till by *some elder masters*, of known honour,
> I have a voice and precedent of peace
> To keep my name ungor'd."

I am not quite sure of this last. By the way, I suspect that one of the two *honours*—the latter—has originated in the other. Merry Wives of Windsor, ii. 1,—

> "'Faith, thou hast some *crotchets* in thy head."

So in Ford, Perkin Warbeck, v. 3, Moxon's edition, p. 121, col. 2,—

> "Death? pish! 'tis but a sound; a name of air;
> A minute's storm, or not so much; to tumble
> From bed to bed, be massacred alive
> By *some physicians*, for a month or two,
> In hope of freedom from a fever's torments,
> Might stagger manhood; here the pain is past
> Ere sensibly 'tis felt."

Clearly *physician*. Tailor, Hog hath Lost his Pearl, iv. 1, Dodsley, vol. vi. p. 379,—

> "—————— ——— If you stay here,
> Your life may end in torture, by the cruelty
> Of *some* wild ravenous *beasts*."

Beast. And so Cymbeline, ii. 1,—"When a gentleman is disposed to swear, it is not for *any standers-by* to curtail his oaths: Ha?" On the other hand, Shirley, Sisters, iv. 2, Gifford and Dyce, vol. v. p. 403,—

> "I've had more lead in bullets taken from me,
> Than would repair *some steeple*."

Perhaps *steeples*. Julius Cæsar, i. 3,—

> "No, it is Casca, one incorporate
> To our *attempts*."

(iv. 1, which I once regarded as corrupt, seems to be right,—

> "———————— and turn him off
> Like to the empty ass, to shake his ears,
> And graze in commons."

I rather think that *in commons* was the established phrase.) Othello, iii. 4,—

> "If my offence be of such mortal kind,
> That nor my service past, nor present *sorrows*,
> Nor purpos'd merit in futurity,
> Can ransom me," &c.

Antony and Cleopatra, ii. 2,—

> "You patch'd up your *excuses*.
> *Ant.* Not so, not so."

I think *excuse* is more Elizabethan. i. 3,—

> "——————— Yet, at the first,
> I saw the *treasons* planted."

King Lear, iv. 6,—

> "When I do stare, see, how the subject quakes."

If this be right, *subject* must refer to Gloster alone. But I think Shakespeare wrote *quake*. *Subject*, more prisco, meaning not *subjectus* but *subjecti;* as we say *the elect*, *the reprobate*. Old writers *passim;* indeed the usage occurs as late as Burke. Winter's Tale, iv. 3, which I once regarded as corrupt, is probably sane,—

> "——————— Here 's flowers for you,
> Hot lavender, *mints*, savory, marjoram," &c.

Quere, whether our ancestors in the time of Elizabeth used *mints* as we do *cabbages*, *parsnips*, and the like? This was certainly the usage in the time of Chaucer; Romaunt of the Rose, p. 176,—I have the quotation from the Encyclopædia Metropolitana, in v. mint. [Fol. 112, ed. 1602],—

> "Tho went I forth on my right hand (*hond*)
> Downe by a litel path I fond
> Of mintes full (*ful*), and fenel greene (*grene*)."

And a passage of Bacon, Essay of Gardens, near the end of the second paragraph, where he associates together "burnet, wild thyme, and watermints," seems to prove the correctness of the received reading in the Winter's Tale. Much Ado, &c., i. 2, near the end,—"*Cousins*, you know what you have to do." *Qu.* See context. Two Gentlemen of Verona, iv. 4,—"the other squirrel was stolen from me by the hangman's *boys* in the market-place." I think *boy* seems more natural, but I doubt much.[88] Tempest, v. 1, fol. p. 18, col. 1,—

"Let vs not burthen our remembrances, with
A heauinesse that 's gon."

Pope (I think it was he) altered this to *remembrance*, for the sake of the metre; rightly; Malone, however, reads and arranges,—

"—— ——— our remembrances
With a heaviness that 's gone;"

ἀμέτρως, Shakespeario saltem judice. Two Gentlemen of Verona, iv. 1,—

"We'll have him: Sirs, a word."

Sir, I imagine; to Valentine. *Ib.*, near the end,—

"Come, go with us, we'll bring thee to our crews."[89]

---

[88] The second folio reads *boy;* Mr. Collier's Corrector, "*a hangman* boy." He evidently knew nothing of the first folio; otherwise he would have read "*the* hangman boys." If Shakespeare wrote *hangman*, *boys* would be more natural, if *hangman's*, *boy*. —*Ed.*

[89] The Old Corrector observed this, and ingeniously read, *cave*, perhaps remembering v. 3,—"Come, I must bring you to our captain's cave." Mr. Collier is, I think, mistaken in supposing that, in iv. 1, the band was present on the stage. Only three outlaws were so.—*Ed.*

Were not *crews* the established reading, every one would perceive at once that it was a solecism. Perhaps Merry Wives of Windsor, iii. 4, near the beginning,—

"Besides these, other bars he lays before me,—
My riots past, my wild *societies*," &c.

Measure for Measure, i. 2,—

"Well, there went but a pair of shears between us.
Lucio. I grant; as there may between the *lists* and the velvet; thou art the list;"

perhaps wrong. ii. 2,—

"———— Heaven give thee moving *graces!*"

Grace? iv. 2,—

"Heaven give your *spirits* comfort;"

perhaps *spirit*, the error having originated in the *spirits* three lines below; yet I very much doubt, for *spirits* seems to be the word required here by Elizabethan usage. Comedy of Errors, i. 1,—

"That by *misfortunes* was my life prolong'd
To tell sad stories of my own mishaps."

Misfortune, surely; and so indeed Ayscough's edition.[90] v. 1,—

"———— that here my only son
Knows not my feeble key of untun'd cares."

Perhaps *care.* Midsummer Night's Dream, ii. 2, *qu.*,—

"I will not stay thy *question;* let me go."

As You Like It, v. 2, read,—

"Speak'st thou in sober *meaning?*"

All's Well that Ends Well, iii. 6,—"he will steal himself into a man's favour, and, for a week, escape a great deal

---

[90] So too the Old Corrector, who, however, seems mistaken in altering *that* to *and.*—*Ed.*

of *discoveries;* but when you find him out," &c. Is this good English? iv. 3, "that he might take a measure of his own *judgments*, wherein so curiously he has set this counterfeit." *Judgment*, of course. 2 King Henry VI. ii. 2, fol. p. 128, col. 1,—

> "What plaine *proceedings* is more plaine then this?"

Vulg., "What —— *are* more," &c. Yet how came *is* to be substituted for *are?* [This is more than I can answer. In fact, *are* is a sophistication, which appears in the Vulgate, the Var. 1821, and some recent editions; the editor of the second folio set matters right by altering *proceedings* to *proceeding*, retaining *is*, and has been followed by the two succeeding folios, the earlier editors down to Johnson inclusive, and Mr. Collier.—*Ed.*] iv. 8,—"In despite of the *devils* and hell, have through the very midst of you! and *heavens* and honour be witness, that no want of resolution in me, but only my followers' ignominious *treasons*, make me betake me to my heels." Some at least of these plurals seem to be wrong. King Henry VIII. iii. 2,—

> "How eagerly ye follow my *disgraces*,
> As if it fed you!"

Clearly *disgrace;* as a dog follows the man who feeds him; and just below, read,—

> "Follow your envious courses, men of malice;
> Y' have Christian warrant for them, and no doubt
> In time will find their fit *reward*."

Titus Andronicus, iii. 1,—

> "O brother, speak with *possibilities*,
> And do not break into these deep extremes."

Ed. 1600, *teste* Var., *possibilitie;* rightly. Timon of Athens,

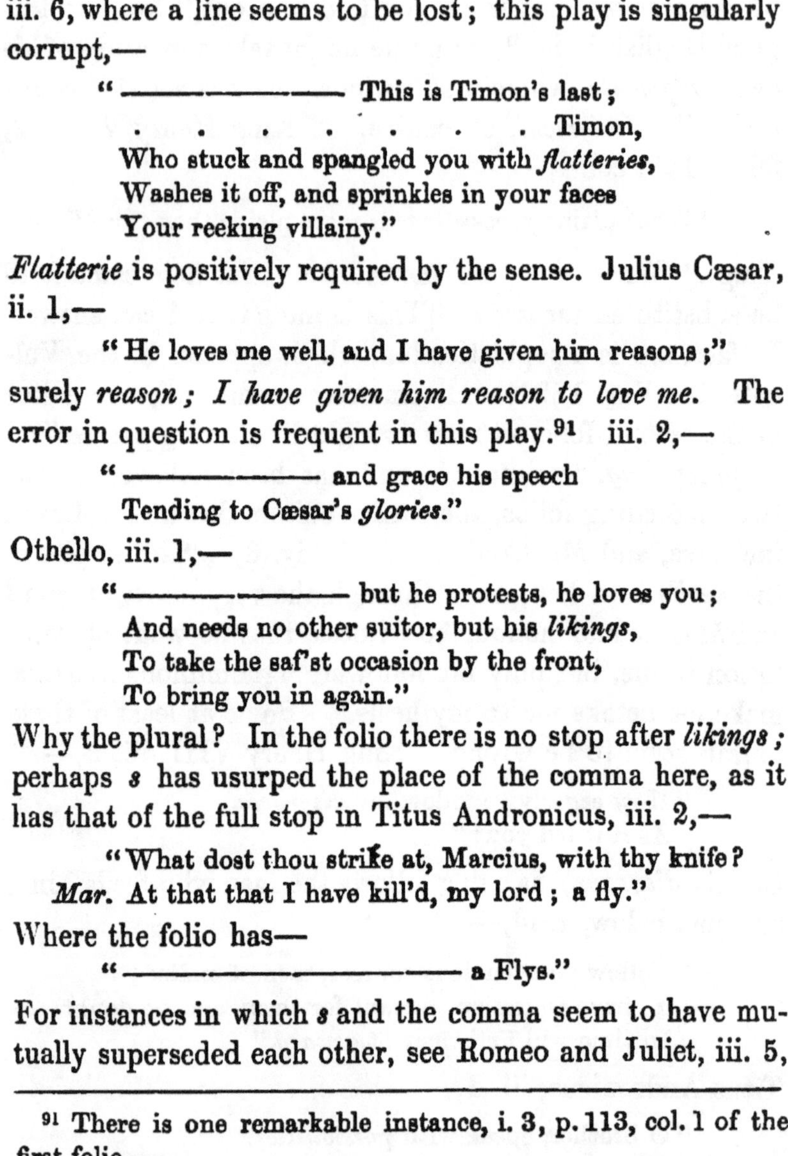

iii. 6, where a line seems to be lost; this play is singularly corrupt,—

> "——————— This is Timon's last;
> . . . . Timon,
> Who stuck and spangled you with *flatteries*,
> Washes it off, and sprinkles in your faces
> Your reeking villainy."

Flatterie is positively required by the sense. Julius Cæsar, ii. 1,—

> "He loves me well, and I have given him reasons;"

surely *reason; I have given him reason to love me.* The error in question is frequent in this play.[91] iii. 2,—

> "——————— and grace his speech
> Tending to Cæsar's *glories*."

Othello, iii. 1,—

> "——————— but he protests, he loves you;
> And needs no other suitor, but his *likings*,
> To take the saf'st occasion by the front,
> To bring you in again."

Why the plural? In the folio there is no stop after *likings;* perhaps *s* has usurped the place of the comma here, as it has that of the full stop in Titus Andronicus, iii. 2,—

> "What dost thou strike at, Marcius, with thy knife?
> *Mar.* At that that I have kill'd, my lord; a fly."

Where the folio has—

> "——————— a Flys."

For instances in which *s* and the comma seem to have mutually superseded each other, see Romeo and Juliet, iii. 5,

---

[91] There is one remarkable instance, i. 3, p. 113, col. 1 of the first folio,—

> "Why Old men, Fooles, and Children calculate."

Read "old men *fool*," if this has not been noticed before.—*Ed.*

fol. p. 70, col. 1 ("Vtter your grauitie ore a Gossips bowles"), and Antony and Cleopatra, iii. 11, fol. p. 357, col. 1 ("Against the blowne Rose may they stop their nose,"). In the latter we should read ***noses***. Donne, Poems, ed. 1633, p. 140, title of a poem, "Obsequies to the Lord Harrington's Brother. To the Countesse of Bedford." For "—— the Lord Harrington, Brother to the Countesse," &c. Chapman, Il. ii. Taylor's ed. vol. i. p. 64, l. 20,

> "Brave Schedius and Epistrophus, the Phocian captains were,
> (Naubolida, Iphitus' sons) all proof [*i.e., all-proof*[92]] 'gainst any fear."
>
> υἱὲς Ἰφίτου μεγαθύμου Ναυβολίδαο,

v. 518. I suspect, "Nauboli*das* Iphitus' sons;" as p. 73, l. 15, "son of *Teutamidas*." At any rate the comma should be expunged. iv. p. 114, l. 35,—

> "————— ——— the Trojans and their *foe*,
> Like wolves on one another rush'd; and man for man it goes."

A couplet. Here however, I think, the comma is in its place, according to the old method of punctuation. Herrick, Clarke, vol. i. clxviii.,— .

> "Have ye beheld, with much delight,
> A red rose peeping through a white?
> Or else a cherry, double grac'd,
> Within a lily, centre plac'd?"[93]

Read, "Within a *lily's* centre plac'd."

Merry Wives of Windsor, iv. 3,—"They shall have my horses, but I'll make them pay; I'll sauce them: they have had my ***houses*** a week at command."—What ***houses?*** Until some satisfactory answer can be given to this ques-

---

[92] This correction is confirmed by Nathaniel Butter's folio.—*Ed.*

[93] The edition 1846, which, I presume, follows the old copy, has "Within a Lillie? Center plac't." *Ed.*

tion, read *house*. This, however, is perhaps rather a case of *contagion*, the printer's eye having been misled by *horses*. Merchant of Venice, iv. 1, point undoubtedly, and, I think, read, as follows,—

> "Cannot contain their urine. For affection,
> *Master* of passion, sways it to the mood
> Of what it likes, or loathes."

At any rate there is no necessity, as far as the *s* is concerned, for reading *maistresse*;—which spelling, moreover, occurs nowhere else in the folio, as far as I recollect. All's Well, &c., v. 1,—

> "——————— I put you to
> The use of your own *virtues*, for the which
> I shall continue thankful."

So Vulg., I believe, and so the folio. Read, I think, *virtue*. Hamlet, iii. 1,—

> "And for your part, Ophelia, I do wish
> That your good *beauties* be the happy cause
> Of Hamlet's wildness; so shall I hope, your *virtues*
> Will bring him to his wonted way again,
> To both your honours.
> *Oph.* Madam, I wish *it* may."

Surely Shakespeare wrote *beauty* [*-tie*], and perhaps also *virtue*. Winter's Tale, i. 1, fol. p. 277, col. 1; and so Vulg., "The Heauens continue their *Loues*. *Arch.* I thinke there is not in the World either Malice or Matter to alter *it*." Read "their *Love*."[94] ii. 3, p. 284, col. 2, near the bottom: and here also the Vulgate follows the folio,—

> "——————— For ever
> Vnvenerable be thy *hands*, if thou

---

[94] So Hanmer; but he is the only editor, as far as I am aware, that detected the error.—*Ed.*

> Tak'st vp the Princesse, by that forced basenesse,
> Which he ha's put vpon't;"

i.e., if thou takest her up as a bastard and outcast, and not with the respect due to the child of thy king. For *upon 't* does not relate to *princess*, but to *hand*—the true reading. Othello, iii. 3,—

> "On horror's head *horrors* accumulate;"

horror. The corruption originated in the preceding *horrors*. Antony and Cleopatra, iii. 1, near the beginning,—

> "——— so thy grand captain Antony
> Shall set thee on triumphant chariots, and
> Put garlands on thy head."

Chariot, surely. 10,—

> "——————————— promise,
> And in our name, what she requires; add more,
> From thine invention, *offers*."

Solœce. Read,—

> "——————————— *and* more,
> From thine invention, *offer*."

1 King Henry IV. i. 1,—

> "On *Holmedon's* plains."

Quære, whether Shakespeare would not rather have written "*Holmedon* plains." 3,—

> "And to your quick-conceiving *discontents*
> I 'll read you matter deep and dangerous."

Discontent? for Hotspur alone seems to be addressed. iii. 1,

> "How 'scapes he *agues*, in the devil's name?"

Perhaps *ague*. Titus Andronicus, v. 2, p. 49, col. 2,—

> "And then Ile come, and be thy waggoner,
> And whirl along with thee about the *globes*."

What globes? *Globe.* Merchant of Venice, ii. 9,—

> "I will not choose what many men desire,
> Because I will not jump with common spirits,
> And rank me with the barbarous *multitudes.*"

Multitude, surely; "the fool multitude, that choose by show," a few lines above. I King Henry VI. i. 1,—

> "Remember, lords, your *oaths* to Henry sworn,
> Either to quell the dauphin utterly,
> Or bring him in obedience to your yoke.
> *Bed.* I do remember *it* ['*t*]; and here take my leave," &c.

Qu. oath; yet does not the old grammar demand oaths?[95] King Henry VIII. ii. 4,—

> "You have, by fortune, and his highness' favours
> Gone slightly o'er low steps."

Perhaps we should read *favour* (and also *lightly.* Is not the construction, *by the favour of fortune and of his highness?*) 1 King Henry IV. v. i.,—

> " ——————— you us'd us so
> As that ungentle gull, the *cuckoo's* bird,
> Useth the sparrow."

What is the *cuckoo's bird?* Read *cuckoo-bird.* King Henry V. v 2,—

> " ——————————————— Peace,
> Dear nurse of arts, *plenties*, and joyful births."

Is *plenties* English? The error arose (*ut sæpe*) from contagion. *Ib.*, near the end of the play,—

> "My lord of Burgundy, we'll take your oath,
> And all the peers', for surety of our *leagues.*"

---

[95] I think not. Compare "Our *mouth* shall show forth thy praise."—*Ed.*

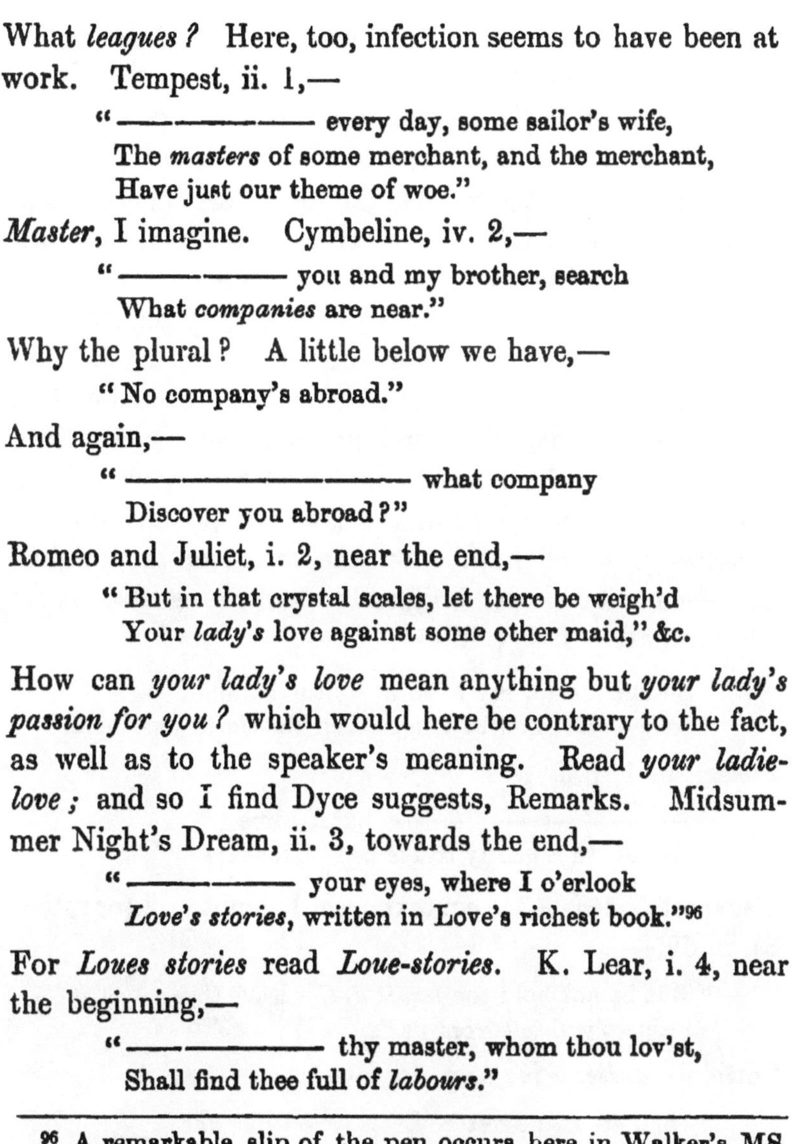

What *leagues?* Here, too, infection seems to have been at work. Tempest, ii. 1,—

"———— every day, some sailor's wife,
The *masters* of some merchant, and the merchant,
Have just our theme of woe."

Master, I imagine. Cymbeline, iv. 2,—

"———— you and my brother, search
What *companies* are near."

Why the plural? A little below we have,—

"No company's abroad."

And again,—

"———— what company
Discover you abroad?"

Romeo and Juliet, i. 2, near the end,—

"But in that crystal scales, let there be weigh'd
Your *lady's* love against some other maid," &c.

How can *your lady's love* mean anything but *your lady's passion for you?* which would here be contrary to the fact, as well as to the speaker's meaning. Read *your ladie-love;* and so I find Dyce suggests, Remarks. Midsummer Night's Dream, ii. 3, towards the end,—

"———— your eyes, where I o'erlook
Love's stories, written in Love's richest book."[96]

For *Loues stories* read *Loue-stories.* K. Lear, i. 4, near the beginning,—

"———— thy master, whom thou lov'st,
Shall find thee full of *labours.*"

---

[96] A remarkable slip of the pen occurs here in Walker's MS. *Loues stories* is written for Love-stories, and *vice versâ*, so that the received reading appears as the proposed correction, and the proposed correction as the received reading.—*Ed.*

The quartos, *labour;* perhaps rightly. 5, near the beginning,—"If a man's *brains* were in his heels, were 't not in danger of kibes?" *Brain* surely, and so Pope and some others.

I feel certain of the truth of the above corrections, except in the instances where I have expressly stated my doubts. Καί μοι τοῦτο τὸ ἔπος ἐχέτω ἐς πάντα τὸν λόγον.

I have not noticed this error as occurring frequently in any other of the early editions of our old poets, so far as I am acquainted with them, except in the collected edition of Daniel's Poems, 1623, and perhaps in Greene's King James IV. In the Second Maiden's Tragedy, as printed (for the first time, so far as is known) in the Old English Drama—in which impression the errors of the original MS. seem to be almost uniformly retained—it also occurs several times. i. 1, p. 3,—

"Beside, I draw my life out, by the bargain,
Some twelvemonths longer than the *times* appointed."

Time. ii. 1, p. 27,—

"———————— but I come
To bear thee gently to his bed of *honours;*"

I suspect *honour;* see context; yet I doubt. 2 (or rather 3), p. 39,—

"But be not bold too far, if *duties* leave thee,
Respect will fall from us."

Certainly *dutie.* iv. 4, p. 70,—

"Thou art an honest boy, 'tis (*it is*) like one
That has a feeling of his master's *passions*,
And the unmatch'd worth of his dead mistress."

Passion? (Write *th' unmatch'd*—pronouncing *mistress* as

a trisyllable (S.V. art. ii. iii. pp. 47 *sqq.*)—or else *the unmatchèd*). Ford, Fancies, &c., iv. 1, Moxon, p. 138, col. 2,

"Sirrah, be sure you show some *reasons* why
You so neglect your duty, quickly show *it*,
Or I shall tame your choler."

Reason, of course. See an earlier part of this article for an instance from Ford, Perkin Warbeck, v. 3, Moxon, p. 121, col. 2. Jonson, Poetaster, i. 1, Gifford, vol. ii. p. 409,—

"O, sacred Poesy, ——————
—————— ——————
What profane violence, almost sacrilege,
Hath here been offered thy *divinities!*"

Evidently *divinity;* there is nothing in the context which can lead us to suppose that the Muses are meant. Day, Isle of Gulls, iii. 1,—"My lady 's in love with thee.—— her amorous glances are her accusers; her very looks write sonnets in thy *commendations*." Should not this be *commendation?* Fletcher, Honest Man's Fortune, i. 1, Moxon, vol. ii. p. 475, col. 2,—

"—————— when all else left my cause,
My very *adversaries* took my part.
Long. Whosoever told you that,
Abused you.
Mont. Credit me, *he* took my part
When all forsook me."

Adversarie.[97] Jonson, Underwoods, Epitaph on Master Vincent Corbet, Gifford, vol. viii. p. 327,—

"No stubbornness so stiff, nor folly
To licence ever was so light,

[97] This conjecture is confirmed by Mr. Dyce's MS., which also restores the decapitated verse that follows. See his excellent edition, vol. iii. p. 351, notes *b* and *c*.—*Ed.*

As twice to trespass in his sight;
His *looks* would so correct it, when
It chid the vice, yet not the men."

Look. Spenser, C. ii. of Mutabilitie, St. x.,—

"Tenne thousand *mores* of sundry sent and hue," &c.

The context—which see—proves that *more* is the right reading. *Frustra omnino Uptonus apud Toddium.*

Machin, &c., Dumb Knight, v., Dodsley, vol. iv. p. 442, *ad fin.*,

Mariana says,—

"Prevention, thou best midwife to misfortune,
Unfold this ugly *monster's treachery;*
And let his birth be ominous, struck dead, [*dele comma*]
Ere it have being in this open world."

Read,—

"Unfold this ugly *monster, treachery.*"

See context. For other instances in which *s* seems to have assumed the place of a comma, see p. 251.

Herrick, The Beggar, Clarke, vol. ii. p. 227, d vii.,—

"Shall I a daily beggar be,
For love's sake asking alms of thee?
Still shall I crave, and never get
A hope of my desired bit?
Ah, cruel *maids!* I'll go my way;"

Maid. Carew, Obesequies to the Lady Ann Hay, Clarke, lxx. p. 91,—

"I heard the *virgins* sigh,"&c.

see context; *virgin* surely.[98] Good Counsel to a Young

---

[98] No doubt. This corruption is found in the first edition, which is also answerable for the interpolated *s* in the two following quotations.—*Ed.*

Maid, xxvi. p. 45, l. 4, *nymphs*, *qu. nymph;* see context. Masque, p. 196,—

"————— This low abject brood,
That fix their seats in mediocrity,
Become your servile *minds*."

Mind? See context. Chapman, Commentary on Il. iii. Taylor, vol. i. page 96, 5 lines from the bottom,—"What touch, then, is it to me to bear spots of *depravations*, when my great master is thus muddily dawbed with it?" *Depravation*, I suspect. Endymion Porter on Donne, edition 1633 p. 406, *ad fin.*,—

"Time hath no soul, but his exalted verse;
Which with *amazements* we may now rehearse."

Amazement? Jonson, Cynthia's Revels, v. 2, Gifford, vol. ii. p. 357; see context,—

"———— that may conform them actually
To God's high *figures*, which they have in power;"

(*in power, i.e., potentially*, as opposed to *actually*). *Figure* surely. Poem in Sidney's Arcadia, iii. 387, 14,—

"Blithe were the *commons* cattle of the field,
Tho when they saw their foen of greatness kill'd."

Common? or shall we point,—

"Blithe were the commons, cattle," &c.

The book is very correctly printed for that age. Chapman and Shirley, Chabot, i. 1, Gifford and Dyce, vol. vi. p. 94,—

"Which will so much increase [*incense*] his precise justice,
That, weighing not *circumstances* of politic state,
He will [*He'll*] instantly oppose it," &c.

Circumstance. ii. 1, p. 103,—

"——— What *commands* of yours,
Not to your expectation obey'd

By him, *is* ground of your so keen displeasure?
Queen. *Commands* of mine?"

Command, surely. Wedding, iv. 4, vol. 1, p. 427,—

"—————————— Would not
Some fearful man or woman, seeing me,
Call this a churchyard, and imagine me
Some wakeful apparition 'mong the graves;
That, for some *treasures* buried in my life,
Walk up and down thus? buried! no, '*twas* drown'd;
I cannot therefore say *it* was a chest;" &c.

Treasure, I imagine. Brothers, v. 3, p. 262,—

"—————————— and [*an?*] if you be
Her friend, advise her to contain her *passions*,
And wisely love one that can entertain *it*."

Passion; at least I know not otherwise how to construe the passage. Court Secret, v. 2, vol. v. p. 506,—

"Clara, I envied, now allow thy happiness,
And will have no more thought upon your *loves*,
But what may be employ'd in hearty wishes
That Manuel may live still to reward *it*."

Love. Fairfax's Tasso, B. xvii. St. xcvi.,—

"See how with gentle beams the friendly sun
The tents, the *towns*, the hills, and dales descries" [*i.e.*, *discovers, shews*].

Town? Orig.,—

"Le tende e'l piano e la cittade e'l monte."

Sackville and Norton, Ferrex and Porrex, iv. 2, near the end, Dodsley, vol. i. p. 158,—

"————— happy he that can in time beware
By others *harmes*, and turne *it* to his good."

Harme.

It is necessary, however, not to be hasty in condemning passages where this error *seems* to have taken place; inasmuch as there are several words, now used in the singular, which were then employed frequently—some of them, perhaps, always—in the plural, with the same meaning. Such were *comforts, wars, spirits, revenges, parts* (in such phrases as *to perform one's parts, I will do my parts*, &c.; mediately or immediately from the Latin *partes*). Such too, I think, are the following. *Commons*, in such places as Julius Cæsar, iv. 1, noticed above,—" And graze in commons." At least I am all but certain that such was the ancient use.

Suits (of clothes). Hamlet, i. 2; see context,—

> " —— customary suits of solemn black."

Massinger, Fatal Dowry, i. 1, Moxon, p. 266, col. 1,—

> " —————————— This obstinate spleen,
> You think, becomes your sorrow, and sorts well
> With your black suits."

Succours is certainly an instance. Massinger, Fatal Dowry, as above,—

> " ———————— that happy age, when justice
> Had no guards to keep off wrong'd innocence
> From flying to her succours."

Fairfax, B. ii. St. xlvii., the King says to Clorinda,—

> " Since on my side I have thy succours got,
> I need not fear in these mine aged days."

Fr. *secours*. So also, I imagine, *virtues;* though of this I am somewhat less confident.

Some light may possibly be thrown on the origin of this error by the fact, that in a few instances a hyphen has usurped the place of the final *s*. 1 King Henry IV. v. 2, folio, p. 70, col. 2,—

> "Vnkle, what *newe-* ?"

2 King Henry VI. iv. 1, folio, p. 70, col. 2,—

"And like ambitious Sylla ouer-gorg'd,
With gobbets of thy *Mother-bleeding* heart."

Browne, Brit. Past., B. i. Song i., Clarke, p. 47; for the error can hardly be attributable to the modern editor,—

"Accounting *women-beauties* sugar'd baits
That never catch but fools with their deceits," &c.;

for *women's beauties*. I have noted above the instances, somewhat more frequent, in which the final *s* has been superseded by a comma.

On the other hand, the concluding *s* is frequently dropt in the folio, though the instances of its omission are not so numerous as those of its interpolation. Timon, v. 5,—

"We sent to thee, to give thy rages balm,
To wipe out our *ingratitude* with loves
Above *their* quantity.".

Read *ingratitudes* (for it is to this that *their* refers, not to *rages*); and so "the modern editors,"[99] *repugnante Malonio.* Mr. Barron Field, in the Shakespeare Society's Papers, vol. ii. p. 58, proposes to read, Midsummer Night's Dream, v. 1,—

"Then know that I, one Snug the joiner, am
A *lion's* fell, nor else no lion's dam."

Perhaps rightly, if *A* can be tolerated. But surely Shakespeare wrote and pointed,—

"Then know that I one Snug the joiner am,
No lion fell, nor else," &c.

---

[99] This emendation is Capell's. As to the modern editors, Walker was misled by Malone's note. In the next example, Rowe and the earlier editors read *No.* Mr. Collier's Old Corrector agrees with Mr. Barron Field. Mr. Singer reads, "A lion-fell." The old copies and Capell have no comma after *joiner.*—*Ed.*

King Henry V. i. 2,—

"——————— or else our grave,
Like Turkish *mute*, shall have a tongueless mouth;"

read *mutes*, as the old grammar requires. Much Ado, &c., iv. 1,—

"——————— Call me a fool;
Trust not my reading nor my observation,
Which with experimental seal doth warrant
The tenour of my *book*," &c.

Books? Measure for Measure, v. 1,—

"——————— O, most kind maid,
It was the swift celerity of his death,
Which I did think with slower foot came on,
That brain'd my *purpose*. But peace be with him!"

Possibly *purposes;* yet an old writer would scarcely have used the plural; *qu.* "But *God's* peace be with him!" the name of God having been omitted in deference to the well-known act. At You Like It, i. 2,—"Monsieur the challenger, the *princess calls* for you. *Orl.* I attend *them* with all respect and duty." Certainly "the *princesses call* for you," as some editions have it. Timon, iii. 6, towards the end,—

"Of man, and beast, the infinite malady
Crust you quite o'er!"

For *maladie* read *maladies;*[100] *infinite* in the sense of *innumerable*, as, *e.g.*, King Henry VIII. iii. 1,—

"Madam, you wrong the king's love with these fears;
Your hopes and friends are infinite."

King Henry VIII. iii. 2,—

"Look'd he o' th' inside of the *paper?*
Cromwell. Presently

[100] So Hanmer.—*Ed.*

He did unseal *them;* and the first he view'd,
He did it with a serious mind," &c.

Papers. *Ib.*,—

"———————— If we did think
His contemplation were above the earth,
And fix'd on spiritual *object*, he should still
Dwell in his musings," &c.

Objects, surely; the same error as above in *mute;* unless indeed *object* had then some meaning, with which we are not now acquainted. v. 2,—

"You were ever good at sudden commendations,
Bishop of Winchester. But know, I come not
To hear such *flattery* now, and in my presence;
They are too thin and base to hide offences."

Flatteries;[101] for it is to this that *they* refers, not to *commendations.* (For *base* read *bare*, as I have corrected elsewhere, and so Dyce also proposes [after Malone], Remarks, p. 141.) Hamlet, v. 2,—"and do but blow them to their *trial*, the bubbles are out." I suspect that, according to the old grammar, we ought to read, with the folio, *trials.* And so Knight. Troilus and Cressida, iv. 4,

"The Grecian youths are full of *quality.*"

What is *quality? Qualities*, I suspect.[102] Perhaps the

---

[101] So Pope, and others down to Malone, who rejected this certain and indispensable correction, believing it *unnecessary.—Ed.*

[102] But compare A Woman Killed with Kindness, Dodsley, vol. vii. p. 239,—

"You 're full of quality and fair desert."

Walker might have added *guift* for *guifts* to the examples of the omission of the final *s* in the first folio. *They 're* for *their* is the certain correction of Rowe. Theobald corrected *gift* to *gifts. Exercise* appears to be the plural. S. V. art. li. It is remarkable that a passage so palpably corrupt as this should not have been tampered with by the Old Corrector.—*Ed.*

whole passage should be read and arranged as follows,—

"Hear why I speak it love; the Grecian youths
Are full of qualities; they're loving, well compos'd,
With gifts of nature flowing, and swelling o'er
With arts and exercise;
How novelties may move," &c.

Pronounce *qual'ties*, S. V. art. xl., and *flow'ing*, *ib.* art. xiii. I suspect, however, that the passage is otherwise corrupt. *Ib.*, a little below,—

"Name Cressid, and thy life shall be as safe
As *Priam* is in Ilion;"

qu., *Priam's*. King Henry V. v. 2,—"Therefore, *queen of all, Katherine*, break thy mind to me in broken English," &c. Read, *queen of all Katherines;* as he calls her before *la plus belle Katherine du monde* (or, as Petruchio hath it, *the prettiest Kate in Christendom*). Midsummer Night's Dream, ii. 2, *init.*,—

"Ill met by moonlight, proud Titania.
Tita. What, jealous Oberon? *Fairy*, skip hence;
I have forsworn his bed and company."

Fairies, surely. There is no comma after Fairy in the folio (p. 148, col. 2); nor, indeed, could there well be one according to the punctuation of the time; probably, therefore, it stood in the MS. *Fairies skip hence;* which might very easily be corrupted into *Fairie*, were it only through the justling of the two *s's*. So at the end of the dialogue she says again, "*Fairies*, away." Love's Labour's Lost, v. i,—"Now understand that the curate and your sweet self are good at such eruptions and sudden breaking out of mirth," &c. Read, *cum quibusdam*, "*breakings* out." Instances in other writers. Browne, Britannia's Pastorals, B. i. Song ii., Clarke, p. 98,—

> "Go, shepherd *swain*, and *wife* all,
> For love and kings
> Are two like things,
> Admitting no corrival."

Read,—

> "Go, shepherd *swains*, and *wive* all," &c.

Marmyon, Antiquary, i. 1, Dodsley, vol. x. p. 11,—

> "———————— What 's this? I dare not
> Trust my own ears, silence *choke* up mine anger."

Of course *chokes*. ii. p. 28,—

> "—————— You were best turn an old ass,
> And meddle with your bonds and *brokage*."

Brokages, metri gratia. Carew, ed. Clarke, cix. p. 148,

> "Admit, thou darling of mine eyes,
> I have some *idol*[103] lately framed,
> That under such a false disguise,
> Our true loves might the less be famed:
> Canst thou, that knowst my heart, suppose
> I'll fall from thee to worship *those?*"

Idols. Cleveland, Ode to Jonson, Gifford's Jonson, vol. v. p. 454, note ‡—

> "For such nice guests ——————
> ——————————————
> In salt *meat* take little or no delight,
> But taste *them* with fastidious appetite."

Meats, of course. Browne, B. P. i. v., Clarke, p. 139,—

> "That man whose mass of *sorrow* hath been such,
> That by *their* weight, laid on his several part,
> His fountains are so dry," &c.

---

[103] This blunder, like several others noticed by Walker in the edition of 1845, is derived from the old edition of 1640.—*Ed.*

Sorrows, surely. Poem in the Arcadia, B. iii. p. 385, 23; see context,—

"This think I well, the beast with courage clad,
Like senators, a harmless empire had."

Beasts, surely. Fletcher, Faithful Shepherdess, ii. 4, Moxon, vol. i. p. 271, col. 2,—

"———————— I charge you, all my veins,
Through which the blood and spirit take their way," &c.

Quære, whether the Elizabethan language does not positively require *spirits?* Chapman, tragedy of Byron, Retrospective Review, vol. iv. p. 373,—

"The very beasts knew the alarum bell,
And, hearing it, ran shuddering to their *home*;".

I *think* the old grammar requires *homes*.

(In Shirley the modern usage begins to appear. Lines on the Death of K. James, Gifford and Dyce, vol. vi. p. 445,

"———— some told me, that did bring,
By torch-light, the dead body of the king,
When every star, like kinsmen to the dead,
That night, close mourners, hid their golden *head*,
And had repos'd that royal burden, where
His people might embalm him with their *tear*."

Sylvester is the only author of an earlier date (among those with whom I am acquainted) in whom it is at all frequent.) Shirley, Poems, vol. vi. p. 474, St. ult.,—

"Meantime, like a pale prisoner at the bar,
Oppressed more with *fear*, than his own chains,
(These of the feet, *those* the head [*i.e.*, *of* the head] troubles are)
Suspecting much her silence, he complains," &c.

Fears? Shirley, Triumph of Beauty, vol. vi. p. 334,—

"———————————— thy acceptance
Of what is in my power, shall make thee scorn

> Those things of care and golden slavery,
> That *fool* and flinty consciences adore,
> And grasp'd, like thieving sands steal through our
> fingers."

Perhaps *fools;* but I think *foul* is very much more probable. P. 336,—

> "—————— all the *pleasure*
> Of these blest shades, they talk of in their songs,
> Shall spread themselves before thee."

Pleasures; only seven lines below, the old edition has *wind* for *winds.* Honoria and Mammon, i. 2, p. 15,—

> *Alworth.* "I am happy
> When you command my *service.*
> *Hon.* Be confident, [*dele comma*]
> I keep a silent register of *all,*
> And shall reward *them.*"

Services. Edwards, Damon and Pythias, Dodsley, vol. 1, p. 256,—

> "For which good tourne, I crave this honour doe me lend,
> Oh frindly *hart,* let me linke with you, to you make me the
> thirde friende."

Harts. Sylvester, Sonnet xxvi. p. 637,—

> "Fortune and fates have chain'd my *fancy* so,
> And thou mayst free *them,* which none else can do."

Fancies, surely.

XXXIX.

Very interpolated.

Taming of the Shrew, v. 2,—

> "You 'are very sensible, and yet you miss my sense."

Dele very. So also iii. 2, above,—

> "——— I cannot blame thee now to weep,
> For such an injury would vex a saint;"

the folio has "a *very* saint;" which the Var., I think, retains. Possibly also All 's Well, &c. iii. 2 (so arrange),—

"Ay, my good lady, he.
Countess. A very tainted fellow,
And full of wickedness;"

very ought to be expunged. 3 King Henry VI. iii. 2,—

"Brothers, you muse what chat we two have had.
Gloster. The widow likes it not, for she looks sad."

Fol., "*very* sad." As You Like It, iii. 5,—

"He is not very tall; yet for his years he 's tall."

Dele very with Steevens. Hamlet, ii. 2,—

"Most welcome home!
Polonius. This business is well ended."[104]

The folio has "*very* well." *Ib.*,—

"Hath there been such a time, (I 'd fain know that,)
That I have positively said, 'Tis so,
When it prov'd otherwise?"

The Hamlet of 1603 has,—

"How? so my Lord, I would very faine know
That thing that I haue saide 'tis so, positiuely,
And it hath fallen out otherwise."

XL.

Metre affected by the pronunciation of *ion* final.

Julius Cæsar, iii. 1,—

"Look how he makes to Cæsar: Mark him.
Cassius. Casca, be sudden, for we fear prevention."

---

[104] The corrupt and imperfect quarto of 1603 has,—

"This business is very well dispatched."

The authentic quartos omit *very*, but otherwise agree with the folio.—*Ed.*

The former line is incomplete, and the latter, to my ear, has not a Shakespearian flow. Arrange,—

"Look how he makes to Cæsar: Mark him.
Cassius. Casca,
Be sudden, for we fear prevention."

And so in Measure for Measure, ii. 2,—

"Heaven keep your honour safe!
Angelo. Amen:
For I am that way going to temptation,
Where prayers cross;"

arrange (and so it stands in some editions),—

"———————————— Amen; for I
Am that way," &c.

1 King Henry VI. v. 4, perhaps; (see S. V. art. lii. p. 268),

"Ay, ay;
Away with her to execution."

Romeo and Juliet, iv. 1,—

"Hold, daughter; I do spy a kind of hope,
That asks as desperate *an* execution,
As that is desperate which we would prevent."

I suspect that *an* is an interpolation. King John, v. 2,—

"My heart hath melted at a lady's tears,
Being an ordinary inundation."

Pronounce *ord'nary*, ut sæpe; so *card'nal*. *Inundation* at the end of a line, with the *tion* undissolved, would not be admissible in this play. Beaumont and Fletcher, Elder Brother, iii. 3, Moxon, vol. i. p. 142, col. 2,—

"She has (pron. *Sh' has*) a wide face then.
Charles. She has a cherubin's,
Cover'd and veil'd with modest blushes.
Eustace, be happy, while poor Charles is patient."

Arrange,—

> "Cover'd and veil'd with modest blushes. Eustace
> Be happy," &c.[105]

On the other hand, Winter's Tale, iii. 2, *ad fin.*,—

> "—————— and tears, shed there,
> Shall be my recreation: So long as
> Nature will bear up," &c.

Arrange (with the folio) and write,—

> "Shall be my recreation: So long as nature
> Will bear up with this exercise, so long
> I daily vow to use it: Come and lead me
> *Unto* these sorrows."

And so Collier and Knight also have arranged, only retaining, with the folio and all the editions, "*To* these sorrows."

XLI.

Littlest; gooder and *goodest; badder* and *baddest.*

Hamlet, iii. 2,—

> "Where love is great, the *littlest* doubts are fear;
> Where little fears grow great, great love grows there."

---

[105] So also Mr. Dyce arranges. The second folio (the first does not contain this play) gives the passage as prose, following, I presume, the quartos. In the passage from the Winter's Tale, all the earlier editors, down to Capell inclusive, follow the *arrangement* of the first folio; but Capell, following Hanmer, inserted *my* before *sorrows* to supply the evident defect of the metre. I should think some adjective—*untimely*, for instance—would be better; but that something is defective, seems certain.—*Ed.*

Beaumont and Fletcher, Queen of Corinth, iv. 1, Moxon, vol. ii. p. 39, col. 2,—

> "————————— to hold
> The poorest, littlest page in reverence," &c.

One might compare *parvissimus*, which, I think, occurs in Lucretius;" [106] but *littlest* in the above passages is not a mere synonym of *least*. (Note, by the way, *gooder* and *goodest*, *badder* and *baddest*, in our old poets. Beaumont and Fletcher, Love's Cure, iii. 4, vol. ii. page 166, col. 2, *ad fin.*,—

> "———— Good faith, sir, I shall prick you.
> *Saav.* In gooder faith I would prick you again."

Jonson, Alchemist. i. 1, Gifford, vol. iv. p. 90,—

> "It is the goodest soul!"

Bartholomew Fair, iv. 2, near the end, p. 481,—"And mistress Justice there, is the goodest woman!" Marston, Antonio and Mellida, P. i. iii. 2,—"'Tis even the goodest lady that breathes." In this last passage it is perhaps a piece of affectation; see context. Poems of Uncertain Authors, Chalmers, vol. ii. p. 431, col. 1, speaking of an ill-matched wife and husband,—

> "A badder match cannot betide."

Heywood, Rape of Lucrece, i. 3,—"—you shall find the baddest legs in boots, and the worst faces in masks." Chaucer has *badder*. Canterbury Tales, 10538.

> "As lewed people demen comunly
> Of thinges, that been made more subtilly
> Than they can in hir lewednesse comprehende,
> They demen gladly to the badder end.")

---

[106] i. 615, 621; iii. 199, ed. Lachmann.—*Ed.*

XLII.

Assure and *affy*.

King John, ii. 2,—

> "It likes us well:—Young princes, close your hands.
> *Austria.* And your lips too; for I am well *assur'd*
> That I did so, when I was first *assur'd*."

It is impossible that this repetition of the same word in a different sense—there being no quibble intended, or anything else to justify it—can have proceeded from Shakespeare. Read "when I was first *affied*," *i.e.*, *betrothed*. Taming of the Shrew, iv. 4,—

> "——— Where then do you know best,
> We be affied; and such assurance ta'en,
> As shall with either part's agreement stand?"

Beaumont and Fletcher, Four Plays in One, Moxon, vol. ii. p. 513, col. 2,—

> "No law nor father hinders marriage there
> 'Twixt souls divinely affied, as, sure, ours were."

Spenser, F. Q. B. vi. C. iii. St. vii.,—

> "For she was daughter to a noble lord,
> Which dwelt thereby, who sought her to affy
> To a great pere."

Note, by the way, that *to affy* is also used in the sense of the Latin *fidere*. Titus Andronicus, i. 1,—

> "Marcus Andronicus, so I do affy
> In thy uprightness and integrity,
> . . . .
> That I will here dismiss my loving friends," &c.

Jonson, Sejanus, v. 10, Gifford, vol. iii. p. 142, Tiberius says in his letter to the Senate, "We affy in your loves and understandings." T. C. Translation of C. iv. of Tasso, ap. Singer's Fairfax, vol. i. p. xlii.,—

"I seek good Godfrey, and in him affy,
Such fame about doth of his bountie fly."

Harrington's Ariosto, B. xxvii. St. x.,—

"And thus the wicked fiend his time espied,
To give the Christians such a fatal blow,
When as these two, in whom they most affied,
Were absent now their prince and country fro."

B. xlv. C. vi.,—

"When in her favour he affied most."

Had this continued in use, it would have supplied the want noticed by Archdeacon Hare in his Victory of Faith, of a word to represent the πιστεύειν of the New Testament. T.C. ap. Singer's Fairfax, vol. i. p. xliii.,—

"Well is thy valure knowne, and as the same
Is lov'd and praysd ev'n by thine enimies:
So it affies, and them invites againe,
Aide at thy hands to beg and to obtaine;"

a different usage still, ὡς δοκεῖ.—Note too, that *to be assured* to a person, is sometimes used in the sense of *being married* to that person. So it is employed, Comedy of Errors, iii. 2,—"To conclude, this drudge, or diviner, laid claim to me, called me Dromio, swore I was assured to her," &c. Compare Dromio's words in the earlier part of the scene: "I have but lean luck in the match, and yet she is a wondrous fat marriage." *Ib.*,—"told me what privy marks I had about me," &c., which none but a wife could know. iv. 1, *ad fin.*,—

"To Adriana! that is where we din'd,
Where Dowsabel did claim me for her husband."

v., near the end of the play,—

> "She now shall be my sister, not my wife."

Lyly, Mother Bombie, v. 3, Old English Plays, vol. 1, 278, —"Come, Stellio, the assurance" [the marriage articles seem to be meant] "may be made to-morrow, and our children assured to-day." They were to be married that day; see Sc. 2. Merry Devil of Edmonton, Dodsley, vol. v. p. 229,—

> "*Clare.* You know, our meeting with the knight Mounchensey
> Is to *assure* our daughter to his heir.
> *Dorcas.* 'Tis without question.
> *Clare.* Two tedious winters have pass'd o'er, since first
> These couple lov'd each other, and in passion
> Glew'd first their naked hands with youthful moisture;
> Just so long, on my knowledge.
> *Dorcas.* And what of this?
> *Clare.* This morning should my daughter lose her name,
> And to Mounchensey's house convey our arms,
> Quarter'd within his 'scutcheon: the affiance made
> 'Twixt him and her, this morning should be seal'd.
> *Dorcas.* I know it should."

Sidney, Arcadia, B. i. p. 17, ll. 35, 38,—"The day of their assurance drew near —:"—"— though few days were before the time of assurance appointed." See context. Merry Wives of Windsor, v., near the end of the play; Fenton says, speaking of his new-married wife,—

> "The truth is, she and I long since contracted,
> Are now so *sure*, that nothing can dissolve us."

By the way, in Macbeth, iv. 3,—

> "———— wear thou thy wrongs,
> Thy title is *affeer'd*;"

folio, *affear'd;*—perhaps we should read *assur'd*, or *affirm'd*. Affear'd may have originated in *feare*, five lines below,—

"I speak not as in absolute fear of you."

XLIII.

Substitution of Words.

This species of corruption—the substitution of a particular word for another which stands near it in the context, more especially if there happens to be some resemblance between the two—a kind of error which, as we have all experienced in writing or transcribing, it is impossible to avoid at all times—occurs frequently in the folio; although how far it is to be attributed to Shakespeare's own manuscript, and how far to the printer, it may be somewhat difficult to determine. For instances in which this has confessedly taken place, even according to the universally received text, see some pages further on. The frequency of the error will justify my boldness in stigmatizing as corrupt a vast number of other passages, in which, as I believe, the same accident has happened. I quote, as usual, from the Variorum of 1821, or sometimes from the Vulgate; but I have also noticed one or two of Knight's errors.

Taming of the Shrew, v. 2,—

"And show more sign of her *obedience*,
Her new-built virtue, and obedience."

In the former line read *submission*. In 1 King Henry VI.

v. 4, *I suspect* the same thing has taken place on a larger scale,—

"Then swear allegiance to his majesty;
As thou art knight, never to disobey,
Nor be rebellious to the crown of England,
Thou, nor thy nobles, to the crown of England."

Hamlet, i. 2,—

"Farewell; and let your haste commend your *duty.*
Volt. In that and all things will we show our duty."

Perhaps, "commend your *service;*" at any rate, duty is wrong. Comedy of Errors, i. 1,—

"Therefore, merchant, I'll limit thee this day,
To seek thy *help* by beneficial help;"

perhaps [with Pope and others], "To seek thy *life.*" Sonnet cxxvii,—

"Therefore my mistress' *eyes* are raven black,
Her eyes so suited; and they mourners seem," &c.

We should read, I imagine, "my mistress' hairs." Comedy of Errors, near the end,—

"The duke, my husband, and my children both,
And you, the calendars of their nativity,
Go to a gossip's feast, and go with me;
After so long grief, such *nativity.*"

This is noticed in the Variorum edition. For the second *nativity*, read, not as is there suggested, *festivity* (this was not the idea likely to occur to Æmilia's mind), but *felicity.*[107] One of the *go's*, too, is wrong; the former, I imagine. King Richard III. ii. 1, l. 3,—

---

[107] So Hanmer, more than a century ago. *Go* occurs twice before in this speech. *Qu.*, therefore,—

"*Hence* to a gossip's feast *along* with me."

Capell approves of Hanmer's correction, in his notes, vol. i. p. 80,

"I every day expect an embassage
From my Redeemer to *redeem* me hence."

Perhaps *recall*. Macbeth, v. 3,—

"Cleanse the stuff'd bosom of that perilous *stuff*,
Which weighs upon the heart."

Tarquin and Lucrece, St. cclxi.,—

"Why, Collatine, is woe the cure for woe?
Do wounds *help* wounds, or grief help grievous deeds?"

"Do wounds *heal* wounds." (Fairfax, B. xx. St. cxxv.,—

"But since all hope is vain, all help is waste,
Since hurts ease hurts, wounds must cure wounds in thee.")

All's Well, &c., i. 3, near the end of the act,—

"———————— he and his physicians
Are of a mind; he that they cannot *help* him;
They, that they cannot help."

Evidently wrong; though I am not sure that "cannot *heal* him" is the true correction. 2 King Henry VI. ii. 1,—

"Come offer at my shrine, and I will *help* thee."

Surely, *heal*. King John, iv. 2,—

"Then I, ——————————————
————————————————
But for myself and them, (but, chief of all,
Your safety, for the which myself and *them*
Bend their best studies,) heartily request
Th' enfranchisement of Arthur."

---

col. 2, though he has kept the old reading in his text. He adds, "the *word* is spoke to herself (Æmilia), and admiringly." He, no doubt, wrote, or meant to write, *line*, not *word*. *Word* occurs three lines above, and *words* two lines below. In the next example, *recall* is another forgotten conjecture of Hanmer's.—*Ed.*

Is it possible that Shakespeare should have written so ungrammatically? *They*, surely. Sonnet xciv.,—

"The summer's flower is to the summer sweet,
Though to itself it only live and die;
But if that flower with base infection meet,
The *basest* weed outbraves his dignity."

Is it *base* that is wrong? or can Shakespeare have written *barest*, in the sense of *poorest, most meagre, scantiest in flowers and leaves? Bare* with him is a "verbum solenne" in describing the ravages made by winter on trees and plants,—which indeed is a somewhat different matter; and the substitution of a letter for the one next to it in the alphabet is a frequent source of error in the folio, as indeed in other books. Love's Labour 's Lost, i. 1,—

"Study is like the heaven's glorious sun,
That will not be deep-search'd with saucy looks;
Small have continual plodders ever won,
Save *base* authority from others' books."

Certainly *bare*. Two N. Kinsmen, i. 2, near the beginning,—

"———— what strange ruins,
Since first we went to school, we may perceive
Walking in Thebes! Scars, and *bare* weeds,
The gain o' th' martialist," &c.

Perhaps *base;* if indeed we ought not to write,—"Scars, *crutches*, and base weeds." King Henry VIII. v. 2 (quoted art. xxxviii. above),—

"They are too thin and *base* to hide offences."

Evidently *bare*. 1 King Henry IV. iii. 2,—

"Such poor, such *bare*, such lewd, such mean attempts," &c.

Base. 2 King Henry IV. iv. 1,—

"———— to dress the ugly form
Of *base* and bloody insurrection
With your fair honours."

Perhaps *bare;* the image seems to require it.[108] Beaumont and Fletcher, Bloody Brother, ii. 2, Moxon, vol. i. p. 524, col. 2,—

> "When he shall brand me here for[109] *base* suspicion;"

bare, I imagine; see context. Richard Brome, A Jovial Crew, ii. 1, Dodsley, vol. x. p. 304; (by the bye, this speech, with the preceding one, and the three following, ought to be printed as prose),—

> "————————— Thou talk'st
> O' th' house: 'tis a *base* melancholy house.
> Our father's sadness banishes us out on 't."

Bare, I suspect. Two Noble Kinsmen, ii. 1 (Fletcher's part), vol. ii. p. 560, col. 1,—

> "——— when the north comes near her,
> Rude and impatient, then, like Chastity,
> She locks her beauties in her bud again,
> And leaves him to *base* briars."

Bare. My emendation, however, of Sonnet xciv. was suggested by the passage itself. The erroneous notion, so prevalent in the last century, of Shakespeare's hasty and slovenly habits of writing, reconciled the commentators to these inelegant repetitions. As You Like It, v. 3,—

> "All adoration, duty, and observance
> All humbleness, all patience, and impatience,
> All purity, all trial, all *observance;*"

I thought of *obedience* in the latter line; and so Malone;

---

[108] We have, besides, "base and abject routs," eight lines above, where probably "*bloody* youth," in spite of Johnson's note, is derived from "*bloody* insurrection" here. Warburton's *heady* seems right.—*Ed.*

[109] The quarto 1639 has *for*, that of 1640 *with*. The latter is adopted by Mr. Dyce, and, if genuine, would authorize *base;* but is it not a sophistication?—*Ed.*

but Ritson reads *obeisance*, which is, I think, preferable. All 's Well, &c. ii. 5,—

> "——————— This drives me to entreat you,
> That presently you take your way for home,
> And rather muse, than ask why I *entreat* you;
> For my respects are better than they seem;" &c.

Read "why I *dismiss* you," or an equivalent word. iii. 4,

> "—————— what angel shall
> Bless this unworthy husband?"

and three lines below,—

> "———————— Write, write, Rinaldo,
> To this unworthy husband of his wife."

(*i.e.*, if the error be not in this line, *this husband unworthy of his wife*. See art. xxvii.) This is a very corrupt play. iv. 3,—"Sir, for a quart d'écu he will sell the fee-simple of his salvation, the inheritance of it, and cut the entail from all remainders, and a *perpetual* succession for it *perpetually*." King John, iii. 4,—

> "And bitter shame hath spoil'd the sweet world's taste,
> That it yields nought but *shame* and bitterness;"

Something is wanting that shall class with *bitterness;* possibly *gall*. King Richard, ii. 1, 3, fol. p. 26, col. 1,—

> "And let thy blows, doubly redoubled,
> Fall like *amazing* thunder on the casque
> Of thy *amaz'd* pernicious enemy.
> Rouse up thy youthful blood, be valiant, and live."

The conjunction of *amaz'd* with pernicious seems unnatural. Var. 1821, "Of thy *adverse*," &c., doubtless from the quartos. The passage is puzzling on account of the metre of l. 4. Possibly Shakespeare wrote,—

> "Of thy pernicious enemy. Rouse up
> Thy," &c.

Yet whence came *adverse? Valiant*, too, seems strange in this place of the line. ii. 2,—

> "Save bidding farewell to so sweet a guest
> As my *sweet* Richard."

Perhaps, "As my *dear* Richard." iv. 1,—

> "That lie shall lie so heavy on my sword,
> That it shall render *vengeance* and *revenge*."

This is probably right. Two Noble Kinsmen, i. 1,—

> "—————— I have heard the fortunes
> Of your dead lords; which gives me such lamenting
> As wakes my vengeance and revenge for 'em."

Fairfax, B. vi. St. lxiv.,—

> "To thee, my beauty,—thine be all these wrongs,—
> Vengeance to thee, to thee revenge belongs."

B. xvii. St. xciii.,—

> "O what revenge, what vengeance shall he bring
> On that false sect and their accursed king!"

But Fairfax is frequently tautological; to which he was led by the law (perhaps a necessary one) of rendering the original stanza for stanza in our more concise language, thus necessitating the introduction of supplementary matter. 1 King Henry VI. iii. 1,—

> "Thy humble servant vows obedience,
> And *humble* service, till the point of death."

Probably "*faithful* service." The affinity of *servant* and *service* rendered the slip easier. 2 King Henry VI. iii. 2,

> "In *pain* of your dislike, or *pain* of death."

3 King Henry VI. iii. 3,—

> "————— I must take like seat unto my fortune,
> And to my humble *seat* conform myself."

State. The old pronunciation of the diphthong *ea* (on which the modern Irish one is grounded) would facilitate the corruption. So in Chapman, Il. xix. Taylor, vol. ii. p. 144, *seat* seems to have superseded *state*,—

> "————————— Dismiss them then to meat,
> And let Atrides tender here, in sight of all his *seat*
> The gifts he promis'd."

Qu., "his *state*;" the princes and nobles surrounding him. Merry Devil of Edmonton, Dodsley, vol. v. p. 229,—

> "For look you, wife, the riotous old knight
> Hath over-run his annual revenue
> In keeping jolly Christmas all the year:
> . . . .
> Besides, I heard of late his younger brother,
> A Turkey-merchant, hath sore suck'd the knight,
> By means of some great losses on the sea;
> That (you conceive me) before God, all's naught,
> His *seat* is weak: thus each thing rightly scann'd,
> You'll see a flight, wife, shortly of his land."

What can *seat* mean here? Unless some intelligible meaning can be attached to it, I would read *state*, *i.e.*, *estate*. *Weak*, unsound, in an impoverished condition; Greene, Friar Bacon and Friar Bungay, Dyce, vol. i. p. 164,—

> "And, as I am true Prince of Wales, I'll give
> Living and lands to strength thy college [*college*'] state."

Green's Tu Quoque, Dodsley, vol. vii. p. 84,—

> "A man must trust unto himself, I see;
> For if he once but halt in his estate,
> Friendship will prove but broken crutches to him."

Beaumont and Fletcher, Wit at Several Weapons, iv. 1, Moxon, vol. ii. p. 345, col. 1, Cunningham says to Mirabel, with (I think) a play upon the words,—

> "Alas, your state is weak, you 'had need of cordials,
> Some rich electuary, made of a son and heir,
> An elder brother, in a cullis, whole;

> 'T must be some wealthy Gregory, boil'd to a jelly,
> That must restore you to the state of new gowns,
> French ruffs, and mutable head-tires."

Shirley, Brothers, i. 1, early in the scene,—

> "——————————— My estate
> Doth walk upon sound feet, and though I make
> No exception to your blood, or person, sir,
> The portion I have fix'd upon Jacinta,
> Beside the wealth her liberal aunt bequeath'd her,
> Is more than your thin younger brother's fortune
> Should lay a siege or hope to."

Merry Wives of Windsor, iii. 4, may also be noticed,—

> "He doth object, I am too great of birth,
> And that, my state being *gall'd* with my expence,
> I seek to heal it only by his wealth."

On the other hand, in the same play, v. 5,—

> "Search Windsor Castle, elves, within and out:
> Strew good luck, ouphes, on every sacred room,
> That it may stand till the perpetual doom,
> In *state* as wholesome, as in state 'tis fit;
> Worthy the owner, and the owner it;"

we ought probably to read *seat*, referring to the healthy situation of the castle.[110] 1 King Henry IV. iv. 1,—

> "——————————— Were it good
> To *set* the exact wealth of all our states
> All at one cast? to *set* so rich a main
> On the nice hazard of one doubtful hour?"

One of the two *sets* must be corrupt. K. Richard II. v. 3,

> "Our prayers do out-pray his: then let them have
> That mercy, which true prayers ought to *have*."

---

110 Hanmer, with his usual acuteness, saw this, and in consequence read *site*, which is an Elizabethan (see Richardson's Dictionary), though not, I think, a Shakespearian word.—*Ed.*

To say nothing else, my ear repudiates this, standing where it does; see context. Read *crave*, I think. *Prayers* in the second line is *precatores*, not *preces*.

Venus and Adonis, St. lxxviii.,—

> "And at his look she flatly falleth down,
> For looks kill love, and love by looks reviveth:
> A smile recures the wounding of a frown,
> But blessed bankrupt, that by *love* so thriveth!"

For *loue* read *losse*. So also Twelfth Night, i. 2,—

> "And then 'twas fresh in murmur (as, you know,
> What great ones do, the less will prattle of),
> That he did seek the love of fair Olivia.
> *Viola.* What's she?
> *Capt.* A virtuous maid, the daughter of a count,
> That died some twelvemonth since, then leaving her
> In the protection of his son, her brother,
> Who shortly also died; for whose dear *love*,
> They say, she hath abjured the sight
> And company of men;"

read *losse*. (I doubt Hanmer's transposition, "the company And sight of men." Is not something lost in the last line but one?) 2 King Henry VI. i. 1,—

> "Or hath mine uncle Beaufort, and myself,
> With all the learned council of the realm,
> Studied so long, &c. ————————
>
> . . . .
>
> And *hath* his Highness in his infancy
> Been crown'd in Paris, in despite of foes?"

So the editions since Steevens. Fol.,—

> "And hath his Highnesse, &c. ————
> Crowned in Paris," &c.

Qu., "And *was* his Highness," &c., the *hath* having originated in the former *hath*. Aliter Dycius, Remarks, p. 127,

But the circumstance of the earlier event (a considerably earlier one) being mentioned after the later ones, seems to demand *was*.[111] Titus Andronicus, ii. 4,—

"Where is my lord the king?
Sat. Here, Tamora, though *griev'd* with killing grief."

I believe we should write *gnaw'd*. iv. 3,—

"Therefore, my lords, it highly us concerns,
By day and night t' attend him carefully;
And feed his humour kindly as we may,
Till time beget some *careful* remedy."

Easeful. So too in Sackville and Norton, Gorboduc, iv. 2, I think we should write *easeful*,—

"Porrex (alas) is by his mother slain,
And with her hand (a woful thing to tell)
While slumbering on his *careful* bed he rests,
His heart stabb'd in with knife is reft of life."

Pericles, iii. 1,—

"Bid Nestor *bring* me spices, ink and paper,
My casket and my jewels; and bid Nicander
Bring me the satin coffer."

Perhaps, "Bid Nestor *fetch* me," &c. (Note, by the way, in this passage, that *simple shells* is the antitheton to *aye-remaining lamps*.) Titus Andronicus, v., near the end of the play,—

"As for that heinous tigress, Tamora,
No funeral rite, no man in *mournful* weeds,
No mournful bell shall ring her burial."

---

111 This remark seems to make against Mr. R. G. White's ingenious conjecture, *had*. In this particular kind of error, the *ductus literarum* is of trifling importance. *Was* was conjectured by Rowe, and adopted by the earlier editors, down to Capell, who first inserted *Been*.—*Ed.*

Timon of Athens, v. 3 (Steevens, too, has noticed this,)[112]

"I met a courier, one mine ancient *friend*,
Whom, though in general part we were oppos'd,
Yet our old love made a particular force,
And made us speak like *friends*."

Locus obscurus; fabula omnium corruptissima. The following instance from the Tempest, i. 2, though not exactly like the other passages here cited, may be classed under the same head,—

"———————— therefore wast thou
Deservedly confin'd into this rock,
Who hadst deserv'd more than a prison."

The nine-syllable line is an alien to Shakespeare. It is possible he may have written,—

"———————— therefore wast thou
Justly confin'd into this rock, who hadst
Deserv'd more than a prison;"

or the like. But, strange as it seems, I cannot help suspecting that *deservedly* has been foisted into the text,—

"———————— therefore wast thou
Confin'd into this rock, who hadst deserv'd
More than a prison."

Note the difference in the flow. King Lear, i. 2,—"though the wisdom of *nature* may reason it thus, and thus, yet nature finds itself scourged by the sequent effects." *Possibly* wrong.[113] Othello, iii. 3,—

"The Moor already changes with my poison:
Dangerous conceits are, in their natures, poisons," &c.

---

112 Steevens noticed "the awkward repetition of the verb *made*;" not *friend* and *friends*. He held the passage generally corrupt. —*Ed.*

113 So Hanmer thought, and instead of the first *nature* read *mankind*. I think *man* would be better; but perhaps *nature* crept

I once thought that we should read "with my practise;" but it would seem that the word required should be similar in termination, or general appearance, to *poison;* for this latter line had dropt out, most probably from that cause, in the quarto 1622. Therefore I conjecture *potion.* Antony and Cleopatra, iii. 9,—

"My very hairs do mutiny, for the white
Reprove the brown for rashness, and they them
For fear and doting.—*Friends*, begone; you shall
Have letters from me to some friends, that will
Sweep your way for you."

Perhaps, "*Fellows*, begone" (*socii*). Two Gentlemen of Verona, iv. 2,—

"Then to Silvia let us sing
That Silvia is excelling;
She *excels* each mortal thing
Upon the dull earth dwelling."

Exceeds? (On the other hand, As You Like It, i. 2,—

"If you do keep your promises in love
But justly as you have *exceeded* all promise,
Your mistress shall be happy."

Read, *metri gratia*, *excell'd.* I think, too, "as y' have *here* excell'd," &c., as an antitheton to *in love*). Cymbeline, i. 6,—

"———————— I will try the forces
Of these thy compounds on such creatures as
We count not worth the hanging (but none human),
To *try* the vigour of them, and apply
Allayments to their act."

---

in from below without displacing any word; *the* or *ye* was a mistake for *yr*, and *of* was purposely inserted to make some sense of "the wisdom nature." Shakespeare perhaps wrote merely "*your* wisdom," as "*your* excellent sherris."—*Ed.*

Possibly *test*. K. Richard II. iii. 2, Scroop's narration,—"*Against* thy majesty"—"*against* thy crown," &c. The four *againsts* seem a little suspicious. Sonnet xix.,—

> "*Devouring* Time, blunt thou the lion's paws,
> And make the earth devour her own sweet brood," &c.

Perhaps *Destroying*. 2 King Henry IV. v. 2,—

> "How might a prince of my great hopes forget
> So great indignities you laid upon me?"

Gross, I think. Titus Andronicus, iii. 1, near the beginning,—

> "For these, these, Tribunes, in the dust I write
> My heart's deep languor, and my soul's sad *tears:*
> Let my tears stanch the earth's dry appetite."

Ib. (Lavinia's tongue)

> "Is torn from out that pretty hollow cage,
> Where, like a *sweet* melodious bird, it sung
> Sweet varied [*sweet-varied*] notes, enchanting every ear."

2,—

> "Thou map of woe, that thus dost talk in signs,
> When thy poor heart *beats* with outrageous beating,
> Thou canst not strike it thus to make it still."

Taming of the Shrew, i. 1,—

> "To suck the sweets of *sweet* philosophy."

Tempest, iii., near the end,—

> "All three of them are desperate: their great guilt,
> Like poison given to work a *great* time after,
> Now 'gins to bite the spirits."

Long. King Richard III. ii. 4,—

> "So long a growing, and so leisurely,
> That, if his rule were true, he should be gracious.
> *Arch.* And so no doubt he is, my *gracious* madam."

At least I think it is the latter *gracious* that is wrong. Titus Andronicus, ii. 1, near the beginning,—

> "Then, Aaron, arm thy heart, and fit thy thoughts
> To mount aloft with thy imperial mistress,
> And mount her pitch, whom thou in triumph long
> Hast prisoner held, fetter'd in amorous chains."

Perhaps "to *soar* aloft." iv. 2, near the end,—

> "I'll make you feed on berries and on roots,
> And *feed* on curds and whey," &c.

Hanmer reads "*feast* on curds," &c. Pericles ii. 5,—

> "Her reason to herself is only known,
> Which from herself (?) by no means can I get.
> 2 *Knight.* May we not *get* access to her, my lord?"

Have, I think. (Here, as in some other places, I have quoted Pericles, Andronicus, and King Henry VI., as among the plays of Shakespeare, without any reference to the question of their total or partial genuineness.) Titus Andronicus, ii. 5,—

> "O, that I knew thy heart!"

See the context. Fol., *hart,* a common mode of spelling *heart.* Read *hurt. Hart* occurs three lines below; whence the error. The following passage may be classed under this head. King John ii. 1,—

> "But, if you fondly pass our proffer'd offer," &c.

The bad English (*proffer'd offer*), the cacophony, and the two-syllable ending, so uncommon in this play, prove that *offer* is a corruption originating in *proffer'd.* Read, I think, *love.* Compare 1 King Henry VI. iv. 2,—

> "But, if you frown upon this proffer'd peace," &c.;

and just below,—

> "If you forsake the offer of their (*our*) love."

3 King Henry VI. ii. 1,—

"Their weapons like to lightning came and went;
Our soldiers', like the night-owl's *lazy* flight,
Or like a lazy thresher with a flail,[114]
Fell gently down, as if they struck their friends."

Merchant of Venice, iii. 2,—

"Thus ornament is but the guiled (?) shore
To a most dangerous sea; the beauteous scarf
Veiling an Indian *beauty*."

Possibly *gipsy*.[115] For *guiled*, compare Tarquin and Lucrece, St. ccxxi.,—

"For even as subtle Simon here is painted,
So sober-sad, so weary, and so mild,
(As if with grief or travail he had fainted,)
To me came Tarquin armed; so beguil'd
With outward honesty, but yet defil'd
With inward vice."

Still I suspect *guiled;* though the following passage from Butler's Satire on the Weakness and Misery of Man, l. 137, makes me think that it *may* be right,—

"Advance men in the church and state
For being of the meanest rate,
Rais'd for their *double-guil'd* deserts,
Before integrity and parts."

Taming of the Shrew, Induction, 1,—

"And burn sweet wood to make the lodging sweet."

---

[114] The old play, which also contains these lines, has "an *idle* thresher," which is probably right. Capell adopted it.

[115] I should prefer *favour*. As to *guiled*, I believe the verb *to guile* is unknown to Shakespeare. However that may be, I have little doubt that the poet was thinking of Raleigh's "Discovery of Guiana," and wrote *guilded*. The error was corrected in the second folio.—*Ed.*

This, however, may possibly be right. Tarquin and Lucrece, St. ccxxxviii.,—

"So here, the helpless merchant of this loss,
With head declin'd, and voice damm'd up with woe,
With sad-set eyes and *wretched* arms across,
From lips new-waxen pale begins to blow
The grief away, that stops his answer so:
But wretched as he is, he strives in vain."

Read, "With *wreathed* arms across," (*i.e.*, "with arms wreathed across," the Latinized construction so frequent in our old poets; see art. xxvii.) Compare Love's Labour's Lost, iv. 3,—

"You do not love Maria? Longavile
Did never sonnet for her sake compile?
Nor never lay his wreathed arms athwart
His loving bosom, to keep down his heart?"

Peele, David and Bethsabe, Dyce second ed. vol. ii. p. 29,

"And at the gates and entrance of my heart
Sadness, with wreathed arms, hangs her complaint."

Fletcher, Faithful Shepherdess, iii. 1, Moxon, vol. i. p. 273, col. 2,—

"An hour together under yonder tree
He sat with wreathed arms and call'd on thee."

King John, iii. 1,—

"A rage, whose heat hath this condition,
That nothing can allay, nothing but blood,
The *blood* and dearest-valued blood of France."

Read, "The *best* and" &c. King Lear, iii. 4,—

"Expose thyself to feel what wretches feel;"

Qu.—Antony and Cleopatra, iv. 10,—

"——— when I am reveng'd upon my charm;"

and nine lines below, without any apparent reason for the repetition of the word,—

"——————— this grave charm;"

wrong, surely; perhaps it is the latter *charm* that is corrupt. *Grave* too looks suspicious. Cymbeline, v. 4, fol. p. 393, col. 2,—

"——————— and so great Powres,
If you will *take*[116] this Audit, take this life,
And cancell these cold Bonds."

I forget whether the Vulgate retains *take*, and have no edition at hand. King John, v., near the end,—

"———— and you, my noble prince,
With other *princes* that may best be spar'd,
Shall wait upon your father's funeral."

Scarcely right; for although Salisbury, Bigot, &c., are called *princes* below,—

"Now these her (England's) princes are come home again,"

and so King Henry V. iv. 1, near the beginning,—

"——————— Brothers both,
Commend me to the princes in our camp,"

the "lords of England," as they are called just below, yet in the present passage the case is different. As You Like It, ii. 3,—

"O good old man! how well in thee appears
The constant service[117] of the antique world,
When service sweat for duty, not for meed!"

I believe that the former *service* is the corrupt one; yet I can imagine Shakespeare having written,—

"When *duty* sweat for duty, not for meed."

---

[116] All the editions that I have seen repeat *take*.—*Ed.*

[117] *Qu.*, "The constant *temper*," &c.—*Ed.*

Troilus and Cressida, v. 3,—

> "Life every man holds dear; but the *dear* man
> Holds honour far more precious-dear than life."

No other word than *brave* will fit the sentence; and so Pope, and all following editors, read, till Johnson (I think it was he) restored *dear*. *Deare* and *brave* are just like enough in appearance to mislead a very careless eye, such as that of the old printer. Knight, too, follows the folio. Julius Cæsar, ii. 1,—

> "Let 's carve him as a dish fit for the gods,
> Not hew him as a carcass fit for hounds."

Is *fit* here the past participle, *i. q.*, *fitted?* So in the Taming of the Shrew, Induction 1, the metre requires us to read,—

> "—————— but, sure, that part
> Was aptly fit, and naturally perform'd."

not *fitted;* and so Cymbeline, v. 5,—

> "—————— and in time,
> When she had fitted you with her craft, to work
> Her son into th' adoption of the crown:" &c.

Fit seems to be the participle, *ib.* iii. 4,—

> "Forethinking this, I have already fit
> ('Tis in my cloak-bag) doublet, hat, hose, all
> That answer to them."

And Jonson, Staple of News, i. 2, *init.*,—

> "What, are those desks fit yet?"

Marmyon, Antiquary, ii. 1, Dodsley, vol. x. page 52,—"Is your disguise fit. *Lionel.* I have all in readiness." Compare *quit*, *rot*, *waft*, and a number of similar past participles which occur in old writers. If this be the case in Julius Cæsar, it seems to lessen the harshness; ἀλλ' ὅμως—.

As You Like It, v. 3, near the end,—"Truly, young gentlemen, though," &c.——"yet the note was very untuneable. *Page.* You are deceived, sir; we kept *time*, we lost not our time." Read, "we kept *tune*," &c. Theobald says "*Time* and *tune* are frequently misprinted for each other in the old editions of Shakespeare." The following may be noticed here. Much Ado about Nothing, i. 1,—

"My love is thine to *teach*; teach it but how,
And thou shalt see how apt it is to learn
Any hard lesson that may do thee good."

Perhaps *use*. As You Like It, iv. 3,—

"He that brings this *love* to thee,
Little knows this love in me."

Love occurs three other times in the course of these fourteen lines; namely, ll. 2, 5, and 13, the above being 7 and 8. Merchant of Venice, iii. 2,—

"There may as well be amity and *life*
'Tween snow and fire, as treason and my love.
Portia. Ay, but I fear you speak upon the rack,
Where men enforced do speak any thing.
Bassanio. Promise me life, and I 'll confess the truth."

League. Measure for Measure, near the end,—

"Well, Angelo, your evil quits you well:
Look that you love your wife; her worth, *worth* yours."

Perhaps, "her worth *work* yours" (*ἀπεργάσηται.*) Romeo and Juliet, iv. 5,—

"But one, poor one, one *poor* and loving child."

Possibly, *dear*. Winter's Tale. i. 2,—

"——————— When at Bohemia
You take my lord, I 'll give *him* my commission
To let him there a month, behind the gest
Prefix'd for 's parting."

You, as I think some editions read.[118] iv. 3,—" He has a son, who shall be flayed alive; then 'nointed over with honey, set on the head of a wasp's nest; *then* stand till he be three quarters and a dram dead; then recovered again," &c.——" then, raw as he is," &c. *There*. Tempest, i. 2,

"—————— Thou best know'st
What torment I did find thee in: thy groans
Did make wolves howl, and penetrate the breasts
Of ever-angry bears: it was a torment
To lay upon the damn'd," &c.

Torture? But perhaps the corruption is deeper, and lies in the other place. T.N.K., v.2, Moxon, vol.ii. p.575, col.2,

"*Torturing* convulsions from his globy eyes *
Had almost drawn their spheres, that what was life
In him seem'd torture."

Or is *torture* the corrupt word? Two G. of Verona, ii. 4,—

"—————— I know the gentleman
To be of *worth*, and worthy estimation," &c.

Palpably wrong. *Wealth*,[119] I think. Merry Wives of Windsor, iii. 3,—" I see what thou wert, if Fortune thy foe were *not* Nature thy friend: Come thou canst not hide it." *Qu., but*. (*Male quidam*, "—— if Fortune thy foe were not; Nature is thy friend," &c.) T. and C., iii. 3,—

"They pass by strangely: they were us'd to bend,
To send their smiles before them to Achilles;
To come as humbly as they *us'd* to creep
To holy altars."

---

[118] So Hanmer, Warburton, Capell, and Johnson. In the next example, Mr. Collier's Old Corrector reads *there*.—*Ed.*

* *Qu.*,

"———— almost from their spheres
Had drawn his globy eyes."

"Make thy two eyes, like stars, start from their spheres."—*Ed.*

[119] So also Mr. Collier's Old Corrector.—*Ed.*

Use, surely. Perhaps this belongs partly to the article on *d* and *e* final. Tempest, iv. 1,—

"—————————— on whom my pains
Humanely taken, all, *all* lost, quite lost!"

Are, surely. Sonnet xcix.,—

"More flowers I noted, yet I none could see,
But *sweet* or colour it had stolen from thee."

Scent; sweet occurs in line 2 of this sonnet, twice; also Sonnet xcviii. ll. 5 and 11, and c. l. 9. xcviii. l. 11, by the bye, is itself suspicious,—

"They were but *sweet*,[120] but figures of delight,
Drawn after you," &c.

Troilus and Cressida, iii. 3,—

"And give to dust, that is a little gilt,
More laud, than *gilt* o'erdusted."

Gold of course; and so I think some editors[121] have corrected it. The following may be noticed here. 2 King Henry VI. iii. 1,—

"My lord, these faults are easy, quickly answer'd;
But mightier [read *weightier*] crimes are laid unto your charge,
Whereof you cannot easily purge yourself."

Wrong, I think; perhaps "*very* quickly," &c. 3 King Henry VI. ii. 6,—

---

[120] Note also the two *buts*. *Qu.* (see context.)
"They were but *fleeting* figures of delight."—*Ed.*

[121] Theobald, Warburton, Hanmer, and Capell, after Thirlby. Compare Honest Whore, Second Part, iii. 2, Dyce's Middleton, vol. iii. p. 184,—

"Believe it, that I know the touch of time,
And can part copper, though 't be gilded o'er,
From the true gold." *Ed.*

"The foe is merciless, and will not pity;
For at their hands I have deserv'd no pity."

Qu.,—

"*Nor* at their hands *have I* deserv'd no pity."

The sense, I think, requires this. *For* begins the fifth line preceding. The turn is like that in i. 4,—

"——I am faint, and cannot fly their fury;
And, were I strong, I would not fly their fury."

King Henry VIII. i. 1,—

"———— but when the way was made,
And pav'd with gold, the emperor thus desir'd,
That he would please to alter the king's course,
And break the foresaid peace. Let the king know,
(As soon he shall by me,) that thus the cardinal
Does buy and sell his honour as he pleases," &c.

Perhaps we should read, "the emperor *then* desir'd," &c. 2,

"———— Please your highness, note
This dangerous conception in this point."

His, I imagine. See context. Troilus and Cressida, v. 2,—

"The fractions of her faith, orts of her love,
The fragments, scraps, the bits, and greasy reliques
Of her o'er-eaten *faith*, are bound to Diomed."

Qu., *truth* or *troth*. 3,—

"When many times the captive Grecians fall,
Even in the fan and wind of your *fair* sword,
You bid them rise and live.

Hector. O, 'tis fair play."

Fair has a specious look, but is quite out of place. Read *fierce*; *faire*—*fierce* or *feirce*. iv. 4,—

"Entreat her fair; and by my soul, *fair* Greek,
If e'er," &c.

Wrong, I think; *fair* occurs again four and seven lines below. v. 3,—

"Spur them to *ruthful* work, rein them from ruth."

Deathful, I imagine. A little below,—

> "Lay *hold* upon him, Priam, hold him fast."

Hand. This is a particularly corrupt part of the folio. In this act, last page but one of the play, col. 2, last line but seven from the bottom, *bed* is improperly repeated, an error corrected in the received text. Other instances occur: i. 1, first page of the play, col. 1, l. ult. ["I would not (as they tearme it) praise *it*," for *her* of the quartos.] ii. 1, 9th page, ["ere *their* Grandsires had nails on their toes," for *your*[122]]. iii. 3, 17th page, col. 1, l. 8 ["That no *may* is the Lord of any thing," for *man* of the quartos]. Coriolanus, ii. 1,—

> "—————— holding them,
> In human action and capacity,
> Of no more soul nor fitness for the world,
> Than camels in *their* war; who have their provand
> Only for bearing burdens, and sore blows
> For sinking under them."

Whose wars? *The.* v. 3,—

> "You have said you will not grant us any thing;
> For we have nothing else to ask but that
> Which you deny already. Yet we will ask,
> That, if *you* fail in our request, the blame
> May hang upon your hardness: therefore hear us."

Clearly *we*. This must surely have been corrected in some edition.[123] Midsummer Night's Dream, ii. 3,—

---

[122] The quartos curiously enough have "*their* grandsires," but omit the words, "on their toes." The next blunder, *may* for *man*, is only a *quasi* example, though no doubt caused by the proximity of *any*.—*Ed.*

[123] Pope corrected it, and was followed by all the editors down to Malone, who restored the corruption. Strange to say, he has found followers. Mr. Collier's Old Corrector has *we*.—*Ed.*

"And run through fire I will, for thy sweet sake.
Transparent Helena! [read *Helen*] nature here shows art,
That through thy bosom makes me see *thy* heart."

My. The old poetical commonplace; *e.g.*, As You Like It, v. 4,—

"That thou mightst join her hand with his,
Whose heart within her bosom is."

Compare Sonnet cxxxiii.,—

"Prison my heart in thy steel bosom's ward."

Pericles, ii., towards the end,—

"I came unto your court for honour's cause,
And not to be a rebel to *her* state."

Your. *Her* occurs 13, and again 18, lines above.

King Richard II. iii. 2,—

"How some have been *depos'd*, some slain in war,
Some haunted by the ghosts they had *depos'd*," &c.

One of these is wrong. Possibly *depriv'd*, and in the latter place. (This, by the way, is the meaning of *depriv'd*, Hamlet, i. 4,—

"And there assume some other horrible form,
Which might deprive your sovereignty of reason."

I have noticed this last elsewhere.) 2 King Henry IV. iv. 4,

"And all thy *friends*, which thou must make thy friends," &c.

Foes, surely; see context. King Henry V. iv. 5,—

"We are enow, yet living in the field,
To smother up the English in our *throngs*,
If any order might be thought upon.
Bourbon. The devil take order now! I'll to the throng."

The repetition is anti-Shakespearian. 1 King Henry VI. iv. 1, *ad fin.*,—

"'Tis much, when sceptres are in children's hands;
But more, when envy breeds unkind division:
There comes the ruin, there begins confusion."

Thence? The following may be noticed here; Timon, iii. 5,

"Why do fond men expose themselves to battle,
And not endure all *threats?* sleep upon 't,
And let the foes quietly cut their *throats*,
Without repugnancy?"

Vulg., "all *threat'nings*, to salve the metre, instead of the folio's *threats*. But surely *endure* requires a different word. 1 King Henry IV. iii. 2, near the end,—

"How now, good Blunt? thy looks are full of speed.
Blunt. So *hath* the business that I come to speak of.
Lord Mortimer of Scotland hath sent word," &c.

Unless this has already been corrected.[124] Timon of Athens, i. 1,—

"Whose present grace to *present* slaves and servants
Translates his rivals."

What is the force of present? Read "*peasant* slaves," &c. This is nearly the converse of the error in the Winter's Tale, iv. 3,—"Advocate 's the court word for a *pheasant;*" where the suggestion of one or two of the commentators, *present*, ought undoubtedly to be received. Timon, *ib.*, 2,

"I weigh my friend's affection with mine own:
I'll tell you true. I 'll call on you."

I. ii. 2,—

"No villainous bounty yet hath past my heart."

Heart occurs three lines below, likewise at the end of a line. Read *hand*, or *hands;* the latter, I think. iv. 2,—

"———— As we do turn our backs
From our companion thrown into his grave,
So *his* familiars to his buried fortunes
Slink all away."

---

[124] Here again Pope corrected the error, which Malone afterwards brought back, and later editors retained. The Old Corrector also set matters right here.—*Ed.*

What is the construction? *Quære, the;* those who were familiar to his—now buried—fortunes. Julius Cæsar, v. 5,

"I shall have glory by this losing day,
More than Octavius and Mark Antony
By *this* vile conquest shall attain unto."

Quære, their. The repetition seems awkward and un-Shakespearian. Macbeth, iii. 4,—

"——————— they rise again,
With twenty mortal murders on their crowns," &c.

Murders occurs four lines above, and *murder* two lines below. This, by the way, would alone be sufficient to prove that *murders* was corrupt. "*Mortal* murders," too, seems suspicious; compare "*deadly* murder," King Henry V. iii. 3, corrected by Steevens after the second folio to *heady*.[125] v. 2,—

"He cannot buckle his distemper'd *cause*
Within the belt of rule."

Wrong. *Causes* occurs thirteen lines above. *Course,* I imagine. 4,—

"For where there is advantage to be *given,*
Both more and less have given him the revolt."

Tane?[126] Hamlet, iv. 7,—

"——————— Sir, this report of his
Did Hamlet so envenom with his envy," &c.

---

[125] *Deadly,* in King Henry V., was, I believe, a conjecture of Malone, who supported it by citing "mortal murders." This was calling Catiline to give a character to Cethegus. Nobody before Walker seems to have suspected the cause of the corruption in Macbeth.—*Ed.*

[126] The Old Corrector saw *given* was wrong, but he was not fortunate in conjecturing *gotten.*—*Ed.*

Is *report* the object or the subject of *envenom?*—if the latter, read *your*. Lover's Complaint, St. xxxvi.,—

"The accident, which brought me to her *eye*,
Upon the moment did her force subdue,
And now she would the caged cloister fly:
Religious love put out religion's *eye*."

Is this an erratum, or an oversight of Shakespeare's? Merchant of Venice, i. 3 (*Qu.*, ought not this speech to be spoken aside?)—

"——— Mark you this, Bassanio;
The devil can cite scripture for his purpose.
An evil soul, producing holy witness,
Is like a villain with a smiling cheek,
A goodly apple rotten at the core:
O, what a *goodly* outside falsehood hath!"

Godly. *Goodly* and *godly*, by the way, and in like manner, *good* and *God*, have been confounded in various passages of our old writers. Davenport, City Nightcap, Lamb's Specimens, vol. ii. p. 208,—

"This hour a pair of glorious towers is fallen,
Two *godly* buildings beaten with a breath
Beneath the grave;"

goodly. So, too, Beaumont and Fletcher, Cupid's Revenge, iii. 2, Moxon, vol. ii. p. 393, col. 1,—

"——— Pray get you hence
Wi' your *goodly* humour!"

See the context. So *ib.*, p. 392, col. 1,—"Grown so godly!" On the other hand, in Chaucer, Legende of Hipsiphile and Medea, ed. 1602, Fol. 192, col. 1,—

"Now was Jason a seemely man withall,
And like a lord, and had a great renoun,
And of his look as royal as a lioun,
And *godly* of his speech and familiere," &c.;

we ought to read *goodly*. Hamlet, ii. 2,—"For if the sun

breed maggots in a dead dog, being a *god* kissing carrion" (undoubtedly the true reading), the folio has "a *good* kissing carrion;" and on the other hand, Coriolanus, iii. 1, p. 15, col. 1, it reads,—

"Shall? O *God?* but most vnwise Particians: why," &c.,

for: "O *good*, but most," &c.; and Troilus and Cressida, i. 3, 6th page of the play, col. 2 (atque ita Eques),—

"Yet *god* Achilles still cries excellent."

King Henry V. iv. 7, fol., p. 89, col. 2,—"I need not to be ashamed of your Maiesty, praised be God, so long as your Maiesty is an honest man. *King. Good* keepe me so;"—the converse error again. Beaumont and Fletcher, Wildgoose Chace, ii. 2, Moxon, vol. i. p. 547, col. 2,—"I have told you enough for your crown, and so *good* speed you." Is this a corruption, or an evasion for "*God* speed you," to avoid the penalties of the profanation act, which in 1647 might have been more strictly enforced than before? Carew, ed. Clarke, civ. p. 105; see context,—

"There none dare pluck thee, for the place is such,
That, save *a good divine*,[127] there none dare touch."

Papæ! *A god divine*, I imagine, in spite of the tautology. Compare *royal king*, *e.g.*, King Lear, i. 1,—

"———————— Royal king,
Give but that portion which yourself propos'd," &c.

Shirley, Arcadia, iii. 3, Gifford and Dyce, vol. vi. p. 212, l. 1,—"*Good* genius!" Dyce's note: "the old copy, *god*." Contention for Honour and Riches, p. 305,—

"And hast so often call'd your great men Gods;"—

Dyce,—"The old copy, *goods*."

---

[127] This ridiculous blunder (for the *place* spoken of is a lady's bosom) is derived from the old copy, 1640.—*Ed.*

Subject of the article resumed.—King Richard II. iii. 4,—

" Why should we, in the compass of a pale,
Keep law, and form, and due proportion,
Showing, as in a model, *our* firm estate [read *state*]?
When our sea-walled garden, the whole land,
Is full of weeds;" &c.

Read "*a* firm," &c. *Our* occurs also four lines previous to this extract. The following may be noticed here. Comedy of Errors, iv. 1,—

" Master, there is a bark of Epidamnum,
That stays but till her owner comes aboard,
And then, *sir*, bears away: our fraughtage, sir,
I have convey'd aboard;" &c.

The folio, p. 93, col. 2, has,—"And then *sir she* beares away." Read, "And then *she* bears away." Merchant of Venice, iii. 2,—

" ——————Therefore, thou gaudy gold,
Hard food for Midas, I will none of thee:
Nor none of thee, thou *pale* and common drudge
'Tween man and man: but thou, thou meagre lead,
Which rather threat'nest than doth promise aught,
Thy paleness moves me more than eloquence," &c.

Stale. (By the way, in Troilus and Cressida, ii. 2,—

" And, for an old aunt, whom the Greeks held captive,
He brought a Grecian queen, whose youth and freshness
Wrinkles Apollo's,[128] and makes *pale* the morning;"

I follow Dyce (Remarks, p. 152), in reading with the folio, *stale.* So also Knight.) I find that Farmer also (Var. 1821, vol. v. p. 84) had conjectured *stale;* except that he, from his punctuation of the line, " thou stale, and common

[128] Does not the construction require us to read *Apollo?—Ed.*

drudge," &c., would seem to make *stale* a substantive. King Richard II. ii. 1,—

> "The commons hath he pill'd with grievous taxes,
> *And quite lost their hearts:* the nobles hath he fin'd
> For ancient quarrels, *and quite lost their hearts.*

Willoughby. And daily new exactions are devis'd," &c.

Can this belong in any way to the present head? or can Shakespeare have written,—

> "The commons hath he pill'd
> With grievous taxes, and quite lost their hearts:
> The nobles hath he fin'd for ancient quarrels:

Willoughby. And daily," &c.

Yet the six-syllable line, thus situated, seems strange in this play. At any rate, the repetition is corrupt. All 's Well, &c., iii. 7, near the end,—

> "————————— which, if it speed,
> Is wicked meaning in a lawful deed,
> And lawful meaning in a *lawful* act;"

Certainly wrong. As You Like It, v. 4,—

> "*Duke.* If there be truth in sight, you are my daughter.
> *Orl.* If there be truth in *sight*, you are my Rosalind.
> *Phe.* If sight and shape be true,
> Why then,—my love adieu."

Read *shape* in l. 2, to which Phebe evidently refers. *Shape* is *dress;* see Gifford's Massinger, vol. iii. p. 301, 2nd ed. Hamlet, i. 3,—

> "But do not *dull* thy palm with entertainment
> Of each new-hatch'd, unfledg'd comrade."

Dulls occurs thirteen lines below. May not Shakespeare have written *stale?* Troilus and Cressida, iii. 3,—

> "The providence, that 's in a watchful state,
> . . . .
> Keeps pace with *thought;* and almost, like the gods,
> Does *thoughts* reveal in their dumb cradles."

Is not one of these wrong? i. 3,—

> "And appetite, an *universal* wolf,
> Thus doubly seconded with will and power,
> Must make, perforce, an universal prey."

Wrong, surely. Midsummer Night's Dream, iii. 2,—

> "Disparage not the faith thou dost not know,
> Lest to thy peril thou aby it *dear*.
> Look where thy love comes; yonder is thy dear."

Possibly *here; (heere—deare)*

(Dyce, Remarks, p. 153, corrects 2 King Henry VI. iv. 9,

> "His *arms* are only to remove from thee
> The duke of Somerset," &c.

I forget (not having the book before me) whether he notices that *arms* recurs six and again eight lines below. Yet may not *arms* possibly be right? v. 1,—

> "——— if thy arms be to no other end,
> The king hath yielded unto thy demand.")

All 's Well, &c., ii. 3,—

> "Good fortune, and the favour of the *king*,
> Smile upon this contract;" &c.

Qu.—"The praised of the king" occurs seven lines above. Much Ado, &c., v. i.,—

> "If such a one will smile, and stroke his beard;
> Cry, 'sorrow, wag!' and hem, when he should groan;"

This is Johnson's emendation; the quarto of 1600 has,—"And sorrow wagge, cry hem," &c.; and so the folio, p. 117, col. 1. *Qu.*, "*Say*, sorrow, wag;" &c. There are three lines in the neighbourhood beginning with *And*. In Hamlet, iii. 4,—

> "For use can almost change the stamp of nature,
> And either *curb* the devil, or throw him out
> With wondrous potency;"

I suspect that the reading "*master* the [*th'*] devil" is the right one; *curb* occurs fourteen lines before.[129] Pericles, v. 1,—

> "First, sir, what is your place?
> *Lys.* I am governor of this *place* you lie before."

iv. Gower's second speech,—

> "Old Escanes, whom Helicanus late
> Advanc'd in time to great and high estate,
> Is left to govern. Bear you it in mind,
> Old Helicanus goes along behind."

Good, I imagine. (For "in time," we should read, I think, "in *Tyre*.") As You Like It, iii. 5,—

> "———— What though you have *no* beauty,
> (As, by my faith, I see no more in you,
> Than without candle may go dark to bed,)
> Must you be therefore proud and pitiless?"

Evidently wrong. *Some*, I think, little as (even when shortened to *som*) it resembles *no*.[130] Marmyon, Antiquary, v. 1, Dodsley, vol. x. p. 83,—"But you 'll object he has *no* means. 'Tis confess'd; but what means has he to keep it?" Here, too, *some* appears to be the true reading.

---

[129] Capell, in his various readings, attributes *curbe* to the quartos and the editions of Rowe and Pope. I know him to be wrong as to the two last, and make no doubt that Mr. Collier is right in stating *master* as the reading of the later quartos, while *either* is that of the earlier. *Curb* is a conjecture of Malone's. When I wrote Note 25 on the "Versification," I had forgotten that Walker had noticed the passage here.—*Ed.*

[130] In this class of errors there is often little or no resemblance between the ejected and substituted word. I believe *som* to be right; but we should also read *had* for *hau*, as the folio prints the word, confounding *d* with the long *u* or *v*. See Mr. Dyce's "Remarks," &c., p. 21, l. 3.—*Ed.*

As You Like It, i. 2,—" Peradventure this is not fortune's work neither, but nature's; who, perceiving our natural wits too dull to reason of such goddesses, hath sent this natural for our whetstone: for always the dulness of the fool is the whetstone of the *wits.*—How now, wit? whither wander you?" *Wise. Ib.*, "I beseech you, punish me not with your hard thoughts; *wherein* I confess me much guilty, to deny so fair and excellent ladies any thing. But let your fair eyes, and gentle wishes go with me to my trial: wherein if I be foil'd," &c. *Qu.*—2 K.Henry VI. ii. 1,

"Sorrow and grief have *vanquish'd* all my powers;
And vanquish'd as I am, I yield to thee,
Or to the nearest groom."

I believe the author wrote *languish'd.* I am pretty sure that I have met with instances of *to languish* as an active verb in this sense, though I do not at present recollect the passages. Cymbeline, i. 7, seems not exactly in point,—

"———————— cries, O!
Can my sides hold, to think, that man who knows
By history, report, or his own proof,
What woman is, nay, what she cannot choose
But must be, will his free hours languish for
Assured bondage?"

(Folio, p. 374, col. 2, "*will's* free houres," &c. Possibly right; *hoürs.*) Nor such as the following:—Sidney, Arcadia, B. iii. p. 382, l. 23, addressing the flowers,—

"Tell me, if husband spring-time leave your land,
When he from you is sent,
Wither not you, languish'd with discontent?"

Astrophel and Stella, lxxxix., he describes himself as

"Tired with the dusty toils of busy day,
Languish'd with horrors of the silent night."

xxxi., "thy languish'd grace." xlii., "languish'd spirits." Milton, Masque, l. 744. Epitaph on the Marchioness of Winchester, 33. Samson, 119. In Richardson and the Encyclopædia Metropolitana, among the meanings of *to languish*, are *to enfeeble*, *to entender;* but no example is given. It is analogous to several other forms which occur more or less frequently in the Elizabethan poets; *e.g.*, *to faint* for *to make faint*, *to cease* for *to cause to cease* (this latter, by the bye, is found in so late an author as Warburton), *to decline*, *to perish*, *to loathe*, *to blast*, *to spring*, *to quake*, &c.; some of them belonging to the ordinary language of the time, others merely poetical coinages. Coriolanus, iv. 3, near the beginning,—"You had more beard when I last saw you, but your favour is well *appeared* by your tongue." *Approved.*[131] *Appear* occurs 24 lines below (24, I mean, in the folio, p. 21, col. 1; where, by the way, another instance of this error occurs,—"Your Noble Tullus Auffidius *well* appear well in these Warres.") Pericles, i. 3, near the end,—

"My message must return from whence they came.
Hel. We have no reason to *desire* it, since
Commended to our master, not to us:
Yet, ere you shall depart, this we desire,—
As friends to Antioch, we may feast in Tyre."

Perhaps *enquire*. 2 King Henry VI. v. 1,—

"Will thou go dig a grave to find out war,
And *shame* thine honourable age with blood?
Why art thou old, and want'st experience?
Or wherefore dost abuse it, if thou hast it?
For shame! in duty bend thy knee to me," &c.

---

[191] So Mr. Collier's Old Corrector. Here, as constantly elsewhere, Walker points out not merely the error itself, but its origin.—*Ed.*

Shame is not the word required. *Staine,* I imagine. All's Well, &c., iii. 2, near the beginning: "—— our old ling, and our Isbels o' th' country, are nothing like your old ling and your Isbels o' th' court." *Qu.* Indeed I suspect that *old ling* is a corruption of some other word or words.[132] 1 King Henry VI. ii. 5,—

"Strong-fixed is the house of Lancaster,
And, like a mountain, not to be *remov'd.*
But now thy uncle is removing hence," &c.

I suspect error here, merely on account of the repetition, for the words themselves are perfectly in place. v. 4 (addressing Charles),—

"Thou shalt be plac'd as viceroy under him,
And still enjoy the regal dignity.
Alen. Must he be then *as* shadow of himself?"

Perhaps an erratum for *a.* 2 King Henry VI. iii., near the end,—

"Look with a gentle eye upon this wretch!
O, beat away the busy meddling [*busy-meddling*] fiend
That lays strong siege unto this wretch's soul," &c.

As You Like It, ii. 4, *ad fin.*,—

"I will your very faithful *feeder* be,
And buy it with your gold right suddenly."

Qu., *factor.* Feed occurs ll. 13 and 16 above. "Your *factor,*" *i.e.*, *your agent in buying the farm.* (I notice this as coming substantially under the present head.) Timon, iii. 5,—

"But, with a noble fury, and *fair* spirit,
Seeing his reputation touch'd to death,
He did oppose his foe," &c.

---

132 *Qu.*, Is not *old ling*, in the second place, a corruption for *youngling?—Ed.*

Fair, except in a modern sense, is inadmissible here.[133] I suspect that for *faire* we should read *free; i.e, single-hearted, generous, ut passim ap. Nostrum.*

That I may not be suspected of rashness in stigmatizing so many passages as corrupt, I will now proceed to cite a number of passages from the folio, in which, even according to the received text—the text recognized in common by myself and my predecessors,—this species of corruption has taken place; from whence it will be evident, that no ceremony need be used in denouncing other passages as similarly vitiated. I believe, however, that in most cases the internal evidence would be quite sufficient, even without this negative support. I have likewise added one or two examples from the Sonnets, and from Pericles of Tyre, which is not in the folio. Titus Andronicus, ii. 1, p. 35, col. 2,—

"———— to wanton with this Queene,
This Goddesse, this Semerimis, this *Queene*,[134]
This Syren," &c.

For *Nymph*. Hamlet, i. 1, p. 153, col. 1,—

"———— which is no other
(*And* it doth well appeare vnto our State)
But to recouer of vs by strong hand
And termes compulsative," &c.

For *As*. i. 3, p. 155, col. 2,—

"———— Perhaps he loves you now,
And now no soyle nor cautell doth besmerch

133 Walker, no doubt, intended to observe here that the following line occurs seven lines below,—

"Striving to make an ugly deed look fair." *Ed.*

134 So, too, the quarto 1611. *Nymph* was first restored by conjecture, by Capell, who was not acquainted with the quarto 1600, which has *nymph.—Ed.*

> The vertue of his *feare:* but you must feare
> His greatnesse weigh'd, his will is not his owne," &c.

For *will*. ii. 2, p. 260 (for 160), col. 2,—

> "My Newes shall be the *Newes* to that great Feaste."

For *fruite*. *Ib.*, p. 261, col. 2,—"I meane the matter you *meane*, my Lord." For *reade*. I have noticed two other instances in the latter part of Hamlet, but, as these may perhaps have originated in other causes, I have not put them down. King Lear, iii. 4, p. 298, col. 1,—"Wine lou'd I *deerely*, Dice deerely;" for *deepely*. Cymbeline, iv. 2, p. 388, col. 2,—

> "—————— O thou Goddesse,
> Thou divine Nature; *thou* thy selfe thou blazon'st
> In these two Princely Boyes."

For *how*. *Ib.*, p. 390, col. 1,—

> "Pisanio might have kill'd thee at the heart,
> And left *this*[135] head on. How should this be, Pisanio?"

For *thy*. v. 5, p. 396, col. 1,—

> "—————— were 't he, I am sure
> He would haue spoke to vs.
> *Gui.* But we *see* him dead.
> *Bel.* Be silent: let 's see further."

For *saw*. Othello, iii. 3, p. 326, col. 2,—

> "—————— Like to the Ponticke Sea,
> Whose Icie Current, and compulsiue course,
> Neu'r *keepes* retyring ebbe, but keepes due on
> To the Proponticke, and the Hellespont."

---

[135] This ridiculous blunder was corrected long ago by Hanmer, who was followed by Warburton and Capell. *This* was restored by Johnson, and has since disfigured most editions. Malone says "*this* head means the head of Posthumus; the head that *did* belong to *this* body." This does not say much for Malone's head.—*Ed.*

For *feels*,[136] (according to the received text. *Feels*, however is wrong; *brooks* would be better, though not, I think, the true word.) Midsummer Night's Dream, i. 1, p. 146, col. 1,—

"The course of true loue neuer did run smooth,
But either it was different in blood.
Herm. O crosse! too high to be enthral'd to *loue*."

For *low*. *Love* occurs again four lines below. Antony and Cleopatra, iii. 11, p. 357, col. 1,—

"—————————— For vs you know
Whose he is, we are, and that is Cæsars.
Thid. So. Thus then thou most renown'd, Cæsar intreats
Not to consider in what state thou stand'st
Further than he is Cæsars."

For *Cæsar*; this, however, may perhaps belong to the class of errata noticed in article xxxviii. Antony and Cleopatra, ii. 2, p. 346, col. 2,—"Say not, *say* Agrippa," for "Say not *so*, Agrippa." iii. 10, p. 356, col. 2,—

"I was of late as petty to his ends,
As is the Morne-dew on the Mertle leafe
To *his* grand Sea."

For *the*.[137] iv. 12, p. 362, col. 2,—

"—————————— How, not dead? Not dead?
The Guard, *how?* Oh dispatch me."

---

136 *Feels*, the conjecture of Pope, is supported by the quarto 1630, and Mr. Collier's Old Corrector; we can scarcely, however, call either of these authorities. Southern read *knows*, a better word than *feels*, but worse than *brooks*.—*Ed.*

137 This self-evident correction of Hanmer's was pronounced arbitrary by Steevens, and is excluded from most modern editions On the next example see Mr. Dyce's "Remarks," p. 249.—*Ed.*

For *hoa*. King Henry V. iv. 5, p. 88, col. 1,—

"Let him go hence, and with his cap in hand
Like a base Pander hold the Chamber doore,
Whilst *a base* slave, no gentler than my dogge,
His fairest daughter is contaminated."

For "Whilst *by a* slave." Pericles of Tyre, ii. 2, Var. vol. xxi. p. 73,—

"'Tis now your *honour*, daughter, to explain
The labour of each knight, in his device.
Thaisa. Which, to preserve my honour, I'll perform."

i. 2, Var. p. 38,—

"For flattery is the bellows blows up sin;
The thing, the which is flatter'd, but a spark,
To which that breath gives heat and stronger glowing."

For *breath*, the old copies have, teste Var., *spark*. (I doubt whether *breath* or *blast* be the true emendation.) King Henry VIII. i. 2, p. 209, col. 1,—

"I told my Lord the Duke, by th' Divel's illusions
The Monke might be deceiu'd, and that 'twas dangerous
For *this* to ruminate on this so farre, vntill
It forg'd him some designe," &c.

For *him*. Taming of the Shrew, iii. 1, p. 218, col. 2,—

"Old fashions please me best, I am not so nice
To charge (*change*) true rules for *old* inuentions."

For *odd*. (By the way, in the Epilogue to Massinger's Bashful Lover, speaking of the author,—

"A strange old fellow this!"

In what sense could *old* be applied to Massinger? Read *odd*.) Midsummer Night's Dream, v. 1, p. 163 (for 161), col. 1,—" —— they may passe for excellent men. Here com two noble beasts, in a *man* and a Lion." For *moon*.

And so Knight![138] Hamlet, v. 1,—"Is this the fine of his fines, &c. to have his fine pate full of *fine* dirt?" *Foule?* Taming of the Shrew, iv. 4, *init.*, p. 225, col. 1,—"*Sirs*, this is the house;" for *Sir; sirs* occurring four lines before. Troilus and Cressida, v. 9, last page but one of the play, col, 2,—

> "My halfe supt Sword, that frankly would haue fed,
> Pleas'd with this dainty *bed*; thus goes to bed."

For *bit*. [The second folio reads *bitt*; the quarto *baite*.] (For the thought, compare Cartwright, Ordinary, ii. 1, Dodsley, vol. x. p. 197,—

> "Sword, sword, thou shalt grow fat," &c.)

Comedy of Errors, ii. 2, p. 89, col. 2,—

> "Dromio, thou *Dromio*, thou snaile, thou slug, thou sot."

For *drone*. Male retinet Knightius *Dromio*.[139] Much Ado, &c., ii. 1, p. 105, col. 1,—"My visor is Philemon's roofe, within the house is *Loue*. *Hero*. Why then your visor should be thatcht. *Pedro*. Speake lowe if you speake Loue." *Love* for *Jove*; nearly the converse error of that noticed by Collier in his "Reasons for a new Edition," &c. Love's Labour 's Lost, iv. 3,—"Or groane for Joane," for *Loue*. Love's Labour 's Lost, i. 1, p. 123, col. 1,—

> "——————— why should proud Summer boast,
> Before the Birds haue any cause to sing?
> Why should I ioy in *any* abortiue birth?"

---

138 Mr. Knight is not singular in this error of his.—*Ed.*

139 Here again Mr. Knight is not singular in his error, palpable as it is. By the way, the 2nd folio omits *thou* before *snaile*, and Mr. Collier's Old Corrector apparently acquiesces in this glaring sophistication, as in many, if not most others, of that edition.—*Ed.*

For *an*. Titus Andronicus, v. 1, p. 48, col. 2,—

"Euen now I curse the day, and yet I thinke
Few come within *few* compasse of my curse,
Wherein I did not some Notorious ill," &c.

For *the*. Hamlet, iii. 1, p. 265, col. 2,—"your Honesty should admit no discourse to your Beautie. *Oph*. Could Beautie my Lord, haue better Comerce then *your* Honestie?" For *with*. 2 King Henry IV. i. 1, p. 75, col. 1,—

"With that he gave his able Horse the head,
And bending forwards strooke his *able* heeles
Against the panting sides of his poore Jade," &c.

For *armed*. In the same speech we have,—

"———— After him, came spurring *head*
A Gentleman," &c.

from the 7th line below,—"With that he gave," &c., as above. As You Like It, iv. 3, p. 203, col. 2,—

"———— and to giue this napkin
Died in *this* bloud vnto the Shepheard youth," &c.

Here the proneness of *this* and *his* to supplant each other might facilitate the error; and the same may be observed of the following; at least *his* for *her* is not unfrequent. v. 4, p. 206, col. 2,—

"That thou mightst ioyne *his* hand with his,
Whose hart within *his* bosom is;"

noticed earlier in this article. All 's Well, &c., ii. 1, p. 236, col. 2,—

"———— not helping, death 's my fee,
But if I helpe, what doe you promise me.
Kin. Make thy demand.
Hel. But will you make it euen?
Kin. I by my Scepter, and my hopes of *helpe*."

For *heauen*. This is among the most incorrect parts of the folio. Twelfth Night, iv. 2, *ad fin.*, p. 271, col. 2,—

"Who with dagger of lath, in his rage and his wrath,
Cries ah ha, to the diuell:
Like a mad lad, paire thy nayles dad,
Adieu goodman *diuell*."

For *drivell*. Hamlet, iv. 5, p. 274, col. 1,—

"Her Brother is in secret come from France,
Keepes on his wonder, keepes himselfe in clouds," &c.

For *Feedes*. Antony and Cleopatra, v. 2, p. 366, col. 2, penult.,—

"—————— I am sure, *mine* Nailes
Are stronger then mine eyes."

Or was this a careless substitution of *mine* for *my* on the printer's part? I have met with one or two other instances of *mine* for *my* in the folio. iv. 8, p. 360, col. 2,

"Mine Nightingale."

1 King Henry IV. iii. 3, p. 64, col. 1,—"Doe thou amend thy Face, and Ile amend *thy* Life;" for *my*. Winter's Tale, iv. 3, p. 295, col. 1,—

"—————— Gracious my Lord,
You know *my* Father's temper:" &c.

For *your*. Comedy of Errors, iii. 1, p. 91, col. 1,—

"Herein you warre against your reputation,
And draw within the compasse of suspect
Th' vnuiolated honor of your wife.
Once this your long experience of *your* wisedome,
Her sober vertue, yeares, and modestie,
Plead on *your* part some cause to you vnknowne;"

for *her*. 2 King Henry VI. iii. 2, p. 134, col. 1,—

"The splitting Rockes cowr'd in the sinking sands,
And would not dash me with their ragged sides,

Because thy flinty heart, more hard then they,
Might in thy Pallace, perish Elianor.[140]
As far as I could ken *thy* Chalky Cliffes,
When from *thy* Shore, the Tempest beate us backe,
I stood vpon the Hatches in the storme:" &c.

Thy occurs again ll. 2, 5, and 6, below. Var., "*thy* c. cliffs —*the* shore;" rather, perhaps, "*the* c. c.—*thy* shore." Cymbéline, ii. 3, p. 377, col. 1,—"it is a *voyce* [and so Knight!] in her eares, which Horse-haires, and Calues-guts, nor the voyce of vnpaued Eunuch to boot, can neuer amed" (*amend*); for *vice*. So Merchant of Venice, iii. 2, p. 174, col. 1, *ad fin.*,—

"There is no *voice* so simple, but assumes
Some marke of vertue on his outward parts;"

for *vice*; *voice* occurs five lines above. Sonnet cx.,—

"Now all is done, *have* what shall have no end."

So the old copy, *teste* Knight; who also reads *have*. Vulg., *save*, rightly. Winter's Tale, iv. 3, p. 295, col. 2,—

"———————— I am put to Sea
With her, who heere I cannot hold on shore:
And most opportune to *her* neede, I haue
A Vessell rides fast by,"

for *our*. Hoc etiam male retinet Eques. All's Well, &c. iv. 5, p. 251 (misprinted for 249), col. 2,—"Indeed sir she was the sweete Margerom of the sallet, or rather the hearbe of grace. *Laf.* They are not hearbes you knaue, they are nose-hearbes. *Clowne.* I am no great Nebuchad-

[140] *Elianor* here is a blunder of the old copies for *Margaret*. Twice besides in this speech *Elinor* is printed for *Margaret*. These blunders were first corrected by Rowe; Capell has not noticed them.—*Ed.*

nezar sir, I haue not much skill in *grace*." For *grass*. King Henry V. iv. 7, p. 89, col. 1,—

"So do our vulgar drench their peasant limbes
In blood of Princes, and *with* wounded steeds
Fret fet-locke deep in gore, and with wilde rage
Yerke out their armed heeles at their dead masters," &c.;

for *their*. King Richard III., near the end, p. 204, col. 2,

"O now, let Richmond and Elizabeth, &c.

———————————————

By Gods faire ordinance, conioyne together:
And let *thy* Heires (God if thy will be so)
Enrich the time to come, with Smooth-fac'd Peace," &c.;

for *their*. Hamlet ii., not far from the end, p. 264, col. 2,

"———— that this Player heere,

———————————————

Could force his soule so to his *whole* conceit," &c.;

for *own*; "his *whole* Function" occurs three lines below. I have inserted this instance, although Knight has restored *whole*; because Knight's text is hardly worth noticing as an exception to the general agreement of the editions. The same may be observed of Hamlet, i. 3, p. 156, col. 2,—

"———————— how Prodigall the Soule
Giues the tongue vowes: these blazes, Daughter,
Giuing more light then heate;" &c.

for *Lends*.[141]

(The following, though not exactly similar, are in point:—Love's Labour 's Lost, v. 2, p. 139, col. 2,—

"————————— Behauiour where wer't thou
Till this *madman* shew'd thee? And what art thou now?
King. All haile sweet Madame, and faire time of day."

---

141 Mr. Knight has adopted these two palpable blunders in defiance of the quartos.—*Ed.*

For *man*. At least if *madman* originated in *Madame*. Timon of Athens, iv. 3, p. 92, col. 2, may be classed under the present head,—

"Had'st thou like vs from our first swath proceeded,
The sweet degrees that this breefe world affords,
To such as may the passiue drugges of it
Freely command'*st*; thou would'st haue plung'd thyself
In generall Riot," &c.).

Instances of the same species of Erratum, hitherto uncorrected, in other Writers.

Selden's Table Talk, ed. 1800, p. 46 [ed. 1856, p. 63], art. *Hell*, paragraph 2,—"*He descended into Hell.* This may be the Interpretation of it. *He may be* dead and buried, then his Soul ascended into Heaven. Afterwards he descended again into Hell," &c. Clearly, "He *was* dead and buried," &c. Chapman and Shirley, Chabot, v. 3, ap. Lamb's Specimens, vol. ii. p. 114,—

"Thus in the summer a tall flourishing tree,
Transplanted with strong hand, with all her leaves
And blooming pride upon her, makes a show
Of spring, tempting the eye with wanton blossoms:
But not the sun with all *her* amorous smiles,
The dews of morning, or the tears of night,
Can root her fibres in the earth again,
Or make her bosom kind, to growth and bearing."

His.[142] (A kind of counterpart to the *he* Philomel, who has chanted in Shakespeare's cii.nd Sonnet, from the first edition down to the present time.) Beaumont and Fletcher, Knight of the Burning Pestle, iii. 1, Moxon, vol. ii. p. 85, col. 1,—

142 *Her* seems a blunder of the printer of the "Specimens;" at least the edition of Shirley by Gifford and Dyce has *his.*—*Ed.*

"———————— I see the god
Of heavy sleep lay on his heavy mace
Upon your eyelids.
Luce. I am very *heavy*."

Is this last *heavy* wrong?[143] Ford, Fancies, v. 3, Moxon, p. 144, col. 2, near the bottom,—

"———— a saint's reward *reward* him!"

"*Attend* him?" Yet it seems possible that *reward* may be right. Massinger, Parliament of Love, v. 5, Moxon, p. 141, col. 1,—

"———— This hungry pair of flesh-flies,
And most inseparable pair of coxcombs."

Bondman, ii. 3, Gifford, vol. ii. p. 50, 2nd ed. Moxon, p. 83, col. 2,—

"——— 'twas odds of strength in tyrants,
That pluck'd the first link from the golden chain
With which that Thing of Things bound in the world."

Where Gifford says in a note,—"A literal translation, as Mr. M. Mason observes, of Ens Entium." A literal translation!—The word *things* occurs four lines below,—

"Or such as know the cause of things pay tribute
To ignorant fools."

Read BEING OF BEINGS. Renegado, ii. 4, Moxon, p. 105, col. 2,—

"And to what end, great lady—pardon me,
That I presume to ask, did your command
Command me hither?"

Perhaps *Summon;* unless the error lies in the former *com-*

---

[143] I should say this *heavy* was the least suspicious of the three. *Qu.*, "*leaden* mace." The writer probably remembered Julius Cæsar, iv. 3,—

"Lay'st thou thy leaden mace upon my boy."—*Ed.*

mand. Play of the Battle of Alcazar (Marlowe's ?) i. Dyce's Peele, ed. 2, vol. ii. p. 96,—

"Then, Bassa, lock the winds in wards of brass,
Thunder from heaven, damn wretched souls to death,
Bar all the offices of Saturn's sons,
Be Pluto then in hell, and bar the fiends,
Take Neptune's force to thee, and calm the seas,
And execute Jove's justice on the world."

Bear. Yorkshire Tragedy, Sc. 2, near the end,—

"————— Has the dog left me then,
After his tooth has *left* me?"

Bit. Peele, David and Bethsabe, Dyce, 2nd ed. vol. ii. p. 71,—

"Salomon, my love, is David's *lord;*
Our God hath nam'd him lord of Israel."

Wrong, I think. [*Qu. choice.—Ed.*] Beaumont on the Marriage of a Beauteous Young Gentlewoman with an Ancient Man, Moxon, vol. ii. p. 706, col. 1,—

"See, see, how thick those showers of pearl do fall
To weep her *ransom*, or her funeral,
Whose every treasured drop, congealed, might bring
Freedom and ransom to a fettered king."

Just below,—

"Hymen, thy pine burns with adulterate fire;
Thou and thy quiver'd boy did once conspire
To mingle equal flames," &c.;

perhaps a mistake for *the.*[144] (This poem looks almost as if it had been left unfinished.) Beaumont and Fletcher, Mad Lover, iii. 4, Moxon, vol. 1, p. 301, col. 2,—

---

[144] Walker here restores by conjecture the reading of the quarto 1640. See Mr. Dyce's note.—*Ed.*

"Live till the mothers *find you*, read your story,
And sow their barren curses on your beauty;
Till those that have enjoy'd their loves despise you,
Till virgins pray against you, old age find you,
And, even as wasted coals glow in their dying,
So may the gods reward you in your ashes."

I cannot correct this. Massinger, Duke of Milan, ii. 1, Moxon, p. 57, col. 2, l. 1,—

"————————— who *but* looks on
This temple built by nature to perfection,
But must bow to it; and out of that zeal
Not only learn to adore it, but to love it?"

"Who *that* looks on," &c. Play of the Merry Devil of Edmonton, Dodsley, vol. v. p. 226, l. 2,—

"O that this soul, that cost so dear a price
As the *dear* precious blood of her Redeemer," &c.

[*Most? Ed.*] P. 236,—

"I have loaded the poor minutes with my moans,
That I have made the *heavy* slow-pac'd hours
To hang like heavy clogs upon the day."

Lazy? P. 265,—

"And did not this good knight here, and myself,
Confess with you, being his ghostly father,
To deal with him about th' unbanded marriage
Betwixt him and that fair young Millisent?"

Confer; (conferre—confesse). *Confessor* occurs 2 or 3 lines before. B. & F., Pilgrim, iv. 3, Moxon, vol. i. p. 609, col. 2,

"He'll come again to-morrow, and bring peascods.
Mast. I'll *bring* your bones."

Bang, verbum solenne in hac re. Fletcher, &c., Two Noble Kinsmen, iv. 2, Moxon, vol. ii. p. 572, col. 2,—

"Your two contending lovers are return'd,
And with them their *fair* knights. Now, my fair sister,
You must love one of them."

For *faire* read *sixe*. Fletcher, Faithful Shepherdess, iv. 5, vol. i. p. 281, col. 2,—

"I do contemn thee now, and dare come near,
And gaze upon thee; for methinks that grace
Austerity, which sate upon *that* face,
Is gone, and thou like others!"

Thy, I strongly suspect. v. 5, p. 286, col. 1,—

"—————————— Great fair, recall
Your *heavy* doom, in hope of better days,
Which I dare promise; once again upraise
Her *heavy* spirit, that near drowned lies
In self-consuming care that never dies."

Wrong, surely. Marmyon, Fine Companion, iv. 6,—

"—————————— I hear she is run mad.
Aur. *Is*, and the cause of her distemperature
Is the reproach you put upon her honour."

Yes. Chaucer, Legende of Hipermestre, l. 86,—

"This Hipermestre cast her iyen doun,
And quoke as doth the leafe of *ashe* grene,
Ded wext her hewe, and like ashen to sene," &c.

Read *aspe*, the old form of *aspen*; a slight variety of the error. All 's Well, &c., ii. 3, may also be noticed under this head,

"Or I will throw thee from my care for ever,
Into the staggers, and the *careless* lapse
Of youth and ignorance," &c.

Perhaps *cureless*; if indeed the passage is corrupt. Chapman's Iliad, vii. Taylor, vol. i. p. 173 (fol. p. 100),—

"But he lies at our crook-stern'd fleet, a rival with our king
In height of spirit; yet to Troy *he* many knights did bring
Coequal with Æacides, all able to sustain
All thy bold challenge can import."

We, sensu postulante. viii., twelve lines from the end,—

"———— ——— fires round about them shin'd,
As when about the silver moon, when air is free from wind,
And stars shine clear, to whose sweet beams, high prospects, and the brows
Of all steep hills and pinnacles thrust up themselves for shows;
And even the lowly vallies joy to glitter in their sight,
When the unmeasur'd firmament bursts to disclose her light,
And all the signs in heaven are seen that glad the shepheard's heart."

Read *The*. (Prospects σκοπιαί· hence it would seem that in old English *prospect* was used for a point commanding a view.) Play of Soliman and Perseda, D 3, p. 2,—

"I dare not stay, for if the governor
Surprise me here, I die by martial law:
Therefore I go. But whither shall I go?
If into any *stay* adjoining Rhodes,
They will betray me to Philippo's hands,
For love, or gain, or flattery."

State, I imagine. Perhaps *state* was mistaken for *staie*, which spelling I notice in Sidney's Arcadia, B. iii. p. 262, l. 17, "a noble *staie*." (As *stay* is here printed for *state*, so *stay* and *state* have both superseded *flawe*, King John, ii. 2, and Cymbeline, ii. 4, l. 6, according to the emendations I have proposed elsewhere.) Song of Davenant's; I quote from Clarke's Helicon of Love, 1844, p. 90,—

"The lark now leaves his wat'ry nest,
And climbing shakes his dewy wings;
He takes *his* window for the east,
And to implore your light, he sings,
Awake, awake, the morn will never rise,
Till she can dress her beauty at your eyes."

(Substitute period for comma after *sings*.)

Your. Herrick, Clarke, vol. ii. ccccxvii.,—

"Dean-bourn, farewell; I never look to see
Dean, or thy warty incivility."

Surely *Thee;* for what can *Dean* be here?

The following may be noticed here; I owe it to a friend, who suggests—rightly, I think—that the latter *but* is only an erroneous repetition of the former. Massinger, New Way, &c. iv. Moxon, p. 306, col. 2,—

"———————— I shall gladly hear
Your wiser counsel.
L. All. 'Tis, my lord, a woman's,
But true and hearty;—wait in the next room,
But be within call; yet not so near to force me
To whisper my intents."

Read,—

"———————— wait in the next room;
Be within call;" &c.

This latter part of Lady Allworth's speech is addressed to her servants. Fairfax's Tasso, B. xvi. St. lxxi.,—

"Nor went she forward to Damascus fair,
But of her country dear she fled the sight,
And guided to Asphalte's [*tes ?*] lake her chair,
Where stood her castle, there she ends her flight:
And from her damsels *fair*[145] she made repair
To a deep vault, far from repose and light," &c.

Wrong. "From her damsels' *face*"? *Face—faire.* So in As You Like It, iii. 2, *faire* has been corrupted to *face*, ὡς δοκεῖ.

"Let no *face* be kept in mind,
But the fair of Rosalind."

---

[145] Mr. Singer's edition has *farre*, the second folio *far;* but both are wrong; see the next line. Walker used Mr. Knight's edition of 1844.—*Ed.*

Browne, Britannia's Pastorals, Clarke, i. i. p. 47,—

> " ——————— But if this cannot move
> Your mind to pity, nor your heart to love,
> Yet, sweetest, grant me *love* to quench that flame,
> Which burns you now."

Leave. Spenser, F. Q., B. v. C. v. St. v., may be quoted here,—

> " Soone after eke came she with *full* intent
> And countenance fierce, as she had fully bent her
> That battels utmost trial to adventer."

Fell; or is it an error of the edition from which I quote? in which I also find, B. i. C. vi. St. xliv.,—

> " So long they fight, and *full* revenge pursue;"

and B. vi. C. iii. St. xlix.,—

> " Yet he him still pursewd from place to place,
> With full intent him cruelly to kill;"

in both which places, I imagine—especially in the former—we ought to read *fell.*[146] The following may be noticed. Browne, Britannia's Pastorals, Clarke, i. v. p. 152,—

> " Oh sacred essence, lightening me this hour!
> How may I *lightly* style thy great power?
> *Echo.* Power."

Rightly. (*Lightening, i.e., enlightening;* as 2 K. Henry IV. ii. 1, *ad fin.*,—" Now the Lord lighten thee! thou art a great fool.") And ii. p. 66; see context,—

> " That giveth most to think of what he had."

Grieveth. Given occurs eight lines below. v., near the end, p. 161,—

---

[146] In these passages Todd reads *full* without a note, except at B. i. C. vi. St. xliv., where he states that the first edition reads *full*, and the second *fell.* The folio of 1611 reads *fell* in the two first passages, and *full* in the last.—*Ed.*

> "These, these in golden lines might write this story
> And make these loves their own eternal glory."

Their, I imagine. *Ib.*,—

> "Yet, when my sheep have at the cisterns been,
> And I have brought them back to shear the green,
> To *miss* an idle hour, and not for need,
> Whose [read *With*] choicest relish shall mine oaten reed
> Record their worths; and though in accents rare
> I miss the glory of a charming air,
> My muse may one day," &c.

T" *amuse.* May, Old Couple, ii. 1, Dodsley, vol. x. p. 404,

> "She wrong'd a worthy friend of mine, young Scudmore," &c.
>
> . . . .
>
> *Freeman.* I must confess, 'twas a foul *cause* indeed;
> And he, poor man, lack'd means to prosecute
> The cause against her."

Course, I suspect. Marmion, Antiquary, i. 1, *ib.*, p. 13,—

> "Settle your mind upon some worthy *beauty;*
> A wife will tame all wild affections.
> I have a daughter, who, for youth and beauty,
> Might be desir'd," &c.

Perhaps *lady*. ii. 1, p. 24,—

> "For flatteries are like *sweet* pills; though sweet,
> Yet, if they work not straight, invert [*convert?*] to poison."

Wrong, I suspect. Browne, Clarke, ii. iii. p. 246,—

> "I have not known so many years
> As chances wrong,
> Nor have they *known* more floods of tears
> From one so young."

Drawn? As King Henry V. ii. 1, fol., "if he be not *hewne* now," for *drawne*. Herrick, vol. ii. p. 210, ccccIxxi.,—

> "I want belief; O, gentle Silvia, be
> The *patient* saint, and send up vows for me."

Wrong; *patron*, I suppose; *patience* occurs four lines below, in Poem cccclxxii.[147] P. 155, ccclvi.,—

"One Cordelion had that age long since,
These three, which three you make up four, brave prince."

This surely. *These* occurs twice in the preceding couplet. Carew, Clarke, xxv. p. 44,—

"My sighs have rais'd those winds, whose fury bears
My sails o'erboard, and in their place spreads *tears*;
And from my tears
This sea is sprung, where nought but death appears."

Fears; see xxi. p. 42,—

"My fearful hope hangs on my trembling sail;"

and context. Richard Brome, A Jovial Crew, ii. 1, Dodsley, x. 300,—

"——— Beggars! are we not so already?
Don't we now beg our loves, and our enjoyings?
Do we not beg to be receiv'd your servants?
To kiss your hands, or, if you will vouchsafe,
Your lips, or your embraces?
Hilliard. We now beg
That we may fetch the rings and priest to marry us.
Wherein are we *now* beggars?"

Not. Chapman, Il. i. ed. Taylor, vol. ii. p. 50, l. 32 [fol. p. 202], may be noticed under this head,—

"——— and his death great Hector's power shall wreak,
Ending his *ends*. Then at once out shall the fury break
Of fierce Achilles."

Labat metrum. Perhaps *evils*; *ends—euils* or *euills*; *i.e.*, *the euils he wrought*. xi. vol. i. p. 250, l. 31 [fol. p. 157],—

---

147 The order is different in Pickering's edition 1846, which, I believe, follows the original, so that the *cause* of the error cannot be what Walker thought; no doubt, however, *patience* is a blunder for *patron*.—*Ed.*

"——— and *at* the fleet of Ithacus he past,
(At which their markets were dispos'd," &c.) ——
———————————————————
He met renown'd Eurypilus," &c.

As. Odyss. x. fol. p. 147,—

"——— But when the haven we found,
. . . .
Our whole fleet in we got; in *whole* receipt
Our ships lay anchor'd close," &c.

Whose; i.e., the haven's. Il. xix., vol. ii. p. 145, l. 20 [fol. p. 271],—

"Let then thy mind rest in *thy* words;"

my; τῷ τοι ἐπιτλήτω κραδίη μύθοισιν ἐμοῖσιν. v. 220.
xxiii. p. 215, l. 23,—

"————— but as a huge fish ———
——————————
Shoots back, and in the *back* deep hides," &c.

black; μέλαν δέ ἑ κῦμα κάλυψεν. v. 693.
Ford, &c. Witch of Edmonton, ii. 2, Moxon, p. 193, col. 1,—"Since Thorney has won the wench, he has most reason to wear her. *Warbeck.* Love in this kind admits no reason *to wear her.*" Read: "admits no reason *near her.*" Massinger, Bondmen, ii., near the beginning,—

"A smack or so for *physic* does no harm;
Nay, it is physic, if used moderately."

Qu.—Sidney, Arcadia, B. iii. p. 297, l. 24,—"His *Impresa* was a Catablepta, which so long lies dead, as the Moon (whereto it hath so natural a sympathy) wants her light. The word signified that The Moon wanted not the *light*, but the poor beast wanted the Moon's light." *Beast?* B. iv. p. 428, l. 43,—

"O light of sun, which is entitled day,
O well thou dost, that thou no longer bidest,
For mourning *light* her black weeds may display."

Night, surely. *For, i.e., in order that.* Astrophel and Stella, p. 540, Sonnet lxiii. 12 (original spelling),—

"For Grammer sayes (ȏ this dear Stella *nay*)
For Grammer sayes (to Grammer who sayes nay)
That in one speech two Negatiues affirme."

Way, i.e., waigh or *weigh.* Perhaps this is too obvious to need noticing. Ford, Broken Heart, iii. 2, Moxon, p. 59, col. 2,—

"*Ith.* How does my lord esteem thee?
Pen. Such an one
As only you have made me; a faith-breaker,
A spotted whore;—forgive me, I am one—
In act, not in desires, the gods must witness.
Ith. Thou dost belie thy *friend.*
Pen. I do not, Ithocles;
For she that 's wife to Orgilus, and lives
In known adultery with Bassanes,
Is, at the best, a whore."

What is *friend* here?[148] I suspect that this is one of the many corruptions of a corrupt play, and that Ford wrote "thy *selfe.*" Chapman, Conspiracy of Byron, Retrosp. vol. iv. p. 368,—

"Vault and contractor of all horrid sounds,
Trumpet of all the miseries in hell,
Of my confusions, of the shameful end
Of all my services; witch, *end*, accurst
For ever be the poison of thy tongue," &c.

Contrary to the context. Read *toad. End* occurs also 12 and 27 lines below, as well as 33, 34, and 41 above. Davenport, King John and Matilda, ii. 1, *ib.*, p. 97,—

"———— but when forty winters more
Shall round thy forehead with a field of snow, &c.

. . . .

[148] *Friendship* occurs seven lines above and 24 below.—*Ed.*

When thy swift pulses shall but slowly pant,
When thou art all a volum of my want,
(That like a *tale-spent* fire thou shall sink,)
Then, John, upon this lesson thou wilt think," &c.

Wrong; *late-spent?* *Tale* occurs 13 lines above. (*Volum* may possibly be an erratum for *model; i.e.*, a *likeness* or *copy of my want;* old Fitzmaurice is speaking.) Chapman, Bussy D'Ambois, *ib.*, p. 351; see context,—

" ———————————— all the forms
That her illusions have impress'd in her,
Have eaten through her *back*, and now all see,
How she is rivetted [*rivell'd*] with hypocrisy."

Bark? we have eight lines above,—

"The too huge bias of the world hath sway'd
Her back part upwards;"

(where by the way, in the words immediately following,—

" ———————————— and with that she *leaves*
This hemisphere, that long her mouth hath mock'd;"

we should read *braves.*)[149] Chapman and Shirley, Chabot, ii. 2, Gifford and Dyce's Shirley, vol. vi. p. 106,—

"I walk no desart, yet go arm'd with that
That would give wildest beasts instincts to rescue,
Rather than offer any force to hurt me.
My innocence *is*, which is a conquering justice,
As wears a shield, that both defends and fights."

I conjecture,—

"My innocence *'tis;* which is a conquering Justice,
And wears a shield," &c.

---

[149] *Braves* is the reading in "Old English Plays," vol. iii. p. 325. We may therefore, perhaps, be indebted to the printer of the Retrospective for *leaves.—Ed.*

Ib., near the end, p. 107,—

" *Mont.* Brave resolution, so his acts be just!
He cares for gain *not* honour.
Chan. How came he then
By all his infinite honour and his gain?"

Not occurs eight lines above. *Nor.* Arcadia, ii. 1, p. 195, "I saw a yellow brightness peeping out o' th' ground, which when I came to examine, *I* proved this metal;" &c. *It.* In the very next page occur the words, "To build *your* hopes on," where Dyce says that the old copy has *to.* Witty Fair One, v. 3, vol. 1, p. 355,—"frequenting of *some* companies had corrupted his nature, and a little debauched him." *Some* occurs 20 lines above, and 8 and 19 lines below. Possibly *loose.* Heywood, Four Prentices of London, Dodsley, vol. vi. p. 432,—

"Princes, my master County Palatine
. . . .
Sends me to know the cause of your arrive:
Or why the arm'd hoofs of your fiery steeds
Dare wound the forehead of his peaceful land?
Godfrey. Dare! *sends* thy lord in that ambitious *key?*"

Sings, I imagine. Edwards, Damon and Pithias, Dodsley, vol. 1, p. 242; see context,—

"*Neare* would I be poled [*polled*] as neere as cham shaven."

Nowe.

END OF VOL. I.

www.ingramcontent.com/pod-product-compliance
Lightning Source LLC
Chambersburg PA
CBHW030859270326
41929CB00008B/486

* 9 7 8 3 7 4 4 7 0 9 4 3 9 *